BROKEN TABLETS

BROKEN TABLETS

LEVINAS, DERRIDA, AND THE LITERARY
AFTERLIFE OF RELIGION

SARAH HAMMERSCHLAG

COLUMBIA UNIVERSITY PRESS / NEW YORK

Columbia University Press
Publishers Since 1893
New York   Chichester, West Sussex
cup.columbia.edu
Copyright © 2016 Columbia University Press
All rights reserved

Library of Congress Cataloging-in-Publication Data
Names: Hammerschlag, Sarah, author.
Title: Broken tablets : Levinas, Derrida and the literary afterlife
of religion / Sarah Hammerschlag.
Description: New York : Columbia University Press, 2016. |
Includes bibliographical references and index.
Identifiers: LCCN 2015039850| ISBN 9780231170581 (cloth : alk. paper) |
ISBN 9780231170598 (pbk. : alk. paper)
Subjects: LCSH: Lévinas, Emmanuel. | Derrida, Jacques.
Classification: LCC B2430.L484 H35 2016 | DDC 194—dc23
LC record available at https://lccn.loc.gov/2015039850

Columbia University Press books are printed on permanent
and durable acid-free paper.

This book is printed on paper with recycled content.
Printed in the United States of America

c 10 9 8 7 6 5 4 3 2 1
p 10 9 8 7 6 5 4 3 2 1

Cover design: Lisa Hamm
Cover image: Decalogue (digital composite)

For Lila and Ryan

ℭℜ

CONTENTS

PREFACE

Poetic autonomy, comparable to none other,
presupposes broken tablets.

—Derrida, "Edmond Jabès and the Question of the Book"

For a long time, for a very long time, I've feared having to say
Adieu to Emanuel Levinas.

—Derrida, *Adieu to Emmanuel Levinas*

The difference between the rabbi and the poet, between religion and literature—already in 1963 Jacques Derrida suggested that it is a matter of how one says à-dieu. It is a difference of interpretation. Commenting on Edmond Jabès's *Le Livre des Questions,* he wrote, "In the beginning is hermeneutics, but the *shared* necessity of exegesis, the interpretive imperative is interpreted differently by the rabbi and the poet. *The* difference between the horizon of the original text and exegetic writing makes the difference between the rabbi and the poet irreducible. Forever unable to reunite with each other, yet so close to each other, how could they ever regain the realm?" (*ED* 102; *WD* 67). The difference is not in the act of writing, but in how the freedom of broken tablets is accepted and negotiated, a difference in how one makes use of the past and how one cultivates the ironies of history and language. For Emmanuel Levinas and Jacques Derrida, the difference was also between how to navigate the demands of the postwar period as Jews and how to think about survival. This book is about Levinas and Derrida's strategies of navigation, but is not a comparative study of two philosophers. Instead it is a book about how Derrida *read* Levinas and ultimately about what it means for us to read both Derrida and Levinas within the context of the study of religion.

One of the first conversations that Derrida and Levinas had face-to-face was about the poet Jabès, whose *Book of Questions* had just been published when Derrida began auditing one of Levinas's classes. For both, the Jewish poet's work was inspiring, but they read him quite differently because of the difference in emphasis each placed on his Jewishness and his position as poet. This was among the first of many encounters between the two philosophers. And yet Levinas would refer much later to their relationship as a chiasmus, a meeting at the crossroads, each headed in a different direction. Derrida, even standing at Levinas's graveside in 1995, insisted on their persistent proximity (*AEL* 11, 1).

The reverberations from their encounters would echo through much of Derrida's later work, in his ongoing commitment to receive, rethink, rewrite, and even deform Levinas's texts, for what Derrida called fidelity to Levinas was often indistinguishable from betrayal. At the same time, however, his ironic homages to Levinas, the recasting of Levinas's claims in language often far from his own, were instantiation of Derrida's meditations on the nature of fidelity, friendship, and politics.[1] Moreover, the very *form* of his relation to Levinas, his subversion of Levinas's thought, arose out of his commitment to Levinas's project, not as Levinas himself conceived it, but as Derrida rewrote it. The way Derrida read and reinterpreted Levinas enacted for Derrida what it meant to rewrite difference as an ethical and ultimately political relation, one not performed in the face-to-face encounter, however, but as the movement of textuality itself, its dissemination and its reception.

This method, while only a matter of reading, has significant philosophical and political consequences. It provided Derrida the means to traverse the chasm between Levinasian ethics and politics, to call into question Levinas's own attempt to locate the political instantiation of what he calls "difficult freedom" in the state of Israel, and finally to advocate for an alternative model of political freedom divorced from sovereignty: to argue indeed for the poet's freedom over the rabbi's.

In the following five chapters I will flesh out each of these claims by engaging with crucial moments in Levinas and Derrida's intertwined histories and by situating them within the larger conversation of post–World War II French intellectual life. Both Jews, both transplants to Parisian philosophical culture, born twenty-five years apart on different continents, Emmanuel Levinas and Jacques Derrida rose to prominence in France at about the same moment, in the 1960s, when World War II was still a live memory but conflicts in Algeria and the Middle East were closer at hand. In reading their work within its historical context, I argue that their choices were not *only* philosophical but also products of and responses to their respective biographies and positions within the French intellectual scene.

My reinterpretation of the textual traces of their dialogue as about the negotiation and imbrication of the categories of religion and literature in the postwar era is a means of thinking through the implications of Levinas's and Derrida's work and their friendship for the academic study of religion. It is not only because of the enormity of their influence on these categories that I see this story as relevant to religious studies but also because within the field a particular narrative of their relation, one that seems predicated on the elision of their significant differences, has predominated.[2] This is perhaps clearest for those who speak of an ethical turn in deconstruction and those who view Derrida as a resource for a minimal, postmodern, or weak theology.[3] But the supposed alliance between Levinas and Derrida is equally central to those who have declared the ethics of alterity itself to be old news.[4] Žižek, Badiou, and their followers have announced their departure from the Levinas-Derrida alliance not by rejecting the centrality of religion for political and philosophical thought but by casting the apostle Paul as a new hero in the race to think constructively about the political-theological nexus.[5] As an intervention in this trend, I return to the supposed consonance between Levinas and Derrida and complicate it. Ultimately I argue that Derrida's own thinking on the relation between religion and literature provides an alternative to recent trends in political theology.

For those theologians and philosophers of religion who have championed a minimal or weak theology, the suturing of Derrida and Levinas secures alterity "*as* religion or in an undeniable relation *with* religion."[6] At the same time, this alterity appears cleansed of anything distastefully dogmatic or conservative. The concept of alterity gleaned from this alliance is supposedly synonymous with a notion of transcendence divested of deter-mination, cut free from metaphysics, yet with a concrete impact on the moral and political sphere.[7] Derrida, even in more subtle religious reap-propriations, is rallied to the side of religion by privileging "the theological moment" of the trace. But such an interpretation, while courted on the sur-face of many of Derrida's texts referencing Levinas, is belied by the details. A close reading of their textual encounters reveals that Derrida pushed hard against the category of "religion" as Levinas had construed it, but also that he insisted on the literary dynamics of Levinas's own texts.

My own reconstruction of their dialogue considers it both through a his-torical and a textual-critical lens and reframes it to put Derrida's substantial differences from Levinas into relief and, furthermore, to frame their differ-ences in terms of the relation between religion and literature. The model I take for this relation is from Derrida's late essays invoking these themes, particularly *Gift of Death* and its last section, "Literature in Secret." In this final section, published in English only in its second edition, Derrida refers to literature as the descendent of Abraham, the inheritor of a testamentary secret, but also its betrayer (*DLM* 205; *GD* 156). It is a model that Derrida obliquely applies to Levinas in the essay itself, but one equally applicable across the terrain of their intertextual relation. In light of this rereading, their alliance can subsequently no longer be framed in such a way that Levinas is read to provide a concretization of Derridean alterity, nor can Levinas's influence be used to construe Derrida as having enacted a turn toward Levinas as a turn to religion or ethics.

What does become clear when their interactions are historically resit-uated is the centrality of the Jewish question for Derrida from the begin-ning of his published writings. Derrida's interaction with Levinas provided a means to address the Jewish question, not in the guise of a temptation or obligation, but as a discourse that could be displaced in and through a reading first of Edmond Jabès and later Paul Celan and Franz Kafka. These writers provided Derrida the means to renegotiate his own relation to Judaism, to transform it from a communitarian context into a diasporic literary form.[8]

While some have suggested that historical inquiry is itself anathema to deconstruction, assuming that such an approach would return us to a prestructuralist hermeneutic in which attention to the authorial intention is again held to be accessible and central to the work of interpretation, I would contend that Derrida's own use of history as a critical force in multiple works and his concern for legacy, particularly in *Politics of Friendship*, as well as his own autobiographical disclosures in late interviews and texts such as *Monolingualism of the Other* and *Circonfessions*, reveals a powerful if complex concern for the determining force of history and context.[9] Even if Derrida explicitly discounted a traditional notion of history as being able to pinpoint causes and effects, he ceaselessly contemplated his own philosophical lineage, recalled his debts and obligations to philosophical forbearers, and traced the lineage of others. He documented the impact of time on meaning and interpretation and attested to the untranslatability of the idiom, thus insisting on the implications of history and language on even the most abstract of philosophical ideas.[10] Furthermore, the recent Benoît Peeters biography and Edward Baring's unearthing of Derrida's youthful writings further highlight the rich and significant historical development of Derrida's thought.[11] Finally, the publication of Levinas's *inédits* in his *Oeuvres Complètes* has multiplied the resources for reconstructing the early stages of Levinas's philosophy. One contention of this book is that Derrida took the task of inheritance seriously, even as he conceptualized it as a necessary betrayal; another is to argue that his relationship to Levinas was itself a testing ground for that concept.[12]

Both thinkers share a concern to consider by means of a phenomenological method that which philosophy could not bring to light. But in shaping and representing a resistance to philosophy they chose not only different vocabularies—religion for Levinas, writing/poetics/literature for Derrida—but different methods. Moreover, Derrida's method functions by theorizing the relation between religion and literature, such that, in commenting on, interpreting, and sometimes defacing Levinas's texts, Derrida rewrites them *as* literary. As he puts it in "Literature in Secret," commenting explicitly on Kafka, "the son is a parasite as literature." It is statement that also aptly describes his relation to Levinas.

This rewriting involves a critique of Levinas's very move both to think alterity as transcendence and to reinscribe it in religious language. Although this critique is announced quite clearly in "Violence and Metaphysics," it has been overshadowed by the general rush to canonize *both* Levinas and Derrida as "saints of postmodernism" and by interpretations of the essays

"How to Avoid Speaking: Denials," "Sauf le nom," and "Of an Apocalyptic Tone Newly Adopted in Philosophy" that try to emphasize the commonalities between negative theology and deconstruction, even as the essays themselves defend the difference between a hyperessentialized concept of God beyond being and Derrida's own negative language concerning the trace.[13]

In the process of locating the consonance between Derrida and theology, readers have sometimes overlooked Derrida's suspicion of even the least dogmatic theological reclamations, seeing his refusal to reject a theological reading of his own work as an implicit acceptance. At the same time, insistence on Derrida's "radical atheism" ignores the fact that Derrida *did* refuse to negate such a reading. At the very least, he never denied the theological specters that deconstruction produces.[14] Literature, I will show here, was a means of owning those ghosts but divesting them of authority.

Reframed as a conversation about literature as the inheritor of an Abrahamic legacy, Derrida's refusal to affirm or deny the theological effects of his own work appears less as an implicit acknowledgment of his theological investments and more as a commitment to the dynamics of deconstruction, which open his own texts to the readings of others, exposing them to their own unworking. It is the literary stakes of this process that philosophers of religion have sometimes overlooked. In reading Derrida, one needs to consider not only the notion of deferral in Derrida's own texts but also its function—the way that a phrase stated in the opening of an essay is turned, twisted, and altered through the course of his essays. From *Writing and Difference* forward, I will show, Derrida's references to religious idioms appear as quotations and repetitions in a procedure of displacement, which I would argue transforms them into literature, as Derrida defines it.

At the same time, it is no secret that Derrida first rose to prominence in the United States not among philosophers of religion—even if they have proved to be some of his most committed readers—but among literary theorists. Through visits first to Johns Hopkins beginning in 1968 and later Yale, Paul de Man's endorsement and correlated method, Gayartri Spivak's translation of and introduction to *Of Grammatology* (1976), and Jonathan Culler's and Frank Lentricchia's framing of Derrida's work as a new key for literary theory, Derrida became in the 1970s and 1980s a darling of literature departments. For literary theory, Derrida's own blurring of the distinction between literary and nonliterary texts opened up a range of textual sources as fair game for interpretation. His method also made reading itself a poetic and political practice: decoding the function of binaries, the working of logocentricism, allowed critics to expose the patriarchial, sexist, and racist implications of texts that may have seemed apolitical on the surface. At the same time, the perceived difficulty of Derrida's prose, its emphasis on play and the undecidable, and his resistance to locating meaning, either as a product of the author's intention or as a reliable outcome of communication, led some to see his theories as an affront to the critical endeavor and others as permission to say anything.

Thus, even as the field of religion and literature would seem like the appropriate site for situating Derrida's work, he has often been treated as a threat to its aims. As a regional field of study within American religion departments and divinity schools, religion and literature is often traced back to Nathan Scott, for whom the field was something closer to theology and literature.[15] Many of Scott's sources were themselves from the same lineage as Derrida's and Levinas's. He found inspiration in Heidegger's discussions of poetry and Gabriel Marcel's concept of mystery and presence. But Scott treats deconstruction, in its critique of the possibility for presence, as an adversary to his enterprise.[16] Even as later theorists in the field moved beyond Scott's Tillichian method, deconstruction continued to be viewed as a nihilating force or as already passé.[17] Where its lasting importance has been acknowledged, it is according to the interpretation pioneered by postmodern theologians and philosophers of religion.[18] What even the most positive accounts of Derrida in the field underemphasize is that Derrida's project was from the beginning concerned specifically with the correlation between religion and literature. It is a project already acknowledged in the choice of Matthew Arnold's famous line from *Culture and Anarchy,* "Hebraism and Hellenism—between these two points of influence moves our world," as epigraph for "Violence and Metaphysics" (*ED* 117; *WD* 79). In fact, as an interpreter of the religious legacy of modern literature, Derrida can be resituated within a lineage of literary theorists that goes back at least as far as Arnold and includes Eric Auerbach, Northrop Frye, Paul Ricoeur, and Frank Kermode, a line of thinkers all invested in the aesthetic and political impact of the biblical forms of irony, mystery, and promise on the constitution of modern narrative.

One reason that Derrida's place in this lineage has been largely over-looked may follow from the fact that neither Levinas or Derrida have been properly contextualized within larger debates over the place of religion and literature after the Second World War. Philosophers of religion have turned to French poststructuralism to think about how religious models can inter-rogate Enlightenment and post-Enlightenmnent theories of subjectivity and rationality and scholars of religion and literature have turned to Hei-degger, Georges Bataille, and Gabriel Marcel for theories about literature's specific mode of accessing the sacred, but a narrative that imbricates these two conversations has not been adequately reconstructed. That reconstruc-tion is not the primary task of this book, but I hope that it can provide at least one brick toward a new edifice.

The opening chapter, in lieu of an introduction, begins at the end of the story, in fact after the end, two years after the death of Levinas and six years before Derrida's, with Derrida's 1998 address to the Colloque des intellectu-els juifs de langue française. Its purpose is to frame the larger issues of the book's constructive argument, articulating them particularly in terms of our thinkers' respective relationships to their Jewish identity and the function of irony in their prose. Irony, I argue here, provides one of the lenses through which the difference between religion and literature can be articulated and was significantly a key trope in Derrida and Levinas's thirty-year friendship. The function of irony is also key, I argue, to considering the political impli-cations of each of their thought.

The second chapter does the work of contextualization, going back before their story's proper beginning. It shows how Levinas's own suspi-cion of literature arose as a product of debates about literature's spiritual function in postwar France. His was a choice, I argue, *for* religion *against* literature as the right means of critiquing the self-sufficient subject of the West. Chapter 3 sets up Derrida on the other side of the debate. It estab-lishes Levinas's importance to Derrida's early conceptualizations of the trace, arguing not only for the importance of "Violence and Metaphysics" (1964), but revealing evidence of an engagement with Levinas already in "Force and Signification" (1963) and "Edmond Jabès and the Book" (1964). The upshot is to show that not only was Derrida in conversation with Levinas in these early works but also that these early essays allow us to frame his project, already in 1963, as one about the relationship between religion and literature—Judaism and literature more specifically—and to show how Levinas's own integration of Judaism and philosophy furnished a provocation for this engagement.

Chapter 4 examines the political implications of both Levinas and Derrida's positions, demonstrating that Levinas's early concern to conceive of a freedom divorced from sovereignty in Judaism developed politically in his engagements with the reality of the Israeli state. Derrida's own rethinking of literature as a means of upending sovereignty sought out a different direction, I argue, one built on a reading of the return of religion in Levinas's texts, but also through a consideration of and critical response to the theological resonances in the work of other philosophers, such as Jan Patocka and Jean-Luc Marion, who sought to return the place of mystery to a prominent position within the philosophical enterprise.

The concluding chapter thus takes up the implications of Derrida's model for recent discussions of political theology. Thus far political theology has itself been predominantly a contest between philosophers, without much attention to the textual dynamics of its sources. What Derrida has done most importantly in linking religion to literature and literature to the democracy-to-come is provide an alternative model to one that advocates for a "return" to the religious sources as an intervention into the politico-theological nexus.

If there is one thing we should have learned in the wake of poststructuralism, it is that a return to some pure beginning is not possible and that indeed the purifying impulse is itself suspect. We can neither unearth a pristine past nor divest ourselves of all of the sediment that stands between us and our sources. The new Paul, hero of universalism, is a fiction, as are Levinas's ethical rabbis and Heidegger's Heraclitus. The question is not only what happens when we acknowledge this—few, I imagine, would not—but when we treat them *as* fictions and cultivate new fictions in their stead.[19]

ACKNOWLEDGMENTS

This book emerged organically out of my first, as an attempt to refine its method and answer some lingering questions. Its earliest instantiations were as conference papers and guest lectures, first at Harvard in 2010, at the "Derrida and Religion" conference organized by Edward Baring and Peter Gordon, then in Bogota, Columbia at the Universidad de los Andes, at the invitation of Carlos Manrique. When Jonathan Boyarin and Shai Ginsburg organized their conference "Jews and the Ends of Theory" I had a chance to crystallize its central argument. Other instantiations and fragments of what would become chapters emerged out of an AAR panel on Derrida's *Passions*, at the Levinas Research Seminar hosted by Oona Eisenstadt, The "Figural Jews" conference at the University of Minnesota organized by Bruno Chaouat and at Jonathan Boyarin and Martin Land's symposium on Derrida's Jewish specters at Cornell University. In the process, I've received terrifically helpful feedback from the conference organizers I've mentioned, but also from Michael Levine, Martin Kavka, Jonathan Freedman, Anita Sokolsky, Andrew Parker, Gil Andijar, Constance Furey, and others.

It was a pleasure working in Special Collections at the University of California, Irvine, and I want to thank both the trustees of the Derrida archives and the terrific librarians there, particularly Alexandra Bisio for her assistance both before and after my visits. Because I wrote this book in the middle of working on another that requires more archival work, I want to thank the Alliance Israélite Universelle, where I have been working intermittently since 2008. Although most of my research from those trips will appear in my next book, my time spent combing through the library's periodicals helped shape my perspective on Levinas's historical trajectory and thus the argument of this book.

Much of my thinking on irony and religion and literature developed out of conversations with my colleague Richard Rosengarten, who also devoted the time and energy to reading early drafts of multiple chapters. His feedback has been indispensable. Conversations with Margaret Mitchell helped hone my thinking on the field of religion and literature and my place in it. I owe a great debt to my students at the University of Chicago who were willing to read with me so many of the texts central to this study and whose interpretive skill and subtlety helped me clarify my ideas. I'm grateful particularly to Maureen Kelly, who not only slogged through those classes but also worked as my research assistant as I put together the final manuscript. Thanks too to Nathelda McGee for her administrative support and to the faculty at the University of Chicago Divinity School, whose scholarly achievements set the highest of bars. Thanks to Jeff Stackert, Dan Arnold, Na'ama Rokem, Leora Auslander, Susan Schreiner, Catherine Brekus, David Tracy, Paul Mendes-Flohr, Jim Robinson, Bill Schweiker, Alireza Doostar, Kris Culp, Cynthia Lindner, and Arnold Davidson for all your kindness and advice in the last few years as I made my transition to Chicago and to Françoise Meltzer, who, though now my colleague, will always be my Doktormutter. I owe a special debt of gratitude to Amy Hollywood whose feedback on the manuscript was spectacularly helpful in its detail, nuance, and precision.

Thanks too to my editors at Columbia, Wendy Lochner, Christine Dunbar, and Susan Pensak. It has been a real pleasure to work with such a responsive and insightful team.

Finally, I want to thank my dear friends and family: my parents for making a life of reading and writing possible; Stephanie and Joe for your support and encouragement; Ali and Micah, Sarabinh and Charlie, Jeff and Dina, Amy and Reed, Dan and Deborah for wonderful conversation and many happy meals.

Finally, it is Ryan and Lila to whom I come home each night. Lila, you are my daily joy. Ryan, as each year passes, we are bound tighter in love and friendship. Thanks for running marathons with me, both literally and figuratively.

ABBREVIATIONS

JACQUES DERRIDA

A   "Avouer—l'impossible: <<retours>>, repentir et réconcilation" in *Comment vivre ensemble? Acts du XXXVIIe Colloque des intellectuels juifs de langue française* (1998), edited by Jean Halpérin et Nelly Hansson (Paris: Albin Michel, 2001) and "Avowing—the Impossible: 'Returns,' Repentance, and Reconciliation," trans. Gil Andijar in *Living Together: Jacques Derrida's Communities of Violence and Peace*, ed. Elisabeth Weber (New York: Fordham University Press, 2013)

AA   "Abraham, l'autre" in *Judéités: Questions pour Jacques Derrida*, ed. Joseph Cohen (Paris: Galilée, 2003)

AC   *L'Autre cap* (Paris: Minuit, 1991)

AEL   *Àdieu à Emmanuel Lèvinas* (Paris: Galilée, 1997) and *Àdieu to Emmanuel Levinas,* trans. Pascale-Anne Brault and Michael B. Naas (Stanford: Stanford University Press, 1999)

AF   *Archive Fever: A Freudian Impression*, trans. Eric Prenowitz (Chicago: University of Chicago Press, 1996)

AO   "Abraham, the other" in *Judeities: Questions for Jacques Derrida*, trans. Bettina Bergo and Michael B. Smith, ed. Bettina Bergo, Joseph Cohen, and Raphael Zagury-Orly (New York: Fordham University Press, 2007)

BTL   "Before the Law" in *Acts of Literature,* ed. Derek Atridge (New York: Routledge, 1992)

D   *Dissemination,* trans. Barbara Johnson (Chicago: University of Chicago Press, 1981)

DLG   *De la Grammatologie* (Paris: Minuit, 1967)

DLL   "Devant la loi" in *La Faculté de juger* (Paris: Minuit, 1985)

DLM   *Donner la Mort* (Paris: Galilée, 1999)

DT   *Donner le temps* (Paris: Galilée, 1991)

ED   *L'Écriture et la différence* (Paris: Seuil, 1967)

FK   "Faith and Knowledge" in *Acts of Religion,* ed. Gil Andijar (New York: Routledge, 2002)

FOL   "Force of Law" in *Acts of Religion,* ed. Gil Andijar (New York: Routledge, 2002)

FS   *Foi et Savoir: suivi de Le siecle et le pardon* (Paris: Seuil, 2000)

GD   *Gift of Death and Literature in Secret,* trans. David Wills (Chicago: University of Chicago, 2008)

GT   *Given Time I: Counterfeit Money,* trans. Peggy Kamuf (Chicago: University of Chicago Press, 1992)

MA   *Mal d'archive: une impression freudienne* (Paris: Galilée, 1995)

MLO   *Monolinguisme de l'autre ou, La prothèse d'origine* (Paris: Galilée, 1996) and *Monolingualism of the Other or, The Prosthesis of Origin,* trans. Patrick Mensah (Stanford: Stanford University Press, 1998)

OG   *Of Grammatology,* trans. Gayatri Spivak (Baltimore: Johns Hopkins University Press, 1974)

OH   *The Other Heading: Reflections on Today's Europe,* trans. Pascale-Anne Brault and Michael B. Naas (Bloomington: Indiana University Press, 1992)

OTN   *On the Name,* Thomas Dutoit, ed. and trans. David Wood, John P. Leavey Jr., and Ian Mcleod (Stanford: Stanford University Press, 1995)

PA   *Passions: "L'offrande oblique"* (Paris: Galilee 1993).

P   *Psyché: inventions de l'autre 1* (Paris: Galilée, 1998) and *Psyche: Inventions of the Other, 1,* ed. Peggy Kamuf and Elizabeth Rottenberg (Stanford: Stanford University Press, 2007)

PG   *Le problème de la genese dans la philosophie de Husserl* (Paris: Presses Universitaires de France, 1990) and *The Problem of Genesis in Husserl's Philosophy,* trans. Marian Hobson (Chicago: University of Chicago Press, 2003)

R   *Rogues: Two Essays on Reason,* trans. Pascale-Anne Brault and Michael Naas (Stanford: Stanford University Press, 2005)

S   *Schibboleth: pour Paul Celan* (Paris: Galilée, 2003) and "Shibboleth: For Paul Celan" in *Sovereignties in Question: The Poetics of Paul Celan,* ed. Thomas Dutoit and Outi Pasanen (New York: Fordham University Press, 2005)

SLN   *Sauf le nom* (Paris: Galilée, 1993)

V   *Voyous: deux essais sur la raison* (Paris: Galilée, 2003)

VP   *La Voix et le phénomène* (Paris: Presses Universitaires de France, 1967) and *Voice and Phenomenon: Introduction to the Problem of the Sign in Husserl's Phenomenology,* trans. Leonard Lawlor (Evanston: Northwestern University Press, 2011)

WD   *Writing and Difference,* trans. Alan Bass (Chicago: University of Chicago Press, 1978)

EMMANUEL LEVINAS

ADV   *Au delà du verset* (Paris: Minuit, 1982)

AE   *Autrement qu'être ou au delà de l'essence* (The Hague: Martinus Nijhoff, 1978)

BJ   "Being Jewish," *Continental Philosophical Review* 40 (2007): 205–10

BTV   *Beyond the Verse: Talmudic Readings and Lectures,* trans. Gary D. Mole (Bloomington: Indiana University Press, 1994)

CC   *Carnets de captivité,* ed. Rodolphe Calin and Catherine Chalier (Paris: Imec/Grasset, 2009)

DE   "De l'évasion," *Recherches philosophiques* 5 (1935–1936): 373–92

DF   *Difficult Freedom,* trans. Seán Hand (Baltimore: Johns Hopkins University Press, 1990)

DL   *Difficile liberté: essais sur le judaïsme* (Paris: Albin Michel, 1963, 1967)

DSS   *Du sacré au saint: cinq nouvelles lectures talmudiques* (Paris: Minuit, 1977)

EE   *De l'existence à l'existant* (Paris: J. Vrin, 1993) and *Existence and Existents,* trans. Alphonso Lingis (Dordrecht: Kluwer, 1978)

EJ   "Être Juif" in *Confluences* 15–17 (1947): 253–64

ELP   *Eros, littérature et philosophie inédits,* ed. Jean-Luc Nancy and Danielle
        Cohen-Levinas, (Paris: Imec/Grasset, 2013)

EN   *Entre nous*: *Essais sur le penser-à-l'autre* (Paris: Grasset & Fasquelle,
        1991) and *Entre Nous: Thinking-of-the-Other*, trans. Michael B. Smith
        and Barbara Harshav (New York: Columbia University Press, 1998)

HS   *Hors Sujet* (Montpelier: Fata Morgana, 1997)

IH   *Les Imprévus de l'histoire* (Montpelier: Fata Morgana, 1994)

NP   *Noms Propres: Agnon, Buber, Celan, Delhomme, Derrida, Jabès,
        Kierkegaard, Lacroix, Laporte, Picard, Proust, Van Breda, Wahl*
        (Montpelier: Fata Morgana, 1976)

NTR   *Nine Talmudic Readings,* trans. Annette Aronowicz (Bloomington:
        Indiana University Press, 1990)

OE   *On Escape,* trans. Bettina Bergo (Stanford: Stanford University Press,
        2003)

OS   *Outside the Subject*, trans. Michael B. Smith (Stanford: Stanford
        University Press, 1994)

OTB   *Otherwise Than Being or Beyond Essence*, trans. Alphonso Lingis
        (Pittsburgh: Duquesne University Press, 1998)

PS   *Parole et Silence et autres conférences inédites au Collège philosophique,*
        ed. Rodolphe Calin and Catherine Chalier (Paris: Imec/Grasset,
        2009)

PN   *Proper Names*, trans. Michael B. Smith (Stanford: Stanford University
        Press, 1996)

QLT   *Quatre lectures talmudiques* (Paris: Minuit, 1968)

SB   *Sur Blanchot* (Montpelier: Fata Morgana, 1975)

TI   *Totalité et Infini: essai sur l'extériorité* (The Hague: Martinus Nijhoff,
        1961) and *Totality and Infinity: an essay on exteriority*, trans. Alphonso
        Lingis (Pittsburgh: Duquesne University Press, 1969)

UH   *Unforseen History*, trans. Nidra Poller (Urbana: University of Illinois
        Press, 2004)

BROKEN TABLETS

1

"WHAT MUST
A JEWISH THINKER BE?"

In her 1994 biography of Emmanuel Levinas, Marie-Anne Lescourret described the scene of the Colloque des intellectuels juifs de langue française, the nearly annual meetings of which Levinas was one of the founding members and arguably its animating spirit. She reproduced the terms of its debates and articulated the aims of its participants: "to use their experience of Judaism, to draw from the Jewish tradition a wisdom, and comprehension of the human predicament." She listed the eminent figures who participated, including Edmond Fleg, Jean Wahl, Vladimir Jankélévitch, and Raymond Aron, and then noted in an aside, "that among attending French philosophers of Jewish origin, one will *never* find there Jacques Derrida."[1]

It must have been with great delight then that Jacques Derrida in early December of 1998 took up the podium at the thirty-seventh meeting of the Colloque des intellectuel juifs de langue française and quoted these lines. The irony being that not only was Derrida standing at the conference in 1998, but that he had already been there in the 1960s, decades before Lescourret had written her book. In 1998 he came with a story to tell about that last visit over twenty years earlier, about a joke Levinas had told him during the 1965 meeting.

The theme in 1965 was "Israel in the Jewish consciousness and that of other peoples."[2] In 1998 the conference convened to ask the question, "Comment vivre ensemble?" How to live together? For Derrida his story was perfectly fitting, for it seemed to call into question the transparency of the conference's greatest spokesman and to make its participants rethink what it was they presumed to share in common. Already a few minutes into his talk, Derrida announced that the story would serve as his preface:

> Before beginning, I recall what Emmanuel Levinas told me on that day in an aside [*en aparté*] and which I also evoked on the day of his death. I recount in the present tense as is done sometimes in the rhetoric of historians in order to make things more tangible for representation. Levinas, on that day says something which resonates otherwise concerning what "living together" might mean *for the Jews*, living or not. André Neher was in the middle of speaking, Levinas whispers in my ear: "You see him, he's the protestant, me, I'm the catholic." This quip [*mot d'esprit*] would call for an infinite commentary.
>
> (A 185–86, 21)

Jacques Derrida, who had, as Lescourret herself rightly tried to communicate, resisted aligning himself with the Jewish intellectual scene, came to the community of which Levinas was a founding member and central figure and revealed an inside joke between the two philosophers, a small ironic quip Levinas had made, one that suggested that even Levinas might occasionally have his tongue in his cheek. The colloquium aimed to develop a particularly *Jewish* mode of addressing universal questions, and, at that meeting in particular, its speakers strived to shore up a perception of Judaism's image and role in the world. Nonetheless, Levinas had joked that their interpretations could be parsed in Christian terms. Derrida responded with a series of questions:

> What must a Jewish thinker be to use this language, with the profundity of seriousness and the lightness of irony that we hear in it? How can he remain a Jew together with himself, while opening himself to another, probable or improbable, Jew, in this case me, who has never felt very Catholic, and above all not Protestant? A Jew who, coming from another shore of Judaism than Neher and Levinas, a Mediterranean shore, immediately remarks in the abyss of these doubles or of this Judeo-Catholic-Protestant triangle, the absence of the Islamo-Abrahamic?
>
> (A 186, 21)

At issue here for Derrida were all the differences the joke opened up, between the Jew and the Protestant, the Jew and the Catholic, but also between the Protestant-Jew, the Catholic-Jew and now the Algerian Jew, who, Derrida admitted, was not even sure he could or should be identified as such (A 186, 21). But at the same time, and perhaps even more importantly, Derrida was concerned with the ironic gesture itself, which, offered up as an aside, in a whisper like a secret, seemed designed to open up a space of intimacy between Levinas and Derrida by excluding the rest of the conference. The gesture would seem to depend upon a shared predetermined understanding, and yet the very joke exposed the fissures that would make such an understanding impossible. Furthermore, when Derrida suggests that the quip would call for an infinite commentary, he was not only referring to the content of Levinas's joke, but to the fact of irony itself, to the fact that the depths of an ironic statement can never be fully plumbed, that the space of indeterminacy it opens cannot ever be satisfactorily closed.

At the same moment that Derrida was inquiring about the nature of irony and its effect, he added to the irony of the situation by revealing the anecdote. Derrida had told this story, he said, as a means of illustrating his own proximity to Levinas. The comment was prefaced by the assertion that Derrida's relation to the colloquium was mediated by his own proximity to Levinas. He had attended the conference in the 1960s, he said, "close to Emmanuel Levinas, near him, perhaps together with him. In truth, I was here thanks to him, turned toward him. That is still the case today, differently" (A 184, 20). But, in the process of making such an assertion, he had in fact betrayed Levinas by revealing something said between the two to the very group from which it had been withheld.

To Derrida's question thus, "What must a Jewish thinker be to use this language, with the profundity of seriousness and the lightness of irony that we hear in it?" We can add, what must this proximity be, this friendship, which is demonstrated by betrayal?[3]

That is the question at the heart of this chapter and indeed at the heart of *Broken Tablets*. The aim of this chapter is to explore the nature of the two thinkers' proximity, which Derrida treats in multiple texts from the period surrounding this address, thus following in the wake of Levinas's death. In beginning with this episode, we begin at the end of the story, after Levinas's death and only six years before Derrida's own. But pregnant in Derrida's own evocation of Levinas there is a history of how each of them negotiated their allegiances to the fact of Jewish identity and to the discourse and discipline of philosophy, a history that went back thirty-five years to their first encounter.

JEWS AND MARRANOS

No doubt their initial friendship arose from what they shared in common. They both came to French philosophy as outsiders. Not only were both Jewish, they both arrived in the *Métropole* to acquire a philosophical education. For both this education was the path toward acclimation into Parisian culture. And for both France and its philosophical tradition were a means toward self-determination and self-formation. Following the 1940 repeal of the Crémieux Decree under Vichy rule in November of 1942, Derrida was expelled from the state-run Lycée Ben Aknoun in Algeria as a consequence of restrictions put on the number of Jewish children allowed in state-run schools, it was his subsequent enrollment at the Jewish Lycée Maïmonide, which he experienced as the most unbearable restriction, a kind of forced inscription, which "mirrored too symmetrically, that *corresponded* in truth to an *expulsion*."[4] Only the discovery of a vocation in philosophy provided an avenue of transformation and transportation to an affiliation with the *Métropole*. For Levinas, a philosophical education took him from Kovno, Lithuana, to the University of Strasbourg and brought him in touch with French culture and intellectual life, which he already associated with the emancipation of the Jews and the victory of "ethics over politics" in the Dreyfus affair. It was philosophical discourse itself that represented the means of translating the experience of the particular into universal terms.[5]

And yet for both Derrida and Levinas there were discourses external to philosophy that came to mediate their relation to the discipline in which both were trained. For Levinas, Judaism never ceased to be an important force in his life. His first professional position in Paris was working for the Alliance Israélite Universelle. Throughout the 1930s he published essays in the Alliance *Bulletin Intérieur* and in other Jewish publications. But, as we will see in the next chapter, the rise of National Socialism also sent him back to the Jewish tradition in ways that are not anticipated by his earliest publications on phenomenology.

For Derrida there was literature. From the beginning, Derrida resisted seeing himself purely within the discipline of philosophy, but came to his vocation in and through literature and his desire to find some way to integrate the two. As an adolescent he had first wanted to be a literary writer and only developed an interest in philosophy in his final year of lycée. Even then, his plan to study philosophy arose only when he discovered that, not having yet studied Greek, he was not eligible to try for the *agrégation de lettres.* His first role model was Sartre, particularly in so far as Sartre had managed to work both as a writer of literary fiction and as a philosopher.[6] As he told an interviewer many years later, "Without giving up on literary writing, I decided that philosophy was, professionally speaking, the better bet."[7] Following in the footsteps of Camus, a fellow Algerian who had become a Parisian intellectual, he decided to enroll in the *hypokhâgne* and to become himself an intellectual.

Thus when Derrida asked in his opening remarks, "What must a Jewish thinker be to use this language?" he was referring to a postwar history that began with Levinas's 1947 essay "Être Juif," a response to Sartre's *Réflexions sur la question juive.* One of Levinas's first essays published after the war, it is less than a dozen pages, but emerged from years in the *Lager* and contains many of the themes and concepts that would occupy him in his major works. In this brief essay he describes Jewish existence as the experience of being riveted to one's being, to an inescapable facticity. But, unlike Sartre, Levinas describes this not as a consequence of the gaze of the other but as the experience of election: "the least rag-seller who thinks himself 'liberated,' the intellectual who thinks himself an atheist, breathes still the mystery of his creation and his election. . . . An attachment to Judaism that remains when no particular idea warrants it any longer."[8] Derrida, who had fashioned himself according to the latter model, could have felt himself fingered by such a statement, called to find himself in its description. In drawing attention to the fractured sense of identity implied by Levinas's joke, told twenty years later, Derrida was also pointing to the dissonance between the joke and Levinas's earlier articulation of Jewish facticity, asking what kind of irony allows for both statements? But also how was he, Derrida, to respond to the earlier statement in "Être Juif," to the claim that, despite his own conceptualization of himself as an intellectual, perhaps even an atheist, despite his own volition, his own articulation of himself as a philosopher and a writer, despite leaving a Jewish community in Algeria where he had never felt at ease, according to Levinas "an attachment to Judaism" would always remain?

For Derrida the tension between these two statements was the tension that he negotiated in his own formulations of his Jewish identity through what he called the literary "comme si." Without denying either of Levinas's assertions, but mobilizing the space between them, Derrida formulated his own notion of the literary marrano, which upset the presumption of election not by denying the facticity of the experience of the call but by calling for a procedure that would suggest that it was "as if [*comme si*] the one who disavowed the most, who appeared to betray the dogmas of belonging" was the one who could *most* claim to be Jewish, to be "the least and the last of the Jews," as Derrida called himself in *Circumfessions* and elsewhere.[9]

In his talk at the colloquium Derrida emphasized both his proximity to Levinas and the sense in which his own formulations of his Jewish identity were reactions against Levinas, against the way in which Levinas's irony often aimed at solidifying alignments.

THE SON IS A PARASITE AS LITERATURE

In both Derrida's address to the colloquium and in the essay "Literature in Secret," published as the last section of *Donner la mort* one year later—a period in which Derrida was occupied by themes of betrayal and forgiveness—he describes moments in which Levinas used irony to solidify his connection to Derrida, and in both cases Derrida then mobilizes irony to betray those secrets.[10] In the process Derrida articulates the ways in which literature can be conceived as a discourse of forgiveness and establishes himself as Levinas's advocate, friend, betrayer, heir, and parasite.

"The Son is a parasite as Literature," Derrida wrote in "Literature in Secret." The straightforward reference in the context of the essay is to Franz Kafka and his "Letter to My Father." But there is another father/son narrative that resonates in Derrida's essay and throughout his late corpus, the story of another betrayal between father and son, one that situates Derrida as the son, as the parasite, as the site of literature, even, and Levinas as the father.

The role of paternity is key to Levinas's treatment of exteriority in his first magnum opus *Totality and Infinity* (1961), where it is considered under the theme of "fecundity," a category that Levinas opposes to the project. Where the project "emanates from a solitary head to illuminate and to comprehend . . . dissolves into light and converts exteriority into idea," fecundity, the son "comes to pass from beyond the possible, beyond projects," one "irreducible to the power over possibles" (*TI* 299, 267). Levinas thus considers paternity as a relation that allows for a true futurity, one not mastered by the subject, not describable in terms of one's potential or capacity. "Paternity is a relation with a stranger who while being Other," Levinas writes, "*is* me, a relation of the I with a self which yet is not me" (*TI* 309, 277). The relation with the son illustrates the self's chance for true transcendence, not a transcendence which would merely materialize the vision of the self, as in the work of art that I produce from my idea. The work of art would not be transcendent. The transcendent comes in the issuing of the son, who would be fully free of the issuer.

Derrida picks up on this theme from *Totality and Infinity* explicitly in an essay first published in *Textes pour Emmanuel Levinas* (1980), "En ce moment me voici." According to Derrida, the conceptual distinction between the son and the work cannot be maintained. Like the son, Derrida counters, the work too is and has a future, one that is not reducible to the "power over possibles," one that cannot be protected from contamination, from *la difference,* a term whose feminine form is already a response to Levinas's masculine description of paternity (*P* 193, 179). In 1980 Derrida develops the implication of this *gendered* difference. He enacts the work's independence by showing the way in which the differential function of language always escapes the intention of the author. Merely by replacing Levinas's name with his initials, EL, its vocalization issues in the pronoun "Elle." For Derrida, this "reading otherwise" is the outgrowth of Levinas's philosophy, the only Levinasian response to the gift of Levinas's text, but it issues, at the same time, from the very working of textuality itself, is "the very process of the trace insofar as it makes a work in a making-work"

(*P* 190, 177). For Derrida, the relation of the Son to the Father is also already the very movement of "the work" of textuality. In the text Derrida dramatizes this parallel by playing the role of the son/daughter and issuing a text whose betrayal, he suggests, is the only possible gesture of loyalty.

In 1992 *Gift of Death* marked a return to the theme of this parallel, a return to the relationship between text and paternity. The essay "Literature in Secret," in which the comment "The Son is a parasite as Literature" appears, was added as an addendum in 1999 to *Gift of Death*. But both developed from a 1991–1992 seminar on the theme of responding to the secret. While Levinas played a fairly central role in *Gift of Death*, his name is mentioned in "Literature in Secret," only in the context of an anecdote. The anecdote calls attention to itself insofar as Derrida oversignifies his efforts not to draw attention to it.

It appears within brackets and is prefaced with a disclaimer: "Although reporting this anecdote is not essential to what I am developing here . . . I remember how one day Levinas, in an aside, during a dissertation defense said to me, with a sort of sad humor and ironic protestation, 'Nowadays, when one says "God," one almost has to ask for forgiveness or excuse oneself: 'God,' if you'll pardon the expression'" (*DLM* 196; *GD* 148).

Derrida set up the comment so that it would be easy to dismiss, except that the phrase, "God, if you'll pardon the expression," is the essay's epigraph, under the title and after the subtitle, "an impossible filiation." As an epigraph it appears without quotes, disconnected from its context, an unattributed citation, a fragment. The essay "Literature in Secret" itself concerns the process by which a word spoken between two can become a quotation, a citation, and then a fragment. It considers what happens when a pledge or a secret is subject to representation. It argues that representation is always already a dissimulation and a betrayal of this relation. Explicitly at issue is the secret that stands between Abraham and Isaac in the Akedah, and the essay proposes that the story of Abraham's sacrifice of Isaac in the Hebrew Bible is already a betrayal of the pact between Abraham and God, as a recounting of what Abraham could not himself tell, what he could not tell Sarah or Isaac. It is the recounting of this story by a third party disseminated to anyone, for any reader.

This drift from covenant to narrative, from the second to the third person, Derrida argues, reveals the connection between modern fiction and the story of Abraham. Modern fiction is the inheritor of a biblical betrayal. Moreover it is something like a sequel, a repetition and reorientation of the religious fable. What separates it from the biblical testament is that it signifies a request for pardon, a pardon for the betrayal of representation. By treating what it represents as fiction, literature refuses to offer up the secret as something revealed. "Pardon de ne pas vouloir dire," or "Pardon for not meaning (to say)," this fragment, according to Derrida, is the formula at the heart of modern literature.

The suspension of the "vouloir dire" in language had been a theme of Derrida's since *La Voix et le phénomène* (1967). The "vouloir dire" or *Bedeutung* is for Derrida, through his reading of Husserl, that element of meaning that expresses the will of the speaker. Its absence correlates to the lack of an animating spirit or "the process of death at work in the signs" (*VP* 44, 34). Derrida's procedure in the text is to reverse the priority between Husserl's two concepts of the sign: expression and indication. Expression for Husserl, a sign with *vouloir dire,* a sign that means, is primary and indication, a sign devoid of intention, but not thus void of signification, is secondary. A close reading of *Logical Investigations I,* particularly of Husserl's description of self-presence, reveals, according to Derrida, that expression is in fact secondary and an effect of indication, thus calling into question the sign's capacity to ever act as a pure expression. Derrida proceeds through an analysis of the function of the "living voice" in Husserl. Here "fiction" is already implicated in the making of meaning, for in speaking to myself, through an internal voice, which should be the site of a pure presence, Husserl suggests that I must proceed by way of a fiction (*VP* 55, 42). Insofar as I speak to myself, I imagine that I use a sign, when in fact the very act of representation would be foreign to the perfect internal solitude of the self. Derrida argues that this necessary "fiction" around which "auto-affection" is imagined is indeed a fiction, but only insofar as he reverses the terms. The activity or movement of the self speaking to itself, which implies a self differing from itself, is the only means by which self-presence can be thought. "But this pure difference, which constitutes the self-presence of the living present, reintroduces into it originarily all the impurity that we had believed we were able to exclude from it" (*VP* 95, 73). The illusion is thus the pure interiority of a self-presence that doesn't involve *re*-presentation, rather than the obverse. At the basis of the speaking subject, thus, there is already what Derrida called "archi-writing," which "is at work in the origin of sense." This dynamic would then implicate the very system of signification, its "meaning" making, which would now be characterized by what Derrida names "supplementarity":

> The structure of supplementarity is very complex. Insofar as it is a supplement, the signifier does not first re-present merely the absent signified. It substitutes itself for another signifier, for another signifying order, which carries on another relation with the missing presence, another relation that is more valuable owing to the play of difference. . . . In this way the indication is not only the substitute which supplements the absence or the invisibility of the indicated. . . . The indicated also replaces another type of signifier, a signifier whose signified (the *Bedeutung*) is ideal.
>
> (*VP* 99, 75–76)

It would thus be fair to say that all discourse for Derrida is in fact supplementing an absence of *vouloir dire*. Thus to speak of the modern institution of literature is not to describe a dynamic of meaning that is any different from language in general. But modern literature provides a means of inhabiting this dynamic differently.[11] Literature says *Pardon* for not having a *vouloir dire*. How so? Fictional literature is characterized by its flaunting of any straightforward expression between the speaker and his *vouloir dire*. A fictional story recounts; it moves the relation between two to the plane of representation, where it becomes a relationship *for* a third. In this sense it inherits the biblical task of revealing the secret, yet alters it by presenting its material under new auspices (*DLM* 196; *GD* 148). The circulation of literature opens up the relationship between two to anyone who can pick up and read. But it replaces the covenantal call with content whose status has itself been called into question by the fact of its context itself having been disrupted. What is key in "Literature in Secret" is that this is a kind of repetition whose function is to undermine the dynamic of election without covering over its own problematic status as representation. At the same time, Derrida argues, literature reinstates the secret but on new ground, not as the site of a covenantal election, a between-two that can in fact be betrayed, but rather through an exposure to interpretation, and resignification, to a slippage in meaning that ironically guards its own secrecy by disrupting the relation between agent and meaning, such that the presumed vertical relation of revelation is replaced by a horizontal drift. As we've seen, this quality is intrinsic to language itself. Thus what marks literature is its avowed parasitic position. It sucks the life out of the covenantal structure of the biblical testament but feeds off its contractual ties.

According to Derrida's interpretation, then, literature is irrevocably tied to the religious testaments of the Abrahamic communities that function within their context as the ciphers of belonging. If, as Paul Ricoeur and André LaCoque have argued, "it is in interpreting the Scriptures in question that the community in question interprets itself," thus founding a dynamic of "mutual election" between community and text, then literature as its heir and betrayer would echo this structure but destabilize the dynamic of election at its heart by calling into question the very relations to the text that allow it to function canonically.[12] At stake in this shift is the function of the text's ironic dimension.

THE IRONIC DIMENSION

As I have already noted, Derrida was keen to highlight the irony at work in Levinas's texts at the same time that he used irony in his own work. But did they each understand and use irony in the same way?

Irony is a touchy subject, its definitions varied, its application and implications widely debated. It is invoked as an instrument of elitism and conservative communitarianism, the shield of the cultured insider, raised to ward off the riffraff and keep outsiders at bay. But it has also been deemed a weapon of subversive political unrest, the skeptic's sword, wielded to cut off both the believer and the rationalist at the knees. It can be a means of invoking intimacy, but also a stance suggesting distance and indifference. It has been viewed as a propaedeutic, a signpost on the way to virtue, and a vice, the calling card of every rogue.[13] The key to its potency as a trope, or the trope of tropes, is the way in which it brings into play the social dimension of linguistic meaning.

In his 1974 book, *The Rhetoric of Irony*, Wayne Booth attempted to refine our conception of irony by distinguishing between literary indeterminacy of all sorts and what he calls stable irony. Booth argues that "in contrast to the general modifications of meaning that all words in any literary context give to all other words in that context," a stable ironic utterance depends upon a tremendous level of understanding, trust, and confidence between the speaker and the audience.[14] For Booth, irony is "the key to the tightest bonds of friendship."[15] In fact, he suggests, one cannot even claim that irony is at work without a highly tuned dynamic of understanding between speaker and audience. For a statement to have an ironic meaning, the speaker or writer must intend something other than what she states; the listener must be able to reject the literal meaning of the statement, either because it lacks an internal logic or is at odds with the situation, with what the listener or reader knows about the speaker or writer. The reader must also reject other explanatory possibilities about the writer or the situation of communication, such as the explanation that the speaker is stupid, deluded, or misinformed. Without all of these features, argues Booth, what you have is not irony but misunderstanding. Irony is only activated in and through understanding; thus it is invoked as a kind of shared experience, a test, even, of a kind of social intimacy.

It follows from this definition that irony would be a tool of community maintenance and a means of community policing. The level of its success would serve as an indicator of social cohesiveness and shared values. Such an interpretation might lead one to believe that the political implications of irony are thus generally conservative, aimed toward maintaining the status quo. Linda Hutcheon, in her book *Irony's Edge*, notes that until the 1980s almost every scholarly treatment of irony identified it as a "conservative force, used to 'shore up the foundations of the established order.'"[16] Of course the same dynamics might equally be used to produce coherence within alternative communities, communities whose very definition involves resisting a hegemonic order. As Hutcheon maintains, "it is less that irony creates communities" than that preexistent "discursive communities . . . provide the context for both the deployment and attribution of irony." I would add that, like dye injected into the social body, irony can make visible certain connections and alliances that might otherwise function unseen. At the same time, however, it may also highlight differences and points of disagreement, for while irony is often used to activate a common bond, it is often also used at the expense of another. Satire, for example, one of irony's most potent forms, is just as much a tool of alienation as it is a means to shore up alliances. Northrop Frye, in the essay "The Nature of Satire," famously refers to it as "intellectual tear gas that breaks the nerves and paralyses the muscles of everyone in its vicinity, an acid that will corrode healthy as well as decayed tissues."[17]

In the case of Derrida and Levinas's two asides, we can risk assuming that Levinas was in fact attempting to cultivate the bond already established between himself and the young philosopher, twenty-five years his junior. In 1965 Derrida he had come to the conference as Levinas's guest, at least this is what Derrida suggests in 1998. They had met almost two years earlier when Derrida had begun attending Levinas's Tuesday night class at the Sorbonne. Derrida had come to the class, according to Benoît Peeters, with his own strategic motivations. Sometime in 1962, when Derrida was an *assistant* in general philosophy and logic at the Sorbonne, he had read Levinas's *Totality and Infinity* on Paul Ricoeur's recommendation. In the summer of 1963 he drafted the first version of "Violence and Metaphysics." It was the first essay devoted to Levinas's magnum opus, which had been published in 1961. In the months leading up to the essay's publication, Derrida began attending Levinas's class and, Peeters reports, "regularly going up to talk to him at the end." His intention, according to Peeters, was to prepare Levinas for what was coming.[18] For the essay, though full of admiration for Levinas, ultimately leverages some very powerful and cutting criticisms. Levinas, as Derrida must have known by then, had a reputation for his prickly nature. But, as he must also have known, Derrida was doing Levinas a great service, for as the first scholarly work devoted explicitly to Levinas it was "of decisive importance in raising Levinas's thought to the forefront of the philosophical scene."[19] Once the two began talking, often after Levinas's lectures, Derrida commenced sending Levinas his own essays. In the letter accompanying these essays he remarked on the peculiar nature of the two philosophers' proximity: "I feel, as always . . . as close to your thought and as far from it as it is possible to be; which is contradictory only in terms of what you call 'formal logic.'" The comment itself reflected both Derrida's scholarly position as well as the very nature of the ethical relation to the Other (*autrui*) that was the theme of *Totality and Infinity*. Only after Levinas had read some of Derrida's other work did Derrida send him the first part of "Violence and Metaphysics."[20] Levinas's response to Derrida's article was warm and gracious, even as it recognized the extent of the critique involved.

Already the role of irony was a touchstone between them. Levinas wrote: "I must tell you of my great admiration for the intellectual power deployed in these pages, so generous even when they are ironic and severe."[21]

From the beginning, the context of their relation was primarily philosophical. Nonetheless, both were far from fully established within the French philosophical community. Levinas did not receive a regular teaching position until the 1964–1965 school year, when he became *chargé d'enseignement* at Université de Poitiers and Derrida was in his last year as an *assistant* at the Sorbonne. But the commonality of their respective ties to Judaism was not absent from the relationship.

For Levinas, Derrida's Jewish background tied him to Levinas's other professional role within the Jewish community, as the director of the École normale israélite orientale and as a member of the colloquium, which was funded by the World Jewish Congress. Soon after Derrida began attending his course, Jacques Lazarus, a delegate for the French Section of the World Jewish Congress, wrote to Derrida's father, Aimé Derrida, to tell him that he had had the chance to tell Levinas about his son and Levinas's own work on Husserl.[22]

Thus, if, as Derrida suggested in 1998, it was at the bequest of Levinas that he attended the colloquium in 1965, we can imagine the aside shared with Derrida as an acknowledgment, on the one hand, of Derrida's own ambivalence in relation to the French Jewish community and, on the other, as an expression of solidarity that positioned Levinas at a distance from the colloquium in a comment marked by its detachment from the contemporary situation. The result was an expression of solidarity that, on the one hand, recognized Levinas's position within the community but, on the other hand, conveyed his capacity to see it *with* Derrida from a position on the margins. Ironically, this meant sharing for a moment in Derrida's own skepticism concerning Levinas's own project. At the moment that Levinas made this joke, he created a scenario in which the participants of the colloquium were its object by taking up the charge to respond to philosophical and political dilemmas with the resources of the Jewish tradition.

Arguably the most scathing critique in "Violence and Metaphysics" is that with which it closes, namely Derrida's argument that any claim to introduce a Hebrew propheticism into the Greek logos as an interruption is always destined to turn down the path toward Christianity:

The history in which the Greek logos is produced cannot be a happy accident providing grounds for understanding to those who understand eschatological prophecy, and to those who do not understand it at all. It cannot be
outside and *accidental* for any thought. The Greek miracle is not this or that,
such and such astonishing success; it is the impossibility for any thought ever
to treat its sages as "sages of the outside," according to the expression of Saint
John Chrysostom. I having proferred the *epekeina tes ousias*, in having recognized from its second word (for example, in the *Sophist*) that alterity had to
circulate at the origins of meaning, in welcoming alterity in general into the
heart of the logos, the Greek thought of Being forever has protected itself
against every absolutely *surprising* convocation.

(ED 227; WD 153)

When Levinas thus described André Neher's biblical interpretation and
his own Talmudic reading in Protestant and Catholic terms, he was, on the
one hand, noting that, like the Catholic tradition, he approached Scripture
through an apparatus and that, like the Lutheran tradition, Neher operated
with the motto of *sola scriptura*. But, on the other hand, he was granting
Derrida's own terms, that any attempt to introduce an exterior voice into the
Greek logos is inevitably domesticated.

But, of course, as is the nature with irony, its capacity to redouble itself
can never be dismissed, not even by Booth, who concedes in a footnote,
"Irony in itself opens up doubts as soon as its possibility enters our heads,
and there is no inherent reason for discontinuing the process of doubt at any
point short of infinity. . . . It is not irony but the desire to understand irony
that brings such a chain to a stop."[23] Thus a further reading beckons, one that
suggests that Levinas's ultimate rebuttal to Derrida's critique in "Violence
and Metaphysics" was in fact to invite him to the colloquium, as a fellow
Jewish philosopher, to confront him with the fact of Jewish intellectuals
working out a response to the Greek tradition. Could Derrida participate
in this meeting and still uphold his conviction that "Jewgreek is greekjew"? (*ED* 228; *WD* 153).[24] Was the irony then that Levinas meant exactly
the opposite of what he said, thus submitting Derrida himself to another
moment of conscription, one that would force Derrida to concede his own
position within the community and to recognize the validity of the colloquium's endeavor?

Conversely, the other anecdote Derrida tells in "Literature in Secret" concerns a moment during a dissertation defense, we can assume, at a later date, though none is given. Here the context is academic, institutional, philosophical. The irony in the comment "Nowadays, when one says 'God,' one almost has to ask for forgiveness or excuse oneself, 'Dieu,' passez-moi l'expression," is less contextual, for it plays on the idea that speaking God's name is to take it in vain, but suggests instead that, within the philosophical context, to introduce God into the picture is to introduce an inadmissible theological dimension. In this scenario, the fact that Derrida was the audience for this ironic comment, one whose irony is unmistakable, would replicate the experience of being on the margins of a community, but this time the community was philosophical. Levinas and Derrida, on the margins, shared in a skepticism concerning its secularity.

Dieu was clearly a word that resonated for Levinas and between Levinas and Derrida, as is evident in the eulogy Derrida gave for Levinas in 1996. It opens: "I knew that my voice would tremble at the moment of saying it, and especially saying it aloud, right there, before him, so close to him, pronouncing this word of *adieu*, this word à Dieu, which, in a certain sense, I get from him, a word that he will have taught me to think or pronounce otherwise" (*AEL* 11, 1). It is surprising in some ways that Derrida didn't tell the anecdote from "Literature in Secret" in the eulogy published in *Adieu*. It is the first place in which he tells the story of the colloquium, referring once again to Levinas's irony, though he did not develop its implications there. But reading the two together, the anecdote from "Literature in Secret" and the opening comments from *Adieu*, is revealing. For together they give new resonance to what it meant for Derrida to have pronounced the words à-Dieu, which Levinas taught him "to think or pronounce otherwise." Levinas's comment at the dissertation defense was the occasion, willed and unwilled, for him to speak the word *God* " aloud, right there before him" (*AEL* 11, 1) In the context of the eulogy it is clear that Derrida is expressing a debt of gratitude, one that he says at the close of the eulogy was "without regret." But it is also difficult to disregard Derrida's use of the phrase "Ma voix tremblerait." For while it is clear in that context—controlling one's emotion is a typical concern of the speaker at a eulogy—trembling is also a theme to which Derrida devoted considerable attention in *Gift of Death* (1992), where it is thematized as that which seems to call into question any act of etiology, any act of saying or pronouncing the word *Dieu*. "I tremble before what exceeds my seeing or and my knowing [*mon voir et mon savoir*] although it concerns the innermost parts of me. . . . In as much as it tends to undo both seeing and knowing, trembling is indeed an experience of secrecy or of mystery" (*DLM* 81; *GD* 55).

One criticism that Derrida was willing to make openly of Levinas was that he was not sensitive enough to the undecidability of what he disclosed through his phenomenology of the ethical encounter. He did not say, "Dieu, passez-moi l'expression." He used irony not as a means of destabilization but as a rhetorical tactic that seemed aimed at solidifying alliances and marking out distinctions in political and theological positions.[25]

While the topic of Levinas's relation to irony is merely mentioned in Derrida's 1980 essay, "En ce moment même dans cet ouvrage me voici," Derrida describes there both the importance of the interruption of thematization in Levinas's work as well as Levinas's attempts to maintain a kind of textual purity:

> Apparently, he likes the tear [*déchirure*] but he detests contamination. Yet what holds his writing in suspense is that one must welcome contamination, the *risk* of contamination, in enchaining the tears and regularly *mending and resuming them* within the philosophical text or tissue of a *récit*. This *mending resumption* [*reprise*] is even the condition on which what is beyond essence may keep its chance against the enveloping seam of the thematic or dialectical. The tear must be saved, and to do so one must play off seam against seam. The risk of contamination must be regularly accepted (in a series) in order for the noncontamination of the other by the rule of the same to still have a chance.
>
> (*P* 167, 162)

In the textual dynamics described here we can see both how and why irony would have been such an important rhetorical tool for Levinas as well as why it would serve as a means by which Derrida would himself "contaminate" Levinas's texts. As Derrida argues in "En ce moment," in order for the relation with the Other to inflect Levinas's text, Levinas requires a means of rending or interrupting the thematic flow of discourse. In order to signal that communication is always buttressed by what Levinas calls

"Le dire," the saying, the text must bear the marks of the ethical relation. Irony would be one means of inflecting the text with that relation. For, in order for irony to function, a meaning must appear that both crosses and supports the discursive plane. Or, as Derrida puts it, "one must play off seam against seam." However, such an endeavor can only take place at the risk of contamination; that risk of an ironic subversion of one's irony is one of the stakes of the game. Yet in Levinas's case the tension between these two, the necessity of risk and the fear of contamination, leaves behind a sardonic aftertaste.

In his eulogy for Levinas, Derrida referred to his irony as a kind of trademark: "the gentle irony, so familiar to us" (*AEL* 25, 12). But was it in fact so gentle? Others have attested to the contrary. Henri Atlan, for example, described Levinas in an interview for *Cahiers d'Etudes Lévinassiennes* as "very '*harif*' (sharp or hot), very acerbic in his critique of everything and everyone and very ironic."[26] Perhaps Derrida comment was itself ironic?

Levinas's irony appears consistently in essays that he wrote specifically for a Jewish audience. These texts, either originally given at the colloquium or similar events or published in Jewish (and occasionally Catholic) journals had a clearly defined intended audience. Often they had a strongly critical edge. Some were caustic in tone, especially if the target was Martin Heidegger, whom Levinas had introduced with fanfare to French audiences in the 1930s, only to become one of his most vocal and vicious critics after Heidegger's infamous 1935 rector's address. An ironic tone appears in the rhetorical questions that Levinas used to parrot (and then debunk) derogatory depictions of Judaism and when he parodied a position he found pedestrian or indulgent. Often his irony seems to be a means of demanding more of his listener or reader. For example, the essay "The State of Israel and the Religion of Israel," published in *Evidences*, a postwar French Jewish journal, Levinas begins, "The idea that Israel has a religious privilege is one that exasperates everyone. Some see it as unjustifiable pride, while to others it looks like an intolerable mystification which, in the name of a sublime destiny, robs us of earthly joys. To live like every other people on earth, with police and cinemas and cafés and newspapers—what glorious destiny!" (*DL* 323; *DF* 216).[27]

The passage concludes with an explanation point, the ultimate sarcastic signifier. The sarcasm is one means to undermine the perspective that Levinas wants to discredit.

We can associate this kind of irony with the Kierkegaardian/Socratic tradition and even view it as a kind of pedagogical tool. For Kierkegaard, the essence of irony is as a feature of the subject, not as a verbal trope. Its primary aspect is as a force of negation, as the "infinite absolute negativity . . . it does not negate this or that phenomenon; it is absolute, because that by virtue of which it negates is a higher something that still is not."[28] As a pedagogical dynamic, it functions to unmask the discrepancy between the real and the ideal by negating the surface reality and, in the process, baiting the student, luring him toward this negation as well, but without offering the assurance or security that he can align himself with the ideal. The ideal itself remains out of reach.

In one of the more vivid passages of *The Concept of Irony*, Kierkegaard describes the ironist as "the vampire who has sucked the blood of the lover and while doing so has fanned him cool, lulled him to sleep, and tormented him with troubled dreams."[29] Irony seems thus a three-step process that ends not in resolution but in desire. It invalidates the present reality, replacing it with the "fleeting but indescribable instant of understanding," which is then "immediately superseded by the anxiety of misunderstanding." One wants to be aligned with the teacher and the teacher's vision, fears being associated with the object of the teacher's ironic gaze, strives to stand with the teacher on the side of rectitude, only to realize that the assumption of mastery that such a move would commence *is* the object of irony. This technique has the effect, on the one hand, of catching the reader sympathizing with the Zeitgeist, but then of reinscribing her into the circle so that, after having been corrected, she can inhabit as well the ironic voice that distances her from "popular" opinion. However, the hearer can never be sure that she successfully occupies that position.

For Levinas, according to this dynamic, the Jewish perspective would thus serve as an interruption to and an agitation of the common culture, but would be effective as interruption only insofar as the reader is realigned in the process with the teacher's perspective. While this may inevitably fail, the result is a *desire* to find one's way to the ideal. This effect is clearest, perhaps, in Levinas's ironic rendition of Heidegger in "Heidegger, Gagarin and Us." "We must urgently defend against this century's technology. Man will lose his identity and become a cog in a vast machine. . . . No one will exist for himself [*pour soi*] . . . " "There is some truth in this declamation," Levinas

continues, only to further denounce this position later in the essay as attrib-
utable to the "pagan recesses of our Western souls," that part of us which
elevates the earth over the other human being (*DL* 347–51, *DF* 231–34).[30]

The reader must thus reject the position, which Levinas consistently
associated with Heidegger, and come to accuse as well "the pagan recesses"
that nonetheless have been attributed to all of us by Levinas's use of the
third-person plural pronoun—Levinas included.

In *A Case for Irony,* Jonathan Lear argues that this type of pedagogical
function is important for modern human life in order to excavate the gap
between pretense and aspiration. "When irony hits its mark, the person
who is its target has an uncanny experience that the demands of an ideal,
value, or identity to which he himself is already committed dramatically
transcend the received social understandings."[31] This for Lear is something
that one can deploy in oneself or cultivate in another as a means of striving
for human excellence.

Lear wants to hold onto the firm distinction between "real" irony and
a derivative irony, which would lead to "an expression of detachment and
lack of commitment rather than an expression of earnestness and commitment."[32] But such a view assumes that one can master one's irony. If there is
irony, and it does issue in the uncanny, couldn't it also function to unfix the
ideal itself? For if one is so sure that one's ideal *is* worthy of commitment,
is the ideal worth striving for, doesn't one risk becoming like Euthyphro in
Plato's dialogue, the one who assumes he *is* the one supposed to know?

As Paul de Man suggests, from its Greek origins the setup of the *alazon*
and the *eiron* resists any assertion of stability. For the minute he thinks
he knows, the minute he plays "the smart guy," he is sure to be shown up
as "the dumb guy," the *alazon*, the target of the *eiron*.[33] One can trace this
dynamic back to *Euthyphro*, in which the target is Euthyphro's certainty
that he knows what piety is. If we assume that Socrates has the answer
and is merely concealing it from Euthyphro, then the very dynamic for
which he faults Euthyphro, assuming that he has wisdom and everyone
else around him is a fool, is one for which Socrates would also be guilty.
Or, if we place ourselves on the side of Socrates as the one who knows
and we laugh along with him when he says of Euthyphro, "You say I make
[words] walk. But in fact it is you who are a good deal more skillful than
Daedalus, for you make them walk in circles," then we are in danger of

being the alazon and thus the butt of the text's joke, the outsider rather than the snugly and smugly complicit insider.[34]

Thus, according to de Man, even Wayne Booth is in danger of being the alazon—a charge de Man knows he can't levy without putting himself in danger of the same assignation. The point is that the ironic status of a discourse is intrinsically undecidable. As even Booth admits, "Any work can be revised, turning the three little pigs into the villians, the wolf into a tragic hero."[35] For Booth, however, cultivating such instability is permitted but ultimately not constructive, especially in comparison to the "rigorously controlled" process he describes under the rubric of "stable irony."

The use of irony for destabilizing purposes has been closely associated with both de Man and Derrida and was key to their relationship to one another as well as to the debate over the status of deconstruction itself. At issue is whether its ironic dimension declassifies it as philosophy. For de Man, the ironic dimension is a challenge to the philosophical operation, unsettling the discursive operation and putting literature as a form of writing that cultivates irony at odds with philosophy, even with those philosophers who want to locate in literature an alternative model of truth.[36] For some, this has been a means of dismissing deconstruction as unsuited to the pursuit of genuine philosophical inquiry. Both Richard Rorty and Hayden White in the 1970s and 1980s asserted as much in their critiques of Derrida.[37] Derrida proceeds to show how . . . "seeing through" is impossible," writes White. "But this disjunction of meaning from Being reveals the favored trope under which Derrida's philosophizing (or antiphilosophizing) takes place. This trope is catachresis, the *ironic* trope par excellence."[38] For White, this championing of false usage is a kind of philosophical sickness, the triumph of absurdist theory.[39] For Rorty, it is a matter of choosing the private over the public, a literary narcissism, which culminates in an endless hall of mirrors, over philosophy, which Rorty suggests, not without some irony himself, "is supposed to be made of sterner stuff and to stay out in the open."[40] While Rorty does not ultimately accept the distinction between philosophy as the public, serious, and political discourse and literature as the private, frivolous and apolitical domain, arguing himself for the role of literature as a means toward inculcating empathy and constructive self-doubt, both Rorty and White's response to Derridean irony maps onto a standard narrative in which irony would be a philosophical tool only insofar as it could be understood in Lear's terms as a propaedeutic, guiding both its target and its audience toward virtue. The peril associated with unstable irony is its supposed lack of orientation.[41] The fear is that a destabilizing irony implies a postmodern renunciation of public normativity.[42]

Thus, between our two forms of irony, one stable, the other destabilizing, we might seem to have two fairly poor options for political engagement: one in which the ironist depends on the stability of her meaning and uses it to establish a space of cohesion, but risks being misunderstood or having her interlocutor use her own irony against her; another in which one grants the instability of irony and embraces its destabilizing powers and thus reduces communication to play, and thus irrelevance. One might argue that Levinas's irony could be faulted for the former, and Derrida for the latter. But the latter is only problematic if we assume that the act of destabilization is ultimately one that necessarily dissolves into free play without limits and thus reduces discourse to a state of indeterminability. If the former irony is also a means of policing cultural boundaries and enforcing a communitarian ethic, might not its destabilization serve an emancipatory purpose?

If the target of irony is indeed the alazon, the one who thinks he has not only the answers but also the right to decide who is on the side of virtue and who is not, then the very fact of irony's destabilizing quality would make it a propaedeutic of another sort, one that operates counter to a will to domination, counter to a will of discrimination, and counter, indeed, to the logic of election, that concept so central to both Levinas's philosophical and Jewish writings, the tie, in fact, that seems to bind the two forms of writing together.[43]

Levinas himself participated in the presumption that Derrida's work ultimately devolves into the less serious aesthetic realm. It was the source of his strongest words against Derrida and a site of difference, which ultimately, he suggested, led to a parting of ways. Derrida, on the other hand, would insist on both his debt to Levinas and his gratitude, while, at the same time, revealing through his readings of Levinas that the dichotomy between stable irony and unstable irony cannot hold. What Levinas understood as a chiasmus, a crossing of the two thinkers, Derrida rethought in terms that imply further imbrication. As Derrida said at the colloquium, he was "close to Emmanuel Levinas, near him, perhaps together with him . . . turned toward him" (A184, 20). But it was, in fact, the very turn of literature that made this proximity a very knowing betrayal, one aimed to dislocate the communitarian tendencies of both Levinas specifically and "religion" generally.

THE CHAISMUS

Although Levinas could certainly be counted among the twentieth-century French philosophers critiquing the tradition of Western metaphysics, and arguing against a "totality which dominates Western philosophy," his critique was never at the expense of truth, but only in favor of an alternate source of truth (TI 5, 21). What was lamentable for Levinas about Derrida's philosophical project was its relentless drive toward subversion. In Levinas's 1973 essay on Derrida's *La Voix et le Phénomène*, "Tout autrement," he delineated his own critical project from Derrida's.

> The desertion of presence, carried out to the point of desertion of the true, to the point of meanings that are no longer held to respond to the summons of Knowledge. Truth is no longer at the level of eternal or omnitemporal truth—but this is a relativism beyond historicism's wildest dreams. An exile or casting adrift of Knowledge beyond skepticism, which remained enamored of truth, even if it did not feel itself capable of embracing it. Henceforth meanings do not converge on truth. Truth is not the main thing! [Ce n'est pas elle la grande affaire!]
>
> (*NP* 68; *PN* 57–58)

Once again we meet with the exclamation point, sarcasm used to reveal the absurdity of the position just outlined. How indeed could truth not be the main thing? Levinas demands in "Tout autrement." This essay continues the tradition of working out a relation of proximity and distance between the two. Like Derrida's "Violence and Metaphysics," it is simultaneously laudatory and scathing. It declares the radicality of Derrida's departure from the tradition, and then, just as Derrida resituated Levinas within the philosophical tradition, Levinas resituates Derrida within a long line of skeptics proper to the discipline of philosophy. Does Derrida represent a new Copernican Revolution, akin to Kant's, Levinas asks? "Is it a new break in the history of philosophy. It would also show its continuity. This history of philosophy is probably nothing but a growing awareness of the difficulty of thinking" (*NP* 65; *PN* 55).

That said, Levinas recognizes Derrida's accomplishment, declaring his "deconstruction" of Husserl devastating. "At the outset, everything is in place; after a few pages or paragraphs of formidable calling into question, nothing is left inhabitable for thought" (*NP* 66; *PN* 57).

But there is a double edge to this high compliment. For mustn't a thought be inhabitable if it is to represent a way forward? Even more ambivalent is the comment "This is, all philosophical significance aside, a purely literary effect, a new *frisson*, Derrida's poetry" (*NP* 66, *PN* 57). Even as it continues to serve Levinas as a source for philosophical reflection in the postwar era, as an end, literature is suspect.[44] It gives off the scent of a morbid frivolity. Eighteen years earlier, in an essay on Blanchot, Levinas had distanced himself from the literary vision as a response to philosophy's ills in similar terms. "The literary sphere into which Blanchot leads us . . . far from elucidating the world, exposes the desolate, lightless substratum underlying it, and restores to our sojourn its exotic essence, and to the wonders of our architecture, their function as makeshift desert shelters." This world, he continued, "is not nihilistic. But, in it, justice does not condition truth" (*NP* 66; *PN* 57). He went further with Derrida, comparing deconstruction to the 1940 exodus, an event that preoccupied Levinas throughout the war, appearing repeatedly in his journals as a moment that signified "not only the end of illusion, but the end of meaning, when meaning itself appeared as an illusion" (*CC* 132). Derrida's deconstruction of Husserl is like a military invasion, unforeseeable and ruinous: "everything is torn down [*déconstruit*] and left desolate: the houses closed up or abandoned with their doors open or emptied of their inhabitants" (*NP* 66; *PN* 57).

The implications are clear. Levinas didn't contest the validity of Derrida's deconstruction of Husserl, but he did wonder whether the metaphysics of presence, the edifice that Derrida tore down, hadn't been the intellectual foundation for civilization. Literature or poetry then would be akin to playing kick the can among the ruins.

In contrast, Levinas had already constructed a way forward, spied an alternate means to retain transcendence and thus truth while still critiquing the autonomous and transparent subject. Like Derrida, Levinas also found in Husserl's analysis of the sign, in the distinction between *expression* [*Ausdruck*] and *indication* [*Anzeichen*], a means for rethinking the metaphysics of presence. Already in 1964, in the essay "Meaning and Sense," Levinas, building off his discussion of signification in *Totality and Infinity*, mobilizes Husserl's distinction to rethink the notion of expression. For Levinas, the function of expression, which "hitherto was taken either to serve as means of communication or to transform the world in view of our needs,"[45] is now rethought as "a relationship with him to whom I express the expression and whose presence is already required for my cultural gesture of expression to be produced."[46] Expression finds its locus of meaning not in what is said but in the act of speaking to another.

The new locus of truth is the Other [*autrui*], not as one present to me, not as the site of a will I can decipher, but as a trace. In the concept of the trace, Husserl's two types of signs—expression [*Ausdruck*] and indication [*Anzeichen*]—converge. For if the meaning of the expression is the Other, the face of the Other also communicates as trace, which, like Husserl's conception of an indication, signifies without pointing to the willed intention of the speaker. The face of the other overflows my intention and points beyond itself to an absence. As trace, the face can be compared to "the fingerprints left by someone who wanted to wipe away his traces and carry out a perfect crime. He who left traces in wiping out his traces did not mean to say or do anything by the traces he left. He disturbed the order in an irreparable way. For he has passed absolutely."[47]

In "Meaning and Sense" Levinas developed this idea in a theological direction through the notion of *illeity*, such that the Other in his transcendence points toward "the God who passed" of Exodus 33. From an analysis of signification, the same source from which Derrida derives his conception of literature, Levinas derives a conception of religion.

Taking up in "Tout autrement" the passage in *La Voix et le phénomène* that states, "In fact, in real communicative, etc. discourse, expression yields its place to indication, because . . . the sense intended by another and, in a general way, the lived-experience of another are not and can never be present in person" (*VP* 99, 76), Levinas demands "whence the sign from which the presence that is lacking to itself is made, or the inassemblable diachrony from which creatureliness is made?" His answer, "It does not begin as a said," but comes from the Other. "What appears truly in deconstructive analysis as a lacking to self is not *the surplus* . . . but the *better* of proximity, an excellence, an elevation, the ethics of before being, or the Good beyond Being, to quote an ancient author" (*NP* 85; *PN* 61).

Thus, in "Tout autrement," Levinas offered his own answer to the question of the nature of the two thinker's proximity. Levinas and Derrida cross paths, in a chaismus at the site of their critique of the metaphysics of presence. But even this description we must read with a view to its irony. For their shared suspicion of presence itself entails the impossibility of the coincidence of meeting. For Levinas, this impossibility of coexistence points beyond, to the transcendence of an absent God. For Derrida, it incites a movement of deferral, one that is not devoid of ethical and political implications.

One of the most striking moments in *Voice and Phenomenon* is Derrida's analysis of Husserl's treatment of the first-person pronoun *I*. Derrida points out that particularly problematic for Husserl's prioritization of expression is the pronoun *I*. Despite the fact that it is supposed to indicate the site of the will, as an "essentially occasional" expression, one that must be reoriented "each time to the occasion, to the person who is speaking, or his situation," it marks a site for Husserl in which indication penetrates. Furthermore, to maintain its status as sign, the pronoun must stand in for a missing object of discourse. But if in this case that missing object is indeed myself as speaker, must I not then refer to my own absence? Thus, Derrida concludes, "writing is not able to come as added onto speech because as soon as speech awakens, writing has doubled it by animating it" (*VP* 108, 83). This element of discourse pointed Derrida toward a principle of hospitality such that language's repeatability must welcome what comes, whether in the form of death or the appearance of the stranger. From here it is not difficult to glimpse Derrida's path toward literature as a discourse that dislocates its relation to fact in order to welcome its occupation by anyone who "picks up and reads." But this is also a site that allows us to see in Levinas the importance of recognizing what he calls, in *Otherwise Than Being*, "le dire," "the saying."

One can almost conclude that Levinas was addressing Derrida when he wrote, in the opening pages of *Otherwise Than Being*, "Saying is precisely not a game. Anterior to the verbal signs that it conjugates, anterior to linguistic systems and to semantic glimmerings—a forward preceding languages [*avant-propos des langues*]—it is proximity of the one to the other, the commitment of approach, the one for the other" (*AEL* 17; *OTB* 5).[48]

He concedes that "the subordination of the saying to the said, to the linguistic system and to ontology is the price that manifestation demands" (*AEL* 17; *OTB* 6). The functioning of signs thus demands that the pronoun *I* refers indeed to the absence of the speaker, but, he insists, language permits us to utter, be it by betrayal, "this *outside of being*, this *ex-ception* to being, as though being's other were an event of being" (*AEL* 18; *OTB* 6). The act of speaking allows us to manifest the face-to-face relation in the act of speaking, to haunt the place of absence signified by the speaking *I* in a scandal that is the animating force of one person speaking to another.

This is not a dynamic that Derrida wished to deny, in fact he insisted, particularly in *Adieu,* on his deep respect for it.[49] At the same time his reading of Levinas illustrates that this dynamic always gives way to a speaking *for* another, or in the place of an other, a dynamic that Derrida himself named *hospitality,* a word that for Derrida in the French already contains the undecidability and interchangeability of the *hôte,* both the guest and the host. Derrida dramatizes this element of language in the *Adieu,* written a year after Levinas's death, by announcing his own intrusion into Levinas's discourse. Again and again we find phrases such as "Levinas never puts it this way" (*AEL* 67, 34) or "Levinas would probably not say it in this way, but could it not be argued that" (*AEL* 54, 25) or "Though Levinas never puts it in these terms, I will risk" (*AEL* 67, 33) What Derrida aimed to illustrate in these pages was that the "third arrives without waiting" (*AEL* 60–61, 29).

Picking up on the term *illeity,* which Levinas used to signal the absent God, the transcendence which returns truth to philosophy after the metaphysics of presence, Derrida exploits the ambiguity of the pronoun to suggest that this third person is always the other other, the absent other, the anyone toward which my discourse always points. What for Levinas is avowedly the scandal of the "the saying" is also a perjury—it implies a claim to be what it cannot be. Derrida already contends in *Voice and Phenomenon* that the *I* is always a perjury; every oath is already corrupted by the fact that I announce my own duplicity the moment that I speak. The implication of this reading on Levinas's thought would suggest that the face to face, even if granted as the scandalous return of expression into language, could never be purified of the drift of indication, of the third person who must be inferred by the occasional quality of language itself, that third person who can always take up and read.

THE LAST WORD

What we have shown so far in this opening chapter is that the proximity between Jacques Derrida and Emmanuel Levinas of which Derrida spoke at the 1998 Colloque des intellectuels juifs was both biographical and philosophical and that this manifested itself in a pointed use of irony on both their parts, even if for different purposes. Philosophically, Derrida and Levinas reached their closest proximity in their respective critiques of Husserl's analysis of signification in *Logical Investigations I*. In many ways this site was a crossroads, sending Derrida toward literary discourse and Levinas toward ethics and ultimately religion. But for Derrida religion and literature could not themselves be separated.

While the biographical and historical dimensions as well as the philosophical and political implications of each thinker's trajectories will be worked out in the coming chapters, what remains to be shown here is that Derrida imposed upon the image of the chiasmus, a further relation, a parasitic subversion that refuses to allow either Levinas or his religion to have the last word.

One can take this quite literally in the case of the 1980 essay "En ce moment même dans cet ouvrage me voici." This text, composed for a volume dedicated to Levinas, ends with a strange dialogue that emphasizes the dimension of address already present in the essay. We can read it as a gesture on Derrida's part toward investing the text with the dimension of the saying. Its very last word would appear to be a command, "Bois [drink]," which is also an act of service, a gesture for the other. However, given that the pronouns in the essay shift from masculine to feminine and the dramatization of the relationship between the speaker and the addressee, it is tempting to think that the speakers have shifted, that suddenly we do not know who is speaking or why. Simon Critchley imagines the scene as one interposed on the essay: "a woman and a man leaning over the grave;

the man, the older of the two, plunges his hands into the earth and takes his stillborn daughter in his arms: Bois [drink]."[50] The dialogue thus fits Derrida's own definition of literature in "Literature in Secret": "Literature would begin wherever one no longer knows who writes and who signs the narrative of the call" (*DLM* 179; *GD* 134).

But the dialogue can also be read as Derrida addressing Levinas and referring to the essay itself in which the dialogue appears: "—Here at this very moment I roll up the body of our interlaced voices faulty consonants vowels accents in this manuscript—I must put it in the earth for you—come bend down our gestures will have had the inconsolable slowness suitable to the gift as if it were necessary to delay the endless falling due of a repetition—it is our mute infant a girl perhaps of an incest stillborn to an incest promised one will never know." The final command that follows, "Bois," could be read otherwise, as a noun and thus *bois* would be translated as "wood," a wooden child, a stillborn. Earlier in the essay Derrida discusses Levinas's "The Name of God According to Some Talmudic Texts," in which Levinas describes the practice of burying a manuscript with a faulty spelling of God's name. If we follow that line, Derrida treats the text itself as their offspring, an incestuous offspring, given that Derrida positions himself as the son. Given that reading, Derrida repeats and distorts Levinas's text. *Bois,* the last word, could indeed indicate the wood pulp of the page, of the manuscript. But the metaphor of the graveside is so vivid that it seems to take over and replace the proper context of the essay.

As John Llewelyn points out in his reading of the passage, what the text dramatizes most clearly is the author's absence, that no one will assist me in getting to the definitive reading.[51] But this is also a gift and a responsibility for the reader, for whom it is left to be taken up and read, by another, by Critchley, Llewelyn, or me, reinvested with an alternative narrative, one in which the drift of indication disallows the last word.

In the position of the name of God, whose burial Levinas described in his Talmudic reading, and which Derrida cites in the essay, Derrida places the trace, *la trace,* about which we can imagine him saying to Levinas in the dialogue that concludes the text, "She does not speak the unnamed one yet you hear her better than me, before me."

For Derrida then, Levinas's work always demanded by its very principle, commentary, distortion, the parasitism of the other reader, of Derrida who performed the role of son implied by Levinas's notion of paternity. This point can be argued on multiple levels: 1. Every text, by the principle of textuality, demands to be read in such a way that its *vouloir dire* is always already compromised. Irony, in some sense, is always already at work. 2. Levinas's philosophy, his notion of the trace, implies the concept of hospitality and indeed requires it by the rigor of its own concepts. 3. Derrida's notion of literature, as the "pardon for not meaning to say," is the inheritor of a biblical covenant whose central concept is election, a principle that it betrays and in so doing asks for forgiveness for its constitutional betrayal. Finally, 4. for Derrida, it was this dynamic between the two thinkers that allowed him to relate to his own Judaism. By exploiting the fissures within Levinas's philosophy, he was able to disrupt its communitarian tendencies and use it as a site to work out a political vision predicated on the deconstructed remains of Levinas's philosophy.

ALL THE REST IS LITERATURE

Eighteen years after "En ce moment même," in 1998, Derrida once again considered the relationship between the name of God and Levinas's ethics by quoting one of Levinas's Talmudic readings, this one given in 1963, also at the colloquium, on the tractate Yoma. "The respect for the stranger and the sanctification of the name of the eternal form a strange equivalence. And all the rest is a dead letter. All the rest is literature. . . . The image of God is better honored in the right given to the stranger than in symbols. Universalism . . . bursts the letter apart, for it lay, explosive, within the letter" (*NTR* 27; *QLT* 61).[52]

Derrida does not quote this passage in order to discuss the role of literature in Levinas's texts but rather to argue that Levinas saw the connection between Jewish universalism and respect for the other. He quotes it in service of suggesting that there is a germ in Levinas's philosophy for understanding the very resistance to community inscription that Derrida felt so profoundly, particularly in Algeria in the 1940s. He quotes it counseling for a kind of vigilance: "Vigilance against all the risks of the 'living together' of the Jews, be they of a symbiotic type (naturalized, birth, blood, soil, nation) or conventional (state juridical, in the modern sense): a certain commu-nitarism, a certain Zionism, a certain nationalism and all that can follow as to the motifs of filiation through blood, appropriation of the place and the motif of election" (A 197, 29). That such a sentiment was far from Levinas's own stated concerns—Levinas who had devoted much of his energy in the postwar period to cultivating Jewish community allegiance, lauding the return by Jewish youth to studying Judaism's great books, arguing for the spiritual exigencies of Zionism—did not seem to trouble Derrida.[53] For the point of Derrida's misreading should now be clear: If, indeed, "all the rest is literature," literature is the space that Derrida chose to inhabit, and, in the meantime, he jostled the stable structures of meaning upon which Levinas depended, transforming Levinas's work *thus* into literature. His essay feeds off of Levinas as a "parasitism" or "vampirism," a process that Derrida describes at length in "Literature in Secret" as a procedure that Kafka himself performed on his father by way of the "Letter to My Father." "It is therefore in the name of the name of the father—a name that is para-lyzed, parasited, vampirized by what the son produces that almost amounts to literature" (*DLM* 185; *GD* 139).[54]

It is striking, in fact, that Derrida subtitles his essay at the colloquium, "a lesson." Levinas himself repeatedly refers to his Talmudic readings as "Les leçons Talmudique." Derrida thus only omitted the canonical referent in his own text, severing the context and thus ironizing the form. In fact, insofar as there is some kind of scriptural referent here, it is Levinas's own readings that occupy the canonical position.

By quoting Levinas's reading from the Babylonian Talmud, tractate Yoma, Derrida himself seems to be imitating and ironizing a rabbinic motif. For, like the rabbis who often quote only a fragment of a prooftext, leaving sometimes the most significant element of it implicit, Derrida too begins his citation of Levinas with an important omission. Levinas's paragraph begins, "To punish children for the faults of their parents is less dreadful than to tolerate impunity when the stranger is injured" (*QLT* 60–61). The child, according to Levinas's reading of the Talmud passage, *can* be held account-able for the sin of the parent. Or, as Derrida no doubt read this line, the child can and will be reinscribed into the tribe to the point of suffering.

Derrida saw himself in the context of both the colloquium and the Jew-ish community more broadly as the child who was held accountable against his will, an Isaac figure. This is a point he makes throughout his presentation at the colloquium. He refers to himself repeatedly as "the Jewish child" and as "the child of whom I speak," emphasizing thus, with his own characteristic irony, his forced inscription into the community and the fact that Lescourret, with her claim that Derrida would never appear at the meeting, had had him disowned (A 186, 195, 22, 27).

But, even as he resisted his reinscription into the community, I want to emphasize that there is a point upon which Levinas and Derrida agree: responsibility precedes accountability. Derrida, for all his distrust of identitarian politics, for all of his resistance to the language of election, agreed with Levinas that one always had to respond to the call of the other, to be responsible even before one has taken account of one's own volition. If this is the centerpiece of Levinasian ethics, then Derrida was its most adamant supporter. It is out of his loyalty to this Levinasian principle, in fact, that he called Levinas's community allegiances into question.

Derrida's point in the lecture given at the colloquium and elsewhere seems to be that without disavowing inscription one can occupy it differently. By mobilizing the element of betrayal that is already as proper to the covenantal relation as the act of inscription, one can activate the aporias that trouble Levinas and make him guard his texts; one can cultivate them and make them work deconstructively. For Derrida, that is exactly the role of literature: "inheritor and traitor," as he writes in "Literature in Secret," parodying the very form of covenant or contract, as every act of literature does according to Derrida:

> Be it understood that literature surely inherits from a holy history within which the Abrahamic moment remains the essential secret (and who would deny that literature remains a religious remainder [*reste un reste de religion*], a link and a relay for what is sacrosanct in a society without God?), but it also denies this history, this appurtenance, this heritage. It denies that affiliation. It betrays it in the double sense of the word: it is unfaithful to it, it breaks with it at the moment of manifesting its "truth" and of unveiling its secret. To know its own filiation: impossibile possibility. This "truth" rests on the condition of a denial whose possibility was already implied by the binding of Isaac.
>
> (*DLM* 208; *GD* 157)

Derrida doesn't refer to the role of irony in this description of literature's religious legacy, perhaps because the notion of irony has multiple trajectories—Socratic, Romantic, Kierkegaardian—some of which he treats in his work. Even in these brief references, however, and in their multiplicity, it is possible to locate a parallel between his claims for what literature does to the covenant and what irony does to its context. "Irony, in particular Socratic irony, consists in not saying anything, in not stating any knowledge, but it means doing that in order to interrogate, to have someone or something speak or think. *Eironeia* dissimulates; it is the act of questioning by feigning ignorance by pretending" (*DLM* 108; *GD* 77).

There is an affinity to the role of literature here: the disjunction from knowledge. Socratic irony, however, would imply that one is still the subject who knows, whose silence has depth and content, a secret that can be revealed. Derrida compares this irony to what Kierkegaard says about Abraham's irony when Isaac asks who will provide the lamb for the burnt offering: "His response to Isaac is in the form of irony, for it is always irony when I say something and still do not say anything."[55] But Abraham's irony, Derrida suggests is "metarhetorical." His is the silence of one who does not know. Nonethless, "his nonknowledge doesn't in any way suspend his own decision, which remains resolute." With the shift from Socratic irony to "metarhetorical" or "Abrahamic" irony, Derrida moved irony from a site of knowledge to nonknowledge. In the process, he situates irony as the condition par excellence of the subject faced with undecidability: "Such, in fact, is the paradoxical condition of every decision: it cannot be deduced from a form of knowledge of which it would simply be the effect, its conclusion or explication. It structurally breaches knowledge and is thus destined to nonmanifestation; a decision is, in the end, always secret" (*DLM* 109; *GD* 78). With this description he also ties himself to Hegel's description of irony in *The Philosophy of Right*, touched on briefly in *Glas*. Hegel's description of ironic consciousness, however, is tied to the subject's capacity to *transcend* the law, to "Virtuosity, Genius." Derrida, in contrast, associates the aporetic decision rather with an anarchic irony, which he links to Antigone, or "'the eternal irony' of the woman."[56]

It was in response to Rorty's accusation that Derrida's work devolves into literature that Derrida is in fact clearest both about the status of irony in his work and the role of literature. At the center of this discussion is the status of the quasi transcendental, the locution that Derrida applies, following Rodolphe Gasché, to his fundamental concepts, such as trace, difference, archi-writing. Derrida uses these concepts to account for the conditions of possibility of experience, and yet he does not assign them transcendental status because they are neither originary nor can they ever be isolated, but only register in their effects. "When I say that quasi-transcendentality is at once ironic and serious, I am being sincere," he writes.[57] And while such a statement in its irony certainly belied its expressed intention, it is clear that Derrida resists treating irony as Rorty does, as a means of disinvolving one-self from the political and philosophical stakes of one's claims. Rather it is a means of taking up one's responsibility. "It is in order to avoid empiricism, positivism and psychologism that it is endlessly necessary to renew transcen-dental questioning. But such questioning must be renewed in taking account of the possibility of fiction, of accidentality, and contingency, thereby ensur-ing that this new form of transcendental questioning only mimics the phan-tom of classical transcendental seriousness without renouncing that which, within this phantom constitutes an essential heritage."[58] This description maps onto the relation we have been tracing between Derrida and Levinas. It is out of a sense of devotion to the principle of election at the heart of Levinas's philosophy that Derrida mimicked it, ironized it, and betrayed it. In this passage, fiction is named as a possibility along the lines of the accidental and the contingent. But, additionally, as an "institution of recent invention," it represents an analogous procedure to irony for relating to the quasi transcendental. In the final pages of "Literature in Secret," Derrida describes literature as "a passive-and-active commitment not-to-be-able-to-mean-to-say," thus echoing his description of Abrahamic irony. Similarly, literature is not romantic freedom from commitment or obedience before the law but bondage to an aporetic reality.

Gift of Death is a text in which Derrida reads Levinas and Kierkegaard against each other in order to expose the aporia at the heart of the ethical relation, but also at the heart of any and every site of election. Can one respond to the demand of election or inscription—one cannot but respond, Derrida insists—and be faithful to the metarhetorical irony of Abraham's response to Isaac? For Derrida this is indeed the promise of literature and the obligation that Derrida took up as a means of expressing his fidelity to Levinas.

"What would literature have to do with the testamentary secret of this "pardon for not meaning (to say) . . . " with the inheritance of this promise and this betrayal, with the forswearing that haunts this oath?" Derrida asks in "Literature in Secret." Rephrased in ethical terms, this question asks, "how can one respond to the illeity that haunts every face-to-face relation?" Derrida's description of literature as "a link to and relay for what is sacrosanct in a society without God," which nonetheless "betrays it in the double sense of the word," is equally a description of Derrida's own relation to Levinas: a betrayal that is equally an act of fidelity.

The implications of this multilevel claim will be developed in what follows. This chapter is neither the first word nor the last on Levinas and Derrida and their relation to each other and to the categories of religion and literature. In the chapters that follow I consider how these categories came to hold their respective significances for Emmanuel Levinas and Jacques Derrida, but also the political implications of each thinker's respective commitments, Levinas's to Judaism *as* religion and Derrida's to literature. At the heart of their decisions, to choose one category over the other, to mobilize one against the other, to use irony in the service of one or the other are different conceptions indeed of what it meant inside and outside the Colloque des intellectual juifs de langue française to be a Jewish thinker. While the implications of such a choice might seem small, as I will show in what follows, their choices have much wider implications for us, not only for how we think about their respective legacies, both philosophical and political, but for how we think more broadly about the categories of religion and literature and their political functions going forward.

2

LEVINAS, LITERATURE,
AND THE RUIN OF THE WORLD

In 1975, eleven years after Derrida published "Violence and Metaphysics," Levinas declared poststructuralism the "ruin of the world." This new "philosophical literature," Levinas wrote "prefers to play with verbal signs rather than to take seriously the system registered in their said" (*EN* 76, 61). However, along with communicating a disgruntled impression that disorder had become the name of the game in politics as well as philosophy, Levinas saw an opportunity in this disorder for a truth perhaps older than the world. "In this rupture, and in this awakening, and in this expiation, and in this exaltation, the divine comedy of a transcendence beyond ontological positions unfolds." Instead of literature, Levinas suggested, the deconstruction of philosophy *could* expose what he would elsewhere call "religion" (*TI* 40, 64, 80, 30, 58, 79).

In making this claim, Levinas did not name Derrida, and he did not credit himself with the insight into a "transcendence beyond ontological positions." The essay was given at the first meeting of the Gabriel Marcel association, and Levinas's explicit purpose was to tie poststructuralism to an earlier twentieth-century movement, which, in critiquing idealist rationalism forty years earlier, had already welcomed in religion as philosophy's other. The essay thus credits Marcel and Jean Wahl as early witnesses to philosophy's end in France and treats them as inaugurators of its new beginnings. In so doing, Levinas framed the relationship between his own philosophy and poststructualism within a larger French philosophical conversation and presented Marcel and Wahl as his original counterparts.

He thus provides us with the outline of a narrative, one that begins with Marcel and Wahl and culminates with Levinas and Derrida's articulation of what constitutes the possible in this postmetaphysical world.

In 1975 the conversation, as Levinas himself asserts in his essay, was taking place after philosophy's closure, the death of God, and the end of the book. But the terms that defined these endings—philosophy, religion, and literature—lived on and continued to be mobilized with and against one another. Levinas and Derrida themselves never ceased to define and redefine them.[1] The very first engagement between these two thinkers in the pages of "Violence and Metaphysics" is already about the potential of religion and literature to occupy positions at the margins of philosophy. Our task in this chapter is thus to retrace the history of a conversation about the relationship between religion, literature, and philosophy. And with Levinas we must return to a historical moment that predates Derrida's arrival on the scene. We do this here not only to build up a sense of historical context but to show that when Derrida came to engage these terms implicitly and explicitly in relation to Levinas it was because Levinas himself had been using, thinking through, arguing about them in a milieu that was itself politically charged. The conversation between Derrida and Levinas, took place thus in the wake of a contest that Levinas had already fought. The very category of religion, I argue here, emerged in Levinas's work in and through a demand to think with many of his contemporaries, Wahl and Marcel among others, about the margins of philosophy and to insist sometimes with and sometimes against them on religion's exigency even after the death of God in a Europe rebuilding its cultural infrastructure after the deluge of World War II. Literature could perhaps reveal a subject with a different relation to power and agency, but only religion, Levinas argued, could ground reason in justice.

PHILOSOPHY BEFORE THE DELUGE

Levinas and Derrida can be situated at the end of a long line of Jews working in the discipline of philosophy in France. It is striking to consider that in the first decades of the twentieth century each of the three most prominent branches of French philosophy had assimilated Jews as their figure heads. Léon Brunschvicg, whose references to "religion" eschew Judaism for Hellenic and Christian sources, was the leading figure in French idealism (*DL* 73; *DF* 43);[2] Emile Durkheim, son of a rabbi, was the leader after Auguste Comte in French positivist thought; and Henri Bergson, whose Jewish background can perhaps only be detected in the vehemence of his rebellion against the legalist nature of Judaism, was the guiding light of spiritualism.[3]

One explanation for the prominence of assimilated Jews in French philosophy in the beginning of the twentieth century was the status of the discipline in the Third Republic. For idealists like Brunschvicg, the exactitude of reason was a replacement for religion.[4] Through its method of abstraction, Brunschvicg suggested, idealist philosophy could provide an ethic and an orientation. And, indeed, if philosophy could replace religion, if it could be the means to a shared humanist project, Jews could not only participate equally in this new faith, but could be its prophets, in and through their absolute willingness to divest themselves of any particularist allegiances. In this version of the quest for truth, wrote Brunschvicg when canvassed on the status of contemporary humanism, "we will be the worthy heirs to the Greeks only in so far as we succeed at being the contemporaries of our civilization as they were of theirs. What good is it to know how to read Plato, if one is incapable of understanding Einstein?"[5]

In the early years of his philosophical career, Levinas seemed to have found philosophy attractive for similar reasons, and he would, even after his philosophical ideals shifted, always praise Brunschvicg for his commitment to universalism, for what he saw as the selflessness or disinterestedness of that position. He seemed, furthermore, to feel buoyed by the position of Jews within philosophy's highest strata. In a 1986 interview with François Poirie, he credited the very mention of the Dreyfus affair by Maurice Pradines, a philosopher and early pioneer of psychology at the University of Strasbourg, with inclining him toward the study of philosophy. When asked why he chose to study philosophy, he replied, "You know among the Jews of Eastern Europe the name of Dreyfus was known everywhere. Old Jews with beards who had never seen a Latin letter in their life spoke of Zola as a saint. And then, suddenly, in front of me, a professor in the flesh chose this as an example."[6]

No doubt the strengthening of the discipline of philosophy was a direct response to the Third Republic's secularization of the state following the Dreyfus affair. If institutionalized religion was to be marginalized, it had to be replaced, the discipline of philosophy inculcated not through churches but through schools. It was to serve as religion's replacement.[7] It is no surprise, then, that the École normale supérieure, the *grande école* for training France's teachers, would rise to extraordinary national prominence during this period, or that philosophy would be its most prestigious discipline, or, in fact, that Jews seeking to cultivate and prove their identification with the nation-state would be inordinately attracted to its universalizing promise.[8] Yet it is all these factors that quickly made the discipline of philosophy and its professors the target of so much criticism in the post–World War I era.

Already during the Dreyfus affair the association between Jews and intellectuals was popularized by Maurice Barrès through his common designation of them as "Les déracineés" (1897). By World War I, the Dreyfusards were seen to have won and to have transformed French culture in the process. In his 1938 book, *De Jaurès a Léon Blum,* Hubert Bourgin associated the rise of socialism after the war with the prominence of the Dreyfusard generation within the École Normale Supérieure. He went as far as blaming the Jewish currents of the school for "the school's transformation and subversion."[9] Bourgin emphasized the Jewish commonality among France's leading intellectuals, describing Henri Berr and Durkheim's rabbinic physiognomy at length, as though it were evidence for their corrupting force,[10] and concluding that the socialist turn of the institution was the consequence of a kind of brilliant but nefarious domination by "des juifs réalistes."[11] Paul Nizan's 1932 *Les Chiens de garde* attacked the leading Jewish figures of philosophy on opposing grounds, not because of their manipulation of the discipline for the sake of politics but because of their very disdain for such pragmatic concerns, because of their dogged commitment to abstract universalism. While salvaging an approach to the discipline of philosophy that would proceed on materialist grounds, he attacked its leading figures for their propagation of the "myth of the mind."[12] As products of bourgeois philosophy, he argued, the philosophers of Paris fashioned "whatever myths this democracy may require."[13] Brunschvicg's idealism was one of his main targets: "Brunschvicg expounds his philosophy without ever mentioning that men suffer, that their private lives are often nothing but a welter of triv-ial, painful or calamitous episodes,"[14] Nizan wrote. But neither Durkheim nor Bergson were exempt from critique. Durkheim was credited with being the first "to produce with such efficiency" . . . "the idealogical ammunition for the defense of the status quo," and Bergson with easing the consciences of the bourgeoisie by allowing them the indulgence of thinking that they have a soul.[15] While Nizan did not directly attack any of the thinkers on the grounds of their religious background, it is clear that what the group had in common was that they were, as Pierre Birnbaum has dubbed a whole gener-ation of Jewish functionaries, "les fous de la République."[16]

By the early 1930s, critiques of academic philosophy began emerging from within philosophy's inner circles and from Jews within it as well. Levinas would come to share in those critiques. The inaugural issue of *Recherches Philosophiques* set itself up as a source for alternative approaches to the disci-pline of philosophy even as it included philosophical mainstays of the previ-ous generation on its *comité de patronage*.[17] In the opening *avertissement* the editors announced their interest in broadening the boundaries of the disci-pline. They acknowledged that the work might "waken" the "resistances" of its readers, but designated it as part of the journal's aim that readers test its theories with their own objections.[18]

The first article was Jean Wahl's introduction to *Vers le concret,* in which Wahl used William James, Alfred North Whitehead, and Gabriel Marcel to establish a countermodel to idealism and abstraction. Wahl was himself an assimilated Jew and would later attend the Colloque des intellectuels juifs de langue française after the war, but like Bergson before the war, he did not identify with Judaism and clearly found the Christian tradition a more compelling resource for his thought. The goal of his early writings was "to reinstate the power of the immediate."[19] This meant that religion as a source for experience that transcended the rational would have a new exigency. But it also involved a turn toward literature. For Wahl, mysticism was the model for thinking about a transcendence that did not resolve into totality or an empty idealism. But Wahl insisted that the model of the soul standing alone before a transcendent other was not exclusively theologi-cal. What he wanted to recuperate from mysticism was the subject's expe-rience of the Other as an experience of individuation. "Nature is no less mysterious than the God of the Orthodox," Wahl wrote in 1937.[20] He saw himself here echoing Heidegger, for whom "transcendence was first of all transcendence toward the world."[21] But in Heidegger, and in Jaspers as well, Wahl recognized "a nostalgia and echo of the religious" that they had not fully surpassed.[22] Existential philosophy was in danger of being too tightly bound to theology and of being too far detached from the concrete given. It was with this dynamic in mind that Wahl spoke of the metaphysical nature of poetry. Were not the artists, the poets, and the writers, Rimbaud, Hölderlin, or Van Gogh, better able to evoke the transcendent nature of existence?[23] Wahl, in asking this question, wanted to set up poetry and religion as two responses to the question of existence and thus to make room for *both* within the purview of an existentialist philosophy arising out of his readings of Kierkegaard, Nietzsche, and Heidegger.

While not as well remembered as many of his contemporaries and successors, Wahl was thus one of the prime agents in the transformation of philosophy in France, key in the articulation of existentialism as a movement and key to the role that literature and religion would play after the war. In Wahl's articulation, existentialism found its origins in Kierkegaard as a protest against Hegel. As a professor at the Sorbonne and a Normalien, he served as an intermediary between the marginal and foreign influences on French philosophy and its central establishments.[24] Levinas himself wrote of Wahl, "during half a century of teaching and research, [he] was the life force of the academic, extra-academic and even, to a degree, anti-academic philosophy" of France.[25]

Equally important to the shift in the philosophical scene of the decade preceding the war, but far more often credited, was Alexandre Kojève, whose famous 1930s seminars on Hegel brought German philosophy to the center stage of the French intellectual scene, making its mark on many of the key figures of twentieth-century France.[26] Although Kojève's reading of the *Phenomenology of Spirit* had a Marxist bent and focused explicitly on the master-slave dialectic, his lectures seemed to have inspired a myriad of philosophical/antiphilosophical approaches, which took combating the Hegelian system as their starting point. In certain versions of the attack, including Levinas's, Hegel's name became synonymous with philosophy and his teleological view of history, the ultimate idol to be deposed.

Levinas and Derrida were both strongly imprinted by the philosophical developments ensuing from Kojève's lectures, Levinas as a follower of the seminar and Derrida as a reader in the 1950s of the thinkers who emerged from the inner circle. Levinas in the 1930s was making his first public forays into Parisian philosophical spheres, establishing a friendship with Jean Wahl, publishing one of his first original essays, "De l'évasion," in the fifth volume of *Recherches Philosophiques,* and attending philosophical lectures, all while maintaining his day job for the Alliance Israélite Universelle.[27] For Derrida, a generation younger, these developments were equally important, but as an already established debate that would inform his earliest writings almost thirty years later.

Levinas in the 1930s was primarily known in Paris as an interpreter and translator of Heidegger and Husserl, but the foundations of his later projects were first laid down in the second half of the decade. The goal of this early work was not so distant from Wahl's: to use the resources of Husserlian and Heideggerian phenomenology to counter German idealism. While Wahl looked to other thinkers such as Whitehead and Kierkegaard for his resources, Levinas began the work of writing his own phenomenological accounts of lived existence. Levinas would always claim a stark distinction between his Jewish and philosophical writings, but during the 1930s that distinction was most clearly in place, with very few references to biblical and other Jewish sources in these early philosophical texts. Nonetheless, Levinas did not lose sight of what it meant to navigate this world as a Jew, nor of the history of that dynamic.

Even as Levinas came to define Judaism as a force of interruption to the philosophical tradition, he was not averse to invoking some of the same arguments as Hubert Bourgin to identify a kind of Jewish undercurrent in the thinking of the Third Republic's philosophers, and as a student at the University of Strasbourg in the mid 1920s, an immigrant who appealed for French citizenship, he seemed to have been attracted to philosophy for the same reasons that the previous generation of Jews found it so liberating. If, as David Carroll has argued, literature as a cultural form in prewar France was treated as an organic entity, linking language to history and territory, philosophy remained free of such regional particularism and thus represented the means to becoming European in the most cosmopolitan sense of the term.[28]

In his 1949 essay on Léon Brunschvicg, Levinas still found something laudable in the cosmopolitan ideal, even as it has been relegated by the war to the past. He presents Brunschvicg as a Jewish countermodel to the Zionist pioneer, seeing in his cosmopolitanism a justification for Diaspora. In Brunschvicg's commitment to social justice, which showed not "the slightest trace of a specifically Jewish" inclination (*DL* 76; *DF* 43), he finds, paradoxically, "the thought of a Jew" or at least one means of inhabiting that identity (*DL* 77; *DF* 45). "Assimilation," thus for Brunschvicg, "proceeded not from betrayal, but from adherence to a universal ideal to which he could lay claim outside of any particularism" (*DL* 76; *DF* 43).

After the war, Levinas no longer endorsed assimilation, but was nonetheless able to gloss it in positive terms by virtue of the fact that it was their commitment to universalism that made Brunschvicg and others of his generation the target of such ire in the 1930s. Here the dichotomy between the Hebraic and the Hellenic that Derrida later identifies in Levinas is not stable. What is clear is that Judaism is positioned as the site of the good whether as interruption to philosophy or its inspiration.

Even as Levinas's own deployment of the distinction between philosophy and religion shifted after the war, he continued to exhibit allegiance to the Jewish philosophers of the Third Republic. Durkheim, for example, is cited as a precursor for Levinas in *Totality and Infinity*. Insofar as "religion" in *Totality and Infinity* is defined as running counter to the realm of light, objectivity, vision, counter in particular to Heidegger, and thus on the side of the Hebraic, then Durkheim is positioned here as well. For where Heidegger, Levinas argues, subordinated intersubjectivity to the "horizon . . . proper to vision," Durkheim was thinking against this logic: "Durkheim already in one respect went beyond this optical interpretation of the relation with the other in characterizing society by religion. I relate to the Other who is not simply a part of a Whole, nor a singular instance of a concept. To reach the Other through the social is to reach him through the religious" (*TI* 64, 68). By defining religion in terms of the social, Durkheim paved the way for a description of "transcendence other than that of the objective" (*TI* 64, 68).

Even after the war, Levinas continued to invoke the assimilated generation of the Third Republic, to forge something of a tradition through a reinterpretation of their thought. But one thing was clear: in this new landscape they were proponents of a worldview that was no longer viable.[29] The relationship between Judaism and philosophy had to be modeled anew.

IN THE *LAGER*

Between the 1930s and 1950s, Levinas's thought underwent a profound shift as the war itself came to serve as a crucible for the development of his own characterization of Being as oppressive. Ironically, during this period the experience of oppression itself becomes the source of escape, when reconceived in religious terms. In developing this view, which would be fundamental to his later ethics, he did not only rely on Jewish prooftexts, but found in literary works, particularly those of French Catholic writers, sources for reconceptualizing the nature of suffering. At the same time, even as these sources seem to have been crucial to his thought, it is never *as literature* that they were valuable to him, but only as descriptions of reality that can and should be recast in more philosophical terms.

Levinas's own sensitivity to the relationship between philosophy, religion, and literature is already evident in his 1935 essay for *Recherches Philosophiques,* "De l'évasion." Here he focuses on preserving philosophy's priority.[30] Levinas's first full-fledged move toward the articulation of an original philosophical project, the essay treats the West's fixation on transcendence as its defining characteristic and primarily presents the portrait of this drama in philosophical terms, arguing that "the need for escape—whether filled with chimerical hopes or not, no matter!—leads us into the heart of philosophy." The essay thus presents literature and religion as poor accomplices in this narrative of failed escape. Levinas discounts the Romantics—Byron and Rousseau by name—as being merely symptomatic and mistaken in a belief that a heroic *I* can break the shackles of "the foreign reality that chokes it (*DE* 373; *OE* 49–50). This romanticism is thus complicit with a bourgeois mentality. At the same time, modern literature and literary criticism might seem to be at least the source for the discovery of Levinas's very theme of escape. He credits his literary contemporaries for the currency of the term itself, but nonetheless insists that literature serves here only as an expression of a cultural malaise, which philosophy grasps at a more fundamentally ontological level. Religion plays an analogous role as symptom: asceticism expresses "the fundamental event of our being: the need for escape" (*DE* 381; *OE* 60). Or, alternately, it too strives futilely for a solution in theology, in the contemplation of and ascendance toward the creator, "as though one could surpass being by approaching an activity or by imitating a work that led precisely to being" (*DE* 391; *OE* 72).

Yet the essay ends enigmatically with the clarion call to blaze a new trail: "It is a matter of getting out of being by a new path, at the risk of overturning certain notions that to common sense and the wisdom of nations seemed most evident" (*DE* 392, *OE* 73). One can only retrospectively wonder if Levinas was not already gesturing toward Judaism as that alternative means in contradistinction to "the wisdom of nations." The very term *the wisdom of nations* is a rabbinic idiom and suggests a contrast between the nations and Judaism and thus harkens to a different relationship between our three terms: religion, literature, and philosophy.[31] But Levinas did not begin to rethink their relation in earnest until the 1940s, during his captivity as a prisoner of war.

Thanks to the recent publication of Levinas's wartime journals, we now have new insight into the ways in which Levinas used sources in the years of his early philosophical germination. These seven notebooks composed between 1937 and 1948 include the period of Levinas's captivity from 1940 to 1945, first in Laval in Western France and then at Stalag 11B, near Hanover, Germany. A member of the French Army and thus protected by the uniform under the 1929 Geneva Convention, Levinas spent these years doing hard labor as a logger in a barrack reserved mostly for French Jewish prisoners.[32] Conditions were harsh, but even those prisoners of war marked as Jews from nations that the Germans deemed useful or from which they feared reprisals subsisted under better conditions than their peers in concentration camps.[33]

One striking feature of these notebooks is their abundance of literary citations, many of which reappear in Levinas's later works, often word for word. In the later works they are cited primarily as artful means of expressing the phenomena that Levinas is describing. Baudelaire expresses an ennui from which the heroic subject cannot escape, Dostoyevsky the experience of a radical guilt that precedes me. Macbeth's cry evinces the futility of suicide.[34] In the notebooks, however, they appear otherwise, as partners in a dialogue, as sources even for his philosophy.

The second notebook, which dates from the time of the captivity, opens with the closing line from the symbolist poet Henri de Régnier's poem "L'ennui," which itself might seem to express the theme of "De l'évasion": the weightiness of being. It describes a kind of longing for an oblivion that will not come and closes with the image of black water that resists one's every stroke, "a weighty river that is not Lethe" (*CC* 61). Levinas continues with notes on Racine's *Phèdre* and once again finds a confirmation that death is not treated here as an escape. "The crime of Phèdre makes visible the fact that she cannot hide. She has assumed the ineffaceable manner of existence. And tragedy is there. It is stronger than death" (*CC* 63). He continues on with Edgar Allan Poe, Ludovico Ariosto's *Roland furieux,* and Dostoyevsky's *Notes from Underground.* Interspersed with quotations and meditations on these texts is the development of a concept of a kind of redemption through the experience of being singled out or called by God, an inflection of the very experience of ennui, of the density of being by a religious resignification: "the happiness of suffering in suffering itself, in its election" (*CC* 64). Thinking with Jankélévitch's *L'alternative* (1938), Levinas reflects that such a redemption requires another. Without the other, the acceptance of suffering is "almost vanity, snobbery" (*CC* 68). He then develops this theme along both religious and literary lines, but in such a way that certain literary sources serve as a means to developing religious concepts.

Thus it is through biblical sources, but also with and against the literary texts of Catholic thinkers, such as Paul Claudel and Léon Bloy, that Levinas begins to formulate his notion of being Jewish. Ironically, this means that Levinas was reading the same sources as the right-wing thinkers of his era.[35] Seán Hand has noticed that at the same time Levinas was reading Bloy, less than fifty miles away, so was Ernst Jünger, the notorious nationalist writer, friend and correspondent of Carl Schmitt and Martin Heidegger.[36] Levinas even listed Alfred Rosenberg, the Nazi ideologue, as one of his objects of philosophical study. The function of all of these thinkers was to serve as a countermodel against which to theorize the nature of being Jewish. But this also entailed a reappropriation of the logic of Catholic-royalist thought, that is to say, a conception of identity built on tradition and heritage. From this point forward, Levinas rejected philosophy as the replacement of religion, as the site of spiritual guidance. Instead, his project entailed a rerooting of philosophy in a religious foundation, and ironically Catholic attempts to do the same provided an important and useful paradigm in this endeavor.

Even Joseph de Maistre played a role in Levinas's thought. Reading Alfred de Vigny's *Stello,* Levinas encountered his denunciation of de Maistre. He comments, "despite all [that is revolting] in de Maistre," there is a plane that goes beyond the subjective and objective that implies a theory of the substitution of suffering, which is paradoxically on the subjective plane and on the objective plane where this would be to misconstrue the subjective character of suffering. One arrives at the ideal plane that I am looking for "in the face of God." While Maistre's theory of substitution justifies the suffering of others, Levinas uses it in his journals to articulate a logic of election that transcends and overcomes the very correlation of guilt and suffering that would seem to be instrumental to Maistre's notion of expiation. Vigny quotes de Maistre: "The nations will continue to buy their salvation forever by the *substitution of expiatory suffering.*"[37] This paradigm is reoriented by Levinas so that this substitution can never be understood as the suffering of another for me, but only of mine for another.[38] In so doing, he later claims, in the essay "Useless Suffering," he overcomes the horror of theodicy. "The justification of the neighbor's pain is certainly the source of all immorality. Accusing oneself in suffering is undoubtedly the very turning back of the ego to itself. It is perhaps thus; and the for-the-other—the most upright relation to the Other—is the most profound adventure of subjectivity, its ultimate intimacy" (*EN* 109, 99). Thus, in a Christian theodicy at its most gruesome, Levinas found a source for an ethics that operates through a reversal of the very logic of theodicy. Through its reworking Levinas discovered a conception of being Jewish.

In commenting on Léon Bloy's letters to his fiancée from 1889–1890, Levinas explicitly highlighted what Bloy had done for Christianity, that he had, without constructing a system, provided an account of mystery in concrete lived experience. For Bloy, Levinas writes, "all of man is put in the categories of Catholicism. . . . While the rest of us remain on the surface of these categories, the Christian, in revealing the meaning of mystery and transcendence, lives these categories at a deeper level. . . . Same work is there to be done for Judaism" (*CC* 151). Bloy's treatment of Catholicism thus provides a model for Levinas in developing a notion of Jewish being.

However, Levinas reworked Bloy's aesthetic of suffering into an ethics. In Bloy the suffering exalted in his work is a feminine suffering, the impoverished prostitute, of whom Mary Magdalene is the archetype. Thus Bloy finds in certain women an instantiation of the theology of the suffering on the cross. In Levinas's journals and, after the war, in the 1947 essay "Être Juif," Levinas reversed the paradigm and suggested that Judaism's theology explicates its facticity. In the notebooks Levinas writes, "Js [Judaism] as category: or individual salvation becomes collective . . . the meaning of the nightmare. Immobile reality—absolutely strange. Night in plain day" (*CC* 86). But this individual move from the experience of election in suffering to the collective paradigm of Judaism can also be universalized and thus serve not only to describe Jewish existence but also as a means to rethink the human condition. As he put it in 1947: "Jewish existence is thus the fulfillment of the human condition as fact, personhood and freedom. And its entire originality consists in breaking with a world that is without origin and simply present. It is situated from the very start in a dimension that Sartre cannot comprehend. It is not situated there for theological reasons, but for reasons of experience. Its theology explicates its facticity" (EJ 263; BJ 210).

Ultimately, in *Otherwise Than Being*, Levinas uses a formulation derived from his description of being Jewish to define religion as a subjection to the Other inflected by God's illeity. In an early notebook he wrote, "In persecution I find the original sense of J[udaism], its original emotion . . . passivity pure by which I become the son of God" (*CC* 179). In *Otherwise Than Being*, then, religion is described in parallel terms: "It is the trace of a relationship with illeity that no unity of apperception grasps, ordering me to responsibility." We can thus trace a line connecting three moments: Levinas's interpretation of Catholic sources during the war, his formulation of Jewish being in 1947, and his definition of religion in *Otherwise Than Being*. This is not to say that the Catholic sources are necessary to the later thought, or to argue for their priority over Jewish sources, but only to reveal the connection between the comments from the notebooks and a mature expression of Levinas's thought.[39]

Given Levinas's initial project, especially as it was first formulated in *De l'évasion* and in *Existence and Existents,* to describe the emergence of the subject from the anonymity of existence, literature could have been, as it was for Sartre and Camus, more than a means to religion for Levinas. Levinas might have harnessed it as the avenue toward his analysis of sociality, as the means to develop a distinction between sociality and the engagement of the subject with objects. This distinction between the social relation and intentionality toward objects would not necessarily seem to necessitate the category of religion. Indeed, there are glimpses in the notebooks that Levinas considered such a possibility.

In the carnets Levinas identifies Marcel Proust's *À la recherche du temps perdu* as a key source for thinking through the dynamics of a social redemption from ennui. Levinas's first mention of Proust is as "the poet of the social—of the very fact that there is for me the other person." Proust reveals the other as other than object, as evanescent, "as a presence made of absence" (*CC* 72). Proust's vision of sociality seems to entice Levinas in its fixation on the inaccessible. Sociality for Proust takes the place of adventure, of the test, of the other novelistic guises of your standard novels. One could say the same for the Other in *Totality and Infinity,* and given his fixation on the Marcel-Albertine relation, may have provided the model for Levinas's conception of the feminine. When Levinas published his reflections on Proust in 1947, he went as far as saying "Proust's most profound teaching— if indeed poetry teaches—consists in situating the real in a relation with what forever remained other—with the other as absence and mystery. It consists in rediscovering this relation also within the very intimacy of the *I* and in inaugurating a dialectic that breaks definitively with Parmenides" (*NP* 122–23; *PN* 104–5).

Yet even as Proust represents another avenue for an exploration of alterity, there is also evidence that Proust may have provided an avenue toward describing sociality in religious terms. Proust himself repeatedly compares his own relation to the other of his desire with religious terminology. He refers to an unexpected response from a lover as a miracle, to the inner sanctum of a home and its supernatural activities. Social rituals are compared to a mass, and even his devotion to the Swanns he relates to a good Catholic's encounter with Ernest Renan's *Vie de Jesus.* Like the believer who comes into contact with a source of demystification, Marcel too must have "banished forever from . . . [his] mind" any corrupting influence.[40] While there is a certain irony in these comparisons, Proust performs a transposition of the ultimate site of mystery into the very being of the other.

Proust would thus be a resource for formulating a metaphysics that implies pluralism, one of the formulations Levinas gives his own project at the conclusion of *Totality and Infinity* (*TI* 322–23, 291–92). Yet when Proust appears in *Totality and Infinity* it is only as his description of a lady's sleeve provides an example of the role of the formal in art, of the facade, of a sensual mode of access fundamentality at odds with the face (*TI* 210, 192). Even in the 1947 essay, Levinas needs to discount the poetic or literary. To teach, literature must be redeemed by criticism.[41] This is a point that Levinas will make more explicitly in his early essays after the war, and there are notes from the later war years that gesture toward this position.

Already by the fourth wartime notebook, Levinas had begun to think methodologically about the relationship of literature to religion. Late in 1943 he wrote, "A literary work—a created world is only valued as the real world by the supernatural of which it leaves a margin and which it makes present: that is the meaning of the symbol and its function." Levinas expanded this notion into a theory of metaphor that was further worked out in his postwar notes and later given as a conference in early 1962 at Jean Wahl's Collège philosophique.

It is striking but not surprising that Levinas never published his paper on metaphor or developed his thinking into a publishable essay. He seems at odds with himself on the topic. On the one hand, metaphor offers a means to identifying transcendence in language. The essence of the metaphor is "the transfer of meaning," the capacity to go beyond the given. Levinas even hints that transcendence could not be understood without metaphor and describes God as the ultimate metaphor. On the other hand, Levinas is in the midst of developing a philosophy that argues transcendence is only possible through the face-to-face relation. Thus in his notes he writes, "How to reconcile my thesis: the speech act [la parole] dispossesses the one who speaks and the thesis the metaphor is the going beyond [dépassement] of signification. How to show that the power of verbal transcendence [du dépassement verbal] is placed in the relation with the Other?" (CC 242). By his 1962 conference, Levinas had solved this dilemma, but we might gather from the fact that he did not publish his thoughts on the topic that it continued to trouble him.

His solution in 1962: "The universally metaphoric quality of language and of signification attests, ipso facto, to the depreciation of transcendence inscribed in metaphor, the beyond itself which is there announced in itself does not represent for language the passage to an alterity that is completely other, for it would be an abstraction, an exit out of context that the universality of metaphor precisely contests. The universalization of metaphor is a condemnation of transcendence" (PS 337). If literary language findstranscendence everywhere; it finds it nowhere. It can all be reduced to play. Artistic life can not point the way to the transcendent. It remains "consequently a transcendence of pure game" (*PS* 338). He even seems to suggest that this element of art leads to the denouncement of religious transcendence. It is as though literature in its constant production of metaphor either fails to be able to see an escape from its game toward a real beyond or the literary arts reject it insofar as it would lead to a conception of art itself as impotence. Levinas then goes on to argue for a more fundamental conception of metaphor, one that transcends its role in signification: "the metaphor absolute" or the interlocutor as that which breaks through worldly signification (*PS* 340). Levinas thus credits metaphor for allowing us to think transcendence, then discounts it as a literary operation in order to rehabilitate the notion in terms that liberate it from the discursive element of signification. It is a feat that recalls Plato's banishing the artist from the republic even while depending on their craft for his own articulation of his political model. This will, of course, be Derrida's argument as well, and we can see in Levinas's fear that metaphor is mere play the early articulation of what would become his critique of Derrida. And yet the crossroads is also evident here, for it seems that Levinas depends on metaphor to reach transcendence.

Given Levinas's denunciation of literary or artistic craft, it is surprising that one further form of literary exploration evident in the wartime journals are Levinas's own literary exploits. When he listed his projects in the wartime notebooks, he divided them between philosophy, literature, and criticism. Proust was to form his critical project. Under philosophy he listed 1. being and nothingness, 2. time, 3. Rosenzweig, 4. Rosenberg. His literary project consisted of two novels of his own, notes for which are interspersed throughout the wartime notebooks. Fragments of the novels themselves are also in the archive and were published in the third volume of the *Oeuvres complètes*. The dating of their composition has not been definitively determined.[42] In his introduction to the volume containing the novels, Jean-Luc Nancy describes the ambiguity surrounding the very question of Levinas and literature as well as the question of the role of these novels as an element of Levinas's overall project. As he points out, the limited nature of Levinas's own engagement with literary themes sets him apart from his contemporaries: from Sartre, Blanchot, and Derrida, but also we can add from Wahl and Marcel At the same time, the fact that Levinas in fact *wrote* novels separates him from other interlocutors of his: from Derrida, Ricoeur, Husserl, Heidegger, and Rosenzweig (*ELP* 9–10).

The novels themselves seem to have provided him the opportunity to explore the wartime world *as* the nonethical world or, more precisely, the world from which social mores and the political structures undergirding morality had vanished. Levinas would later remember the fall of France in 1940 in exactly these terms, as the dropping away of all forms of culture. "There was no longer any measure to contain monstrosities," Levinas wrote in the essay "Honneur sans drapeau."[43] The image itself goes back to a passage from the notebooks: "The drapery which falls. The world which appears without its contors <naked?> . . . the fall of the drapery—the defeat. To describe in the scene of Alençon the rhythm of this fall. There was nothing left of the official. There was no more official" (*CC* 112).[44] This is the world of the novel that Levinas entitled "Triste Opulence" in the notes which refer to it in the wartime notebooks and "Eros" in the notebooks that contain its fragments. A world where "there was no more France [*plus de France*]. It had departed in a night like an immense circus tent, leaving a clearing strewn with debris" (*ELP* 43). This is the world to which he would much later compare Derrida's "philosophical literature." He even transcribed a scene from the novel into the later essay on Derrida. A barber gets drunk because nothing has any value anymore and, in a play on the old joke, the barber hangs a sign outside his door that says, "Demain on rase gratis," offering free shaves to passing soldiers, "and suddenly it was today" (*NP* 67; *PN* 56).[45] It is a world that has lost its meaning, yet also a world "from which all the fog had lifted. One reaches the things in themselves," Levinas wrote in the novel fragment. Here anything is possible, and Levinas even describes a scene of wanton abandon: erotic desire resurfaces in the forgotten corner of the trenches with a schoolgirl "feeling with joy reborn in him desire without ambiguity, without feeling, like purity itself" (*ELP* 44).

But the novel is not a sustained effort. It is fragmented, without developed characters, without a stable place or time, and ultimately the notebooks containing its fragments pass into philosophical reflection on eroticism, on being Jewish as suffering.

The second novel, entitled "La Dame de chez Wepler," also explores the theme of a world devoid of moral subjectivity, devoid of humanity, a man whose wife is hospitalized wanders around Paris during the war without direction, without purpose, and in this world the reading of literature, erotic desire, and the very experience of materiality in its weightiness—with its smells and close corridors—subsist unredeemed. Levinas's own literary attempts thus seem to confirm his view of literature itself, and the view he associates with Blanchot's novels that literature exposes the underside of being, but it cannot "break open the definitiveness of eternity." As Levinas put it in 1966, "Two beings locked in a room struggle with a fatality that brings them too close together or sets them too far apart to find a door. No novel, no poem—from the *Illiad* to *Rememberance of Things Past*—has done anything other than this" (*SB* 39; *PN* 147).

This claim concerning literature's futility, its reduction to immanence, developed already during the war from Levinas's own attraction to literature. It also determined his thinking against it. It is a critique that gained in its adamancy as Levinas discovered in the postwar context that the war had only elevated the importance of literature as a counterdiscipline to philosophy.

LITERATURE—AFTER THE DELUGE

One has merely to scan an array of philosophical and literary journals from 1946 to discover that the war was perceived as a profound break in the French philosophical tradition. Even when trends from the 1930s reappeared, they reappeared with the understanding that they had to be thought anew in light of a new historical reality. Jean Wahl's *Deucalion* provides a case in point.

The journal, which appeared for the first time in 1946, takes the flood as its central motif, but only by way of a Greek-Latin-French translation of the event. No doubt the biblical narrative resonates in the title, but Wahl chose to transpose it into a Greek mythological referent for the philosophical nature of the journal and for its humanist bent. The epigram itself is a retelling of the Greek myth by Stéphane Mallarmé by way of Ovid. In this version, instead of Noah as God's chosen one, Deucalion gives the orders, prays to Zeus, and brings back the human race by tossing stones, the bones of his mother behind him. The poem concludes, "The stones . . . became men and women and so began the hard life of labor which is ever since the lot of humanity." Wahl presented the journal as a kind of ground clearing.

He commenced the *présentation* by writing, "The upheavals in the midst of which we find ourselves are accompanied by profound modifications of thought, perhaps even its very essence. It is necessary to know what has disappeared and what has survived."[46] The journal begins with the presupposition that, insofar as they are to be reinterpreted, philosophical concepts will occur through philosophy's interaction with other human activities, literature and art in particular.[47] In this, existentialism is seen to lead the way.

Wahl was indeed one of the most explicit thinkers in the postwar moment to associate literature and religion, not only in *Deucalion* but also in a book of essays composed during the war and published in 1948.[48] As Wahl saw it, science had itself overturned the basic assumptions of classical mechanics; the categories of time and space had burst. The philosophies of Bergson, Heidegger, and Whitehead had attempted to respond. But what they missed was poetry's power to rewrite our sense of perception. The twentieth century was a moment like that of the romantics responding to Kant, yet again one saw the association of metaphysics and poetry. And poetry has the advantage of being able to manipulate the categories of time and space. In this sense it goes beyond metaphysics and is indeed a form of spiritual exercise.

It was in Wahl's *Deucalion* that Levinas published what would become the centerpiece of *Existence and Existents*, the essay "Il y a," a philosophical description that makes the atmosphere of the *Lager* an archetype for being. But, even as Levinas's essay was intended as a rebuttal to Heidegger, Heidegger was still clearly the central figure around which new thought would emerge. The journal includes an essay by Alphonse de Waehlens on Heidegger and Sartre, one by Wahl himself on Sartre's notion of nothingness, and an essay by Roland Caillois on time in Husserl and Heidegger. An emphasis on literature is notable by the second issue's inclusion of a poem by Wallace Stevens, with whom Wahl had become acquainted while teaching at Mount Holyoke College during the war, an essay on Kafka, and an essay by Levinas on Proust.[49] Georges Bataille contributed to the second issue of *Deucalion* as well, even as he began his own journal *Critique* in the same year, with a similarly international emphasis and a commitment to thinking together the philosophical, the literary, the political, the historical, and the economic. It was also clear in *Critique* that literature would allow philosophy to rethink its purview, with essays on Henry Miller, Sade, Kafka, the poet René Char, and Rilke.

The attention by philosophers to literature in the years immediately following the war is striking. Given the immanent concerns of food and energy shortages, war orphans, and the unearthing of Nazi atrocities, it might seem surprising that something as seemingly frivolous as literature would become such a point of concern, but the question of literature arose in the wake of a spiritual vacuum that made the reconstruction of culture as crucial as the rebuilding of political and physical infrastructure. The journals themselves make clear that France's postwar intellectuals set themselves the task of reimagining the human being in the wake of its destruction.[50] Levinas published in both *Les Temps Modernes* and *Deucalion* and was reviewed in *Critique*. Thus he was no doubt a part of this conversation. While he too saw the need to re-evaluate the function of culture and to rethink the position of rationality in our conception of the subject, he resisted the turn to literature and vocalized his objections. To understand how Levinas established his resistance and how and why he inserted Judaism, sometimes under the more general category of "religion," into this debate, we must consider all of the debate's angles.

WHAT IS LITERATURE?

Only the year before the publication of the first issue of *Deucalion*, Jean Paul Sartre, philosophy's most dominant voice by the end of the war, launched *Les Temps Modernes* out of the conviction that other journals, whatever their importance, were "inadequate to express the age we were living in."[51] Literature would be one of the primary means of this mission.

In the introduction to *Les Temps Modernes,* and in subsequent essays on the topic, Sartre presents literature as the instrument for creating a new mythology for a new era.[52] "Literature's only chance" is "Europe's chance, the chance of socialism, of peace, and of democracy . . . We must play it." The aims are linked. Literature would help forge this new world, even as its possibility was dependent on the emergence of peace and democracy. The very form of literature understood as an expression of embedded freedom would be the instantiation of these principles and ideals. Sartre's interests here are both political and philosophical. In the introduction to

Les Temps Modernes, Sartre insists that the journal itself will resist staking claims in terms of political parties, but he does not deny that there were clear political stakes to the essays ultimately collected under the title *Qu'est-ce que la littérature?* For Sartre argued that, by its very nature as an expression of the world in which the writer writes, literature is always already political. "The writer is *situated* in his time; every word he utters has reverberations. As does his silence. I hold Flaubert and Goncourt responsible for the repression that followed the Commune because they didn't write a line to prevent it," he declared.[53]

Sartre understood himself to be writing his manifesto at a crucial point in France's literary history. In the "Situation of the Writer in 1947" he traces out the previous fifty years, dividing it into three generations. The first were those that came of age before 1918 and forged a connection between literature and the bourgeoisie. Here Sartre writes of writers such as Claudel, Proust, and Gide, whom he groups with Barrès for Barrès's bourgeois version of a monarchist sensibility.[54] The second generation is best represented by the surrealists, whom Sartre attacks for an adolescent sensibility. The third generation is his own, for whom literature does not offer a means of escape or amusement but rather a means of reconstruction. "The flood has come. What remains to be destroyed?" he writes.[55] In this essay Sartre thus renders the history of the first half of the twentieth century as a history of literature, thus making its future literary too.

It is no surprise then that the question of literature's essence, its relation to philosophy, to ethics, and to politics, generated multiple responses. Among them were Georges Bataille's, Maurice Blanchot's, and Emmanuel Levinas's. It was the conversation between these three thinkers that determined Derrida's own position on literature and indeed his reading of Levinas. Bataille was one of Derrida's clear forerunners in raising the profile of literature as a means of resisting philosophy's hegemony. Sartre, in his series of essays on literature, disparages Bataille as a feeble echo of surrealism.[56] Perhaps this is because of the very threat he posed.[57] Bataille's journal *Critique* was *Les Temps Modernes*'s main rival. But Bataille would not be so easily dismissed. He became one of the key interlocuters in the debates that followed Sartre's essays. Suzanne Guerlac has argued that it is Bataille's conception of literature that largely shaped its later politicization in the 1960s in the journal *Tel Qel*.

In 1943 Bataille lauded poetry in terms starkly opposed to those for which Sartre championed literature after the war. Instead of functioning as "tools of useful acts," poetry performs a sacrifice "in which words are victims."[58] This is exactly what made poetry significant for Bataille as a spiritual practice.[59] It is a form of destruction and through that destruction a kind of rescue practice, a restoration. Like a horse put out to pasture, words can be released from service. "Poetry is only a havoc which restores. It gives to time, which eats away, that which a dull vanity removes from it; it dissipates the false pretenses of an ordered world."[60] It is by definition the antithesis of philosophical discourse insofar as it takes language out of its servitude to reason.

But part of what made it significant for Bataille is its vanity, for of course poetry can't fully succeed in the venture of sacrificing meaning; even in poetry words continue to mean, especially inasmuch as they become the object of critique. But this again is poetry's virtue, for if it fully succeeds it then replicates the structure of project. To be conceived as sacrifice, it has to fail. As Derrida puts it in the essay "From Restricted to General Economy," "The poetic or the ecstatic is that *in every discourse* which can open itself up to loss of its sense," but in so doing, he continues, "poetry risks letting itself be domesticated, 'subordinated' *better* than ever" (*ED* 384; *WD* 261; my emphasis).

Bataille first responded to Sartre's conception of engaged literature in the third issue of *Critique* in a review of Jacques Prévert's volume of poetry, *Paroles*. Here he aligns himself momentarily with Sartre's introduction to *Les Temps Modernes* with the desire to rescue literature from the rut into which it had fallen, to take it out of bourgeois circulation.[61] But, to the charge of irresponsibility that Sartre makes in the opening lines of his introduction, Bataille responds, "Poetry dresses in red, finds the anguished note . . . but it does not suffice to say to the poet, what event do you express . . . It expresses the event . . . it is change . . . it is nothing but the condition of change."[62] And he concludes, "In truth society is vulgar, made by men fleeing from themselves, and it hides itself under decoration. But poetry evokes this society not by being content to describe it: it is its negation."[63] Bataille thus places the political gesture of literature on a different plane. He insists that it is not through representation that it is relevant in the world as action, but through the negation of the referential dimension itself, as a kind of laying bare of what the very act of reference, of representation hides. Literature is thus seen to expose being as it precedes illumination.

It is on these grounds in fact that Bataille identified a point of alliance between Levinas's first major publication after the war, *De l'existence à l'existant*, and his own theorizing of literature. But in a move that Derrida's own analysis in "Violence and Metaphysics" later echoes, this is an alliance forged at the expense of Levinas's own expressed intentions. In *De l'existence à l'existant* Levinas in fact formulates an understanding of art that seems even to borrow from Bataille's own formulations. He describes painting and poetry as preserving exoticism insofar as they "removed from represented objects their servile function" (*EE* 89, 47). But Levinas associates this operation with returning materiality to an impersonal state, to the rustling of the *Il y a*. In this context art and poetry are identified with primitivism and against the hypostasis of the subject in subjectivity. Levinas did not laud the activity of the artist. Rather he told a coming-of-age story of the subject coming out of this primitive space into the illumination of subjectivity and finally moving toward the exteriority of the other. Levinas was not yet explicitly judgmental about literature or art in *Existence and Existents*. Yet Bataille recognized already a kind of rivalry in Levinas's work between art and religion before it had even explicitly appeared. It is this same rivalry that Derrida exploits in his own readings of Levinas.[64]

In a review essay in *Critique* Bataille focused on the description of the *Il y a* in the text. Levinas's attempt was to describe being in a different register than Heidegger did, as a kind of horrific rustling in which there is an absence of subject and object, an impersonal anonymous force of existence. Bataille here foreshadows Derrida's critique of Levinas in "Violence and Metaphysics" when he points out the very tension between the philosophical discourse in which Levinas writes and that which he describes: "Ultimately, the discourse that does not wish to oppose to the *there is* a sentence that speaks about it (which would distance it, due to the very fact that once enunciated, discourse limits the one who enunciates it to the clear world) ceasing to speak of it, therefore in order to reach it, translates an inability not to betray its intention by a mortal disorder."[65] But Bataille credits Levinas with seeing the link between art and literature and the *Il y a,* identifying art or poetry as that which "destroys the meaning of the thing," thus "returning it to the last silence: that which it reveals is matter and 'matter is the very fact of the *there is*."[66]

Bataille would thus seem to be developing points of consonance with Levinas. But, in fact, Bataille suggests, he cannot follow Levinas as far as he will go. For, first of all, if the *Il y a* is a space of nonknowledge, what is to allow us to read it as harrowing as opposed to ecstatic, anguished as opposed to joyful? Furthermore these states themselves can only be described in and through a recourse to "formal effects," among which are modern painting and surrealist art. But Levinas can only reach them from the outside.[67] What Levinas seemed to miss, Bataille suggests, is the *activity* itself of art and poetry, the fact that they aren't merely renderings of the world without subjects, but activities performed by subjects attracted by the prospect of dissolution, of letting go, of expenditure without return. Poetry is the "end of the one who knows," but it cannot reveal to us existence without existents, only the time of expenditure, the sacrifice of recompense.

The philosophy of existence has posited subjectivity, but it is to the extent that this positing necessarily implies the ruin of the subject posited that this philosophy is worthy of interest. Furthermore, it had to forge part of the way itself. Already the existence of the philosophy of Levinas is no longer that of the subject. It is existence given independently of all subject and object, although still approached by way of the subject. But the objective way introduces a decisive change: the servitude of the operations of knowledge—the substitution by philosophy of known existence (of an intellectual approach) for naked existence—arises at the very moment in which *intimacy* comes into play. The method poses in principle the impossibility of *knowing* the instant with which intimacy is identified. The outside is only given to knowledge by the fact of the appurtenance of things to duration. Thus it leaves open a chance to experience poetry or rapture, supposes a downfall and the suppression of knowledge, which are not given in anguish. *This is the sovereignty of poetry*—at the same time, a hatred of poetry *because it is not inaccessible.*[68]

This account of Levinas's philosophical project on the one hand locates it as a tremendous achievement, but unwittingly. Levinas reveals the subject's temptation for dissolution whether in religion or art. But rendering this dissolution means abandoning oneself to nonknowlege. "Nothing remains that is up to reason, but reason no longer renders an account of the fact of a world up to reason." Levinas's anxious efforts to distinguish a dissolution of the subject that would precede it in art from a dissolution of a subject in religion is, Bataille suggests, "an unavoidable necessity," an attempt at a kind of recuperation of meaning. "The futile—and guilty—aspect of crucial moments is justified—and is affirmed *as a face*."[69] Bataille thus affirms the immorality of art, but only by rendering the ethics of alterity as a kind of guilty effect of the temptation of dissolution.

Whether or not Levinas ever read the review, he only bolstered his attack on art after its appearance, working even harder to render a distinction between what he calls "religion" and art.

Three of Levinas's postwar essays take up this theme, two of which can be read as debates over Sartre's question, "What is literature?" The first is "L'autre dans Proust," published in *Deucalion* in 1947. Following from Levinas's wartime reading of Proust, it is the most positive of the three. Its disclaimer, "if indeed poetry teaches," becomes the argument for his next essay, "Reality and Its Shadow," in which Levinas argues that literature requires criticism to tear "the artist out of his irresponsibility" (*IH* 126; *UH* 90).

"Reality and Its Shadow" was published in *Les Temps Modernes* in November of 1948.[70] Levinas's very choice to publish the essay there suggests that he intended it as a response to Sartre, but it is perhaps also in response to Bataille, Jean Wahl, and later to Heidegger that Levinas felt it necessary to intensify his critique. "Reality and Its Shadow" develops the argument not explicitly in relation to literature but in relation to art. As Martin Jay argues, the insistence on the visual here is tied to a denigration of art in terms of image, a Jewish anti-iconic argument, which further solidifies the opposition between religion/Judaism and art/literature.[71] But in 1948 Levinas most explicitly accused Sartre—though not by name—of returning after the death of God to "artistic idolatry" when he came to see himself as both critic and artist, believing in his "mission as creator and revealer" (*IH* 127; *UH* 91).

The editors of *Les Temps Modernes* clearly understood Levinas's essay as a response to Sartre and prefaced it with a note suggesting that the essay showed that Levinas had only "partially considered Sartre's ideas on the engagement of literature."[72] In the essay Levinas argues that, in its essence, art is "dégagée" (*IH* 109; *UH* 77). "Does not the function of art consist in not understanding? The obscurity of art, does this not provide it with its very element and its achievement *sui generis*, foreign to the dialectic and the life of ideas?" (*IH* 109–10; *UH* 77).[73] Levinas goes on to further develop his argument from *Existence and Existents,* but also to engage Bataille's critique by insisting on the difference between transcendence and literary immanence. Transcendence, he argues, is defined by communication and understanding. "Isn't the function of art to not understand?" He asks rhetorically (*IH* 109–10; *UH* 77).[74]. If they are both on the margins of knowledge, their directionality is in tension. He seems thus to have accepted Bataille's account of poetry as a form of sacrifice, and to borrow from its definition as activity, when he writes, "To use theological terms that permit, however roughly, the definition of ideas with regard to current conceptions, we will say that art does not belong to the order of revelation. Nor does it belong to the order of creation, whose motion is pursued in exactly the opposite sense" (*IH* 110; *UH* 78). In distinguishing so adamantly between art and religion, Levinas not only refutes Bataille's reading of his project, he refutes what he sees as the cultural turn toward art. After denouncing art in perhaps his starkest terms, he acknowledges, at least obliquely, the way in which his own critique is an attack on the recent fascination for the aesthetic as a new route to the spiritual.[75] "It is outrageous to denounce the hypertrophy of art in our times, when almost everyone identifies it with spiritual life" (*IH* 125; *UH* 90).

One figure surprisingly unmentioned in *Reality and Its Shadow* is Maurice Blanchot. He was himself a prominent player in the "What is literature?" debate and Levinas's clearest intellectual fellow traveler, going back to their student days at University of Strasbourg.[76] Blanchot had himself directly responded to Sartre's essays in "La Règne animal de l'ésprit" and "La littérature et la droit à la mort" published in late 1947 and early 1948 in Bataille's journal *Critique*.[77]

Blanchot too proposed an aesthetics of disengagement or *désoeuvrement,* as he came to call it. His focus was more specifically on literature as opposed to art, and he developed its relation to what he called the neuter specifically in terms of Levinas's notion of the *il y a*. But for Blanchot the worklessness of literature is only to be denigrated as a means toward recognizing it as a form of resistance. "It is not a question of abusing literature, but rather of trying to understand it and to see why we can only understand it by disparaging it."[78] Staging an attack on Sartre for his attempt to co-opt writing as another form of meaningful activity in the Hegelian sense,

Blanchot found in writing a subject to be understood by Hegelian analysis, but harnessed against it. In his essay "Literature and the Right to Death," literature's nonpower is lauded for its resistance to instrumentality. Thus the analysis is developed in exactly the opposite direction from Sartre's description of writing as an expression of will and freedom, and yet his aims are no less political. As opposed to Sartre's definition of writing as instrument, "a means of extending one's hand to the highest branch,"[79] Blanchot offers us writing as Lazarus's stinking corpse.[80] Thus Blanchot too allies religion and literature.[81] But literature is not a parallel form of transcendence as it was for Wahl, rather it reveals death's immanence. Language's materiality points us toward what is left over after the concept emerges from my encounter with a particular object. It thus disrupts the productive movement of history. As Blanchot puts it, "by turning itself into an inability to reveal anything, literature is attempting to become the revelation of what revelation destroys."[82] To express this, Blanchot borrowed the terminology of Levinas's description of existence without existents, describing literature as "*my* consciousness *without me*, the radiant passivity of mineral substances, the lucidity of the depths of torpor."[83]

Blanchot, Bataille, and Levinas thus all align in an analysis of literature at odds with Sartre. But Bataille, Blanchot, and Sartre all align against Levinas in a rehabilitation of literature as a political and spiritual resource. For Sartre, literature is developed in the service of action, and for Bataille and Blanchot it is developed as resistance to work or project. For Blanchot, in particular, its political exigency emerges from its disruptive function, a disruption that is passive, disengaged from the working of force. It ruins action by introducing deceit and mystification into communication, and yet it does so with complete honesty. When lined up, "Reality and Its Shadow" and "Literature and the Right to Death" reveal a powerful consonance, but with opposing valorizations. Yet Blanchot and Levinas's friendship was clearly the source of these resonances. Levinas had himself quoted Blanchot's *Thomas the Obscure* in developing the notion of the *il y a,* and then Blanchot referenced the *il y a* in developing the relationship between literature and worklessness. Ironically it was exactly the social dynamic of such a textual relationship that redeemed it for Levinas. As he'd written in "Realité et son ombre," critique "integrates the inhuman work of the artist into the human world" (*IH* 126; *UH* 90). Art must be made to speak, as he elaborates in the 1949 essay on Michel Leiris's "The Transcendence of Words." Also published in *Les Temps Modernes*, in this essay Levinas argues, "criticism, which is the word of a living being speaking to a living being, brings the image in which art revels back to the fully real being. The language of critique takes us out of our dreams, of which artistic language is an integral part" (*HS* 202; *OS* 149).[84] Levinas's position on criticism points toward an ambivalence, a refusal to relinquish his own relationship to literature as source for philosophical analysis, while he at the same time pursues a strategy of vanquishing it as religion's rival. Blanchot provided the friendliest site to work out this rivalry, and Heidegger the unfriendliest.

AWAY FROM THE HEIDEGGERIAN WORLD

Heidegger's own turn to poetry had begun in the 1930s, not long after the rector's address. And, as Philippe Lacoue-Labarthe argues, it is tied intrinsically to the political project developed over the 1930s and 1940s.[85] Already in the "Origin of the Work of Art," Heidegger describes poetry as the "the fable of the unconcealment of beings," one that unfolds in and through history and thus is linked to the expression not only of individuals, but the expression and destiny of historical peoples.[86] To read Hölderlin, thus, was a national project, one tied to the enactment of a German ethos from which "mere residents of the soil" were excluded.[87] It is not surprising then that in his attempt to define himself against the thinker who he had himself helped to introduce to France in the late 1920s, Levinas would associate the poetic with the pagan and define himself insistently against it. Heidegger's work on poetry continued into the 1940s and 1950s with essays on the relation of poetry, language, and thought, which were in themselves a mature expression of Heidegger's "turn" away from philosophy toward "thinking. "During this same period, Heidegger's influence in France grew steadily. It was impossible to separate Sartre's existentialism from its Heideggerian roots, and after Sartre's famous 1946 essay, "Existentialism Is a Humanism," and Heidegger's epistolary response, published as "A Letter on Humanism," Heidegger furthermore became a resource for thinking against Sartre.[88] At the same time, this growing attraction was not without its ambivalence. *Les Temps Modernes* published two accounts of visits with Heidegger by seekers attempting to gauge his involvement with the Nazi Party. [89] The upshot, published in its fourth postwar issue in early 1946, was an attempt to salvage the thinking while condemning the thinker. "Occasionally philosophers are unfaithful to their best thinking when it comes to political decisions," the editors wrote in the preface, while insisting that one nonetheless needed to read the texts of this thinker to discover its vulnerabilities to political weakness.[90] The harshest of the two accounts concludes, "Whatever his genius, how could one not measure the contrast between the demands of his philosophy and the evasive attitude of "l'homme en situation"?[91] Jean Wahl, who, as a Jew, had himself taken refuge in New England during the war, gave a course on the thinker in 1946 and referred only once to Heidegger's political errors. "One can conclude [On est amené à dire] that Heidegger as a man was inferior to Heidegger as a politician, at least at a certain moment."[92]

Levinas, from the very beginning, did not take the same tack. He resisted the postwar French romance with a poetics infused by Heideggerian "thinking."[93] Thus, in 1956 in a review of Blanchot's *L'Espace littéraire*, Levinas took up the Parisian attraction to the post-turn Heidegger. "Everyone seems to think this century is the end of philosophy!" he wrote in one of his characteristically ironic passages (*SB* 9–10; *PN* 127). This has translated, he suggests, into an exaltation of submission, but to what? "A strange nothingness, that does not keep still but 'nihilates,' a silence gifted with speech, an essential speech even" (*SB* 10, *PN* 128). Levinas then points in the essay to the commonality between Heidegger and Blanchot, that they both name this speech as poetic or literary. Without explicitly allying himself with Blanchot, he describes Blanchot's project in terms consonant with his own attempts to grapple with alterity. "How can the other . . . appear, that is, be for someone without already losing its alterity and exteriority by that way of offering itself to view? How can there be appearing without power?" (*SB* 14; *PN* 130). Blanchot and Heidegger share in common an attempt to answer this question after the gods have departed and to find in the poetic or the literary the answer to that question. Literature is thus once again positioned as religion's replacement, one that, like Levinas's own writing on the encounter, reverses the direction of the gaze. "The gaze is seized by the work; the words look at the writer" (*SB* 16; *PN* 132). But what is disclosed by this reversal of power? Here is where Levinas marks the contrast between Blanchot and Heidegger and finds in Blanchot at least the occasion for a path forward. For Heidegger, poetry's disclosure is the "truth of being," and it shines (*SB* 19; *PN* 134). Blanchot's is a "nontruth," and its darkness is unwavering (*SB* 19; *PN* 134). This is its virtue, its capacity to uproot. Ironically through the same turn to literature, sometimes even to the same texts that Heidegger read, Rilke and Hölderlin, Blanchot led the exodus from "the Heideggerian universe," exposing a portrait of being that "call[s] us away from the Heideggerian world" (*SB* 26; *PN* 139). And yet, Levinas asks, is this enough? What can it show us? "Does not the poet, before the 'eternal streaming of the outside' hear the voices that call away from the Heideggerian world?" (*SB* 26, *PN* 139). Whose voices? Levinas will not say in positive terms. Instead he concludes by characterizing the Heideggerian world itself: the world where "man dwells poetically" is one in which "justice does not condition truth," one "which remains forever closed to certain texts, a score of centuries old, in which Amalek's existence prevents the integrity of the Divine Name—that is, precisely, the *truth of being*" (*SB* 26; *PN* 139).

While Levinas does not literally oppose religion to literature in this essay, we can nonetheless read it as a plea for another spiritual response to the death of God, another means of opposing the "*being able [à pouvoir]*" of philosophy (*SB* 16, *PN* 132). For Levinas, that response was religion. In claiming this term explicitly, Levinas was once again taking a stand against Heidegger. Heidegger's poetic turn, which, as Lacoue-Labarthe points out, involved its own sort of piety, was itself a response to the eclipse of religion, As Heidegger wrote in the 1946 essay "Why Poets?": "the default of God means that a God no longer gathers men and things to himself visibly and unmistakably and from this gathering ordains world-history and man's stay in it."[94] In place of religion, in place of this visible gathering together, Heidegger saw the vocation of the poet as the one who speaks not from a site of transcendence but from within the "destiny of the age," but speaks so that other men can listen. Thinking with the poet means entering into "a dialogue engaged with the history of being."[95] Poetry is thus religion's replacement, speaking the destiny of an era without claiming transcendence to it or an exigency outside of it, opposing as well the objectivizing voice of science. Poetry is a voice at risk, which nonetheless holds a relation to the holy, but as beckoning.

Against Heidegger Levinas doggedly insisted on maintaining the term *religion*. But Levinas reconfigured it idiosyncratically, maintaining the principle of transcendence, but in such a way that it was consistent with the death of God. Religion indeed thus came to mean for him, in *Totality and Infinity*, a justice that conditions truth.

RELIGION AFTER

It is something of a truism in Levinas studies that it was the Catholics who first discovered Levinas *as* philosopher. While this account undervalues his position within the postwar Jewish community as well as the prominence of his role in Jean Wahl's College de philosophie, it is nonetheless clear that, as Lescourret puts it, for those "practicing Religion *and* philosophy," the Catholics were the most prominent interlocutors for even a Jewish philosopher in France.[96] Levinas had himself made this conversation one of his prime political projects after the war. As he wrote in the preface to *Difficult Freedom*, "To find oneself a Jew in the wake of the Nazi massacres . . . meant once more taking up a position with regard to Christianity" (*DL* 10; *DF* xiii). While this new relation involved a reclaiming of Jewish sources from Christian interpretation and thus an effort to define the Jewish message, often against the Christian one, it is clear, as we've already seen from Levinas's wartime journals, that Levinas found the model, if not the resources, for his own project in Catholic sources. Moreover, it was in Emmanuel Mounier's personalism, Gabriel Marcel's Christian existentialism, and in the movements surrounding them that religion was most prominently represented in the first decade after World War II as a means of social and philosophical critique.

But it is also the case that more diffuse conceptions of religion were at play in postwar attempts to rethink and revalue the scope and nature of human activity and interaction. Bataille's journal *Critique,* which defined its mission expansively as "wanting to provide, insofar as it was possible, the least incomplete overview of the diverse activities of the human spirit," gave almost equal space to religious themes as it did to literature.[97] It included an essay on T. S. Eliot as spiritual poet and a review by Mircea Eliade suggesting that "Western philosophy maintained itself in a sort of 'provincialism,' which disallowed it from acceding to the other great currents of human thought (the primitive, the East, and the Far East)."[98] In a review essay concerning the relationship between religious ecstasy and intoxication, Bataille, clearly aligning his own project with the religious, writes that "the experience of intoxication defines the domain of religion . . . [It] is rightly tied to the overcoming of self, to the leap beyond the limit of the real."[99] The journal even allowed for an alliance between such an endeavor and those of theologians rethinking the church's potential role for the left. A review of Henri de Lubac's *Proudhon et le Christianisme* points toward de Lubac's attempt to establish commonalities between Pascalian antihumanism and Proudhon's antitheism, thus paving a way for a Christian response to social injustice, which began from a starting point of human humility.[100] Given, however, the historical associations between the Catholic Church and France's right-wing movements, as well as the dominance of the French Communist Party (PCF) after the war, the Catholic establishment had its work cut out for itself in defining a position that made it a legitimate interlocutor on the left.

The most prominent figure in the recalibration of Catholicism's position after the war was Emmanuel Mounier. Mounier's movement, personalism, and his journal, *Ésprit,* were themselves born of a reorientation of the Catholic mainstream in France after the Holy Office in 1926 placed the right Catholic review *Action française* on the index of books forbidden to Catholic readership.[101] In the power vacuum that opened up after right-wing leaders were ousted from positions of Church power in France, Mounier carved out a prominent position for himself and his journal by returning to Charles Péguy's opposition between *mystique* and *politique*. Despite having been the child of a pharmacist in Grenoble, Mounier followed in Péguy's footsteps and built his ethos by claiming humble peasant origins and developing a critique of bourgeois culture founded in a call for spiritual renewal.[102] Trying at first, with Jacques Maritain, to find a way for French Catholicism to position itself above politics, he ultimately cut a crooked path toward a leftist Catholic position through a two-decade long oscillation that took the journal *Esprit* and the movement from a centrist skepticsm of both right and left political poles into a semicollaborative relation with Vichy and ultimately toward an avowed leftist stance.[103] After the war, Mounier's journal became a major platform on the left, one that brought together and published prominent

Catholic figures such as Gabriel Marcel, Jean Lacroix, and Jean-Marie Domenach, along with Paul Ricouer, Maurice Merleau-Ponty, and Levinas. Even Louis Althusser was a significant figure at *Esprit* in his early years. Mounier's capacity to create conversations that linked Christian existentialism, phenomenology, Sartre's existentialism, and Marxism arose from his concern for movements and thinkers that were combating philosophical idealism and bourgeois liberalism. In the discourse of humanism, Mounier and other figures on the Catholic left, such as Domenach and Lacroix, were able to locate if not a common position for each of these groups then at least some common points of critique and a question that put Catholics, existentialists, and Marxists in conversation.[104] For Mounier, the importance of existentialism was its capacity to return religion's most powerful questions to the center of philosophical discussion. This was particularly crucial for Mounier after the "death of God," when people found themselves unmoored from tradition and religious infrastructure. For Mounier, "all religions, even if 'atheist,' contributed to the progress of personalism," that is to say to the protection of the person as a being of absolute value against the varying threats of modernity that sought to degrade it.[105]

One advantage that Christian existentialism in particular had in this battle and the larger cultural renegotiation of reason's autonomy was its appeal to mystery. The leading figure of Christian existentialism in France was Marcel, who was even credited with having coined the term *existentialism* in early 1943.[106] Marcel was a prominent member of Wahl's circle in the 1940s and one of the subjects of Wahl's *Vers le concret* (1932). In Marcel, Wahl found a fundamentally antisystematic thinker, a proponent of a philosophy of invocation, for whom metaphysics was not a dry objective philosophy. Rather, discoveries about the nature of being followed from the exigencies of the subject in Marcel's *Journal Métaphysique*, the structure of which, a series of dated meditations, reoriented the very form of what one understood by metaphysics. Marcel's work, too, crossed the lines between philosophy and the literary arts. He was also a playwright who found in the theater a means to explore the relationship between subjectivity and knowledge's capacity to "transcend objectivity."[107] A convert to Catholicism in 1929, Marcel was also one of Levinas's earliest Catholic theological interlocutors. In the 1930s it was at both Wahl's College and Marcel's Friday night salons that Levinas and Marcel first exchanged ideas about subjectivity and alterity and where Levinas had the chance to encounter Wladimir Jankélévitch, Jacques Maritain, and Eugène Minkowski. After his conversion to Catholicism in 1929, Marcel's work began to develop around the central node of mystery. Experience, he would argue in *On the Ontology of Mystery*, comes first, and thought and explication after, and only inadequately.[108] Marcel criticized the reduction of human existence to functions and sought to reveal and expose in existence that which was not reducible to function, that which called the human being, but to which no formulation could ever adequately respond.

In the postwar context Marcel's Christian existentialism offered an antidote to Sartre's formulation of human freedom as pure unfounded self-projection. Marcel described human transcendence "towards a supra-human experience," one that could not be claimed, possessed, or even understood by the subject.[109] Mounier contrasted the two visions of existentialism this way. For Christian existentialism,

> Individual liberty is surrounded and envisaged by a Being, who for not having the logical immobility of objectified substance overflows no less in all dimensions the outpouring of the individual existence. Freedom for him is an infinite sovereignity, but it is freedom before God or better in God ... [It] places action in a tension between a creative superabundance and a purifying meditation. For existentialism *inexistentialiste* [Sartre's existentialism] the tension is between an ethic of action for action's sake, indeterminate, passionate, that which the heroes of Malraux or Hemmingway try to exercise and an unavowed assent, almost a constraint, in the face of the necessity of the world, which means before the necessity of a world which is not necessary, the necessity of the absurd and the preposterous. Man, useless passion, cultivates action in vain.[110]

For Mounier, both Sartre's existentialism and Heidegger's philosophy of being offered no recourse to judge human action, no recourse to a transcendent plane of value. In contrast, Christian existentialism provided a vantage point above the fray. It emphasized human freedom, but placed it within the context of divine abundance and goodness.

Although neither Christian existentialism nor personalism is remembered as *the* dominant movement of the period, it is clear that in the late

1940s and early 1950s they held a powerful hold on the minds of many young intellectuals in France attracted by the capacity to furnish a site of historical critique, one that distanced itself from the right, but nonetheless held onto its prewar suspicion of liberalism and capitalism without succumbing to Marxist determinism. As numerous historians have shown, there was even a kind of fluidity in the late 1940s between the Catholic, Marxist, and existentialist positions, before battle lines were drawn by the 1949 papal decree that excommunicated members of the Communist Party.[111]

While Levinas never fully denounced Marx, stressing on multiple occasions the materialist elements of his own thought, Levinas insisted with the Christian existentialists on the fundamental need for thinking of transcendence against the heteronomy of reason, but also specifically in the postwar context, when it was imperative to find a site of judgment rooted outside history. His championing of "religion" over against "literature" was a means of staking a claim on one side of contemporary debates about the power of reason, the extent of human freedom, and the source of our powers for moral and political judgment.

On the one hand this meant aligning with the dominant Catholic thinkers of his day, but often it also meant defining religion in such a way that Christianity would always fall short for not providing a conception of transcendence that broke with logos or with being. In a 1971 review of Jean Lacroix's *La crise intellectuelle du catholicisme français* (1970), *Le sens de l'athéisme moderne* (1970), and *Spinoza et le problème du salut* (1970), Levinas considered the capacity of an apologetic Catholicism to provide a conception of religion that was not complicit with philosophy's hegemony. The review, which treats Lacroix's books as separate prongs in a single argument, can be read as a summary diagnosis and ultimately a dismissal of the Catholic foray into debates over humanism. Lacroix, one of the pioneers of socialist humanism, was himself one of the founding members of *Esprit*, the philosophy columnist for *Le Monde,* and one of the major proponents of dialogue between the Catholic and non-Catholic left; he thus served effectively as a mascot for a movement that by 1970 had clearly run its course.[112]

By 1970, the left-leaning Catholics had a new profile and a renewed cultural legitimacy subsequent to the Second Vatican Council, for which many of the left-leaning French intellectuals had been instrumental.[113] At the same time, in the aftermath of May 1968, they faced a new leftist student politics and a new intellectual challenge in structuralist antihumanist arguments coming from the human sciences.[114] In response to these events, Lacroix argued for a renewed synthesis of reason and faith, "the resurgence of a state of mind that we have perhaps not seen since Saint Thomas Aquinas," as Levinas described it (*NP* 99; *PN* 85).[115] This position *seemed* at least like a reversal, Levinas suggests. "M. Jean Lacroix formerly contemplated a philosophy of insufficiency, or a necessary insufficiency of philosophy, which was to leave a place for faith. He now believes that position untenable, and that one must, in philosophy, go on to the end" (*NP* 103; *PN* 89). Lacroix thus tried to think a Spinozist theology. Levinas does not lament this shift in position so much as he points to its fundamental consonance with the Christian existentialism of the past. His point is that a theology of being is always already in cahoots with logos. Whether in Marcel or in the move of Jean Beaufret toward Heidegger's philosophy of being, Levinas saw only totality. "Does not there exist for modern consciousness . . . an alternative that does not come down to a choice between reason and incommunicable meaning, between theology and mysticism?" Levinas asked (*NP* 99–100; *PN* 86).

Two alternatives present themselves, Levinas suggested. One was literary. In a move that echoes Levinas's opposition between Blanchot and Heidegger in "The Poet's Vision," Levinas turns to Blanchot's analysis of literature to suggest an ominous force within or behind "totalized totality." He goes as far as pointing toward literature's disruption of logos. "Transcendence, in contemporary poetry (but probably perennially) may disrupt and bewilder *apophansis*, which is unable to embrace its *epos* in terms that, delayed in relation to their writing [*écriture*] do not rejoin their identity" (*NP* 100; *PN* 86). Literature is thus raised as an interruption, an antithesis to Lacroix's religio-philosophical synthesis. But Levinas only raises it here to supersede it. Only a *religious* transcendence can provide interruption without becoming taxed by nihilism, he insists in the following paragraph. In what could be read as him a co-opting and reorienting himself to Derrida's "Violence and Metaphysics," Levinas writes,

> Literature, writing, ataxia, audacity proximity: these are not experiences of literature, disorder or proximity. Experience would still be knowledge, still opening on being, already ontology, already philosophy, already totalization.

Transcendence arises again, from behind every experience of transcendence, which tries to surround, circumscribe, fasten or bring transcendence. For this binding, the cord is not too short or too frayed. But the concern here is with meanings that arouse totally different shivers [*frémissements*] of the human.

(*NP* 101; *PN* 87)

In "Violence and Metaphysics" Derrida argues that Levinas's own resorting to the terminology of empiricism and thus to experience cannot extract him from the metaphysics of presence. Here Levinas makes the same argument about literature. Two years later he referred to Derrida's *frisson*, his poetry as another form of disruption. Here he wants to distinguish between a shivering or a quaking, a φρικη, that is literary from one that is religious (*NP* 101; *PN* 87).[116] He thus confirms the religious way, but rejects both a Spinozist philosophy of substance "in itself and . . . conceived through itself" and a theology of being, which placed "however high, would not prevent its immediate agglutination [*s'agglutine*] to the totality it transcends." The only manifestation of transcendence left standing is "the excessive expenditure of the human, in *the-one-for-the-other*, destroying the balance of accounts" (*NP* 101; *PN* 88). Only a religion understood as ethics can disrupt economy. Levinas thus reclaimed the banner of antihumanism not to side with Foucault or Derrida but to suggest that in the wake of an antihumanist critique of autonomy "that denies the *I* that takes its own security for an ontology" one might find another form of heteronomy (*NP* 102; *PN* 88).

Thus in the essay on Lacroix, Levinas sided, at least momentarily, with those ruiners of the world, if only to discredit the trajectory of Christian existentialism, whereas in his 1975 essay on Marcel, with which we began, he situates himself, at least momentarily, with the Christian existentialists in order to suggest that poststructuralism had lost sight of religion.

RELIGION OR JUDAISM?

Throughout this chapter I have sought to establish Levinas's discourse concerning both religion and literature as a part of a historical and cultural conversation about how to upset philosophical ontology. This establishes that the debate between Levinas and Derrida was already an intervention in an ongoing conversation and shows how Levinas's choice for religion was distinctly a choice against literature. For Levinas, formulating his relationship to the discourse of philosophy was always a matter of a choice between an above and a below. As Levinas himself put it in an essay on Jeanne Delhomme: "It is as if behind being [*l'être*], one could hear the sarcastic laughter of irresponsibility, for which the freedom within being is not free enough; but beyond being [*l'essence*] there would extend the goodness of unbounded responsibility, for which that freedom is not generous enough" (*NP* 58; *PN* 54). Thus, for Levinas, the choice between literature and religion was a choice between upsetting the hegemony of the autonomous I by embracing its nether regions, of embracing a world in which "everything is permitted," or choosing justice. The choice was thus a political choice between chaos or order, between the prioritization of freedom or justice. And for Levinas, it was clearly only religion that could offer the right response to a world in which the draperies had already fallen. Especially when, Levinas insisted, one only had to listen carefully in order to hear again the "chilling wind [that] sweeps through the still decent or luxurious rooms, tearing down tapestries and pictures, putting out the lights, cracking the walls, reducing clothing to rags and bringing with it the screaming and howling of ruthless crowds" (*NP* 145; *PN* 123).

But was it indeed religion that he was after? Along with an insistence on a distinction between religion and literature, Levinas distinguished between the Christian and the Jew, between that which was complicit with Athens, and thus with being, and that which was not. Are there other kinds of political stakes to such a distinction? Does such a choice imply different risks, perhaps by virtue of the very act of insisting that Jerusalem stands on the side of justice? These are the questions I think Derrida's work poses to Levinas, as we'll see in the next chapter. But there is one further question we must develop by considering Derrida's own writings on the question of religion or literature. Is it possible to reconceive of the relationship between literature and politics, perhaps by rethinking the relation of religion and literature not as competing claims to a postphilosophical discourse but in such a way that the latter is intrinsically tied to the former, as heir and betrayer, as legacy and as parasite?

3

BETWEEN THE JEW
AND WRITING

However we read the relationship between Derrida and Levinas, the lasting impact of Derrida's first encounter with Levinas's work is hard to dispute. Even in his final years, Derrida treated it as one of his life's decisive turning points. In a letter written to Paul Ricoeur in January of 1996, less than two weeks after Emmanuel Levinas's death, Derrida recalled its importance by reminding Ricoeur that it was he who first introduced Derrida to the thought of the Lithuanian phenomenologist.[1] It was 1961 or 1962, Derrida recalled, and they were walking in Ricoeur's garden. *Totality and Infinity* had just been published, and Ricoeur was one of Levinas's examiners for his habilitation. It was a day, Derrida wrote to Ricoeur, "which I imagine you have forgotten." Derrida had not yet read Levinas's magnum opus, but was motivated enough by Ricoeur's description to make it the focus of future work. "I in turn read *Totality and Infinity*," he wrote to his mentor in 1996, "and started to write one long article, then another—and his thought has never left me since."[2]

The years 1962 and 1963 were pivotal for Derrida. His translation of and introduction to Husserl's *Origins of Geometry* appeared as his first publication, and, almost instantly, he began to receive recognition: notes of congratulations from Foucault and Canguilhem and invitations to speak at Jean Wahl's College philosophique and to write for *Critique*. Wahl's College and Bataille's journal were the intellectual foci of the previous generation of thinkers testing the boundaries between philosophy, literature, and religion. The leaders of these forums took note of Derrida as a young, up-and-coming philosopher whose work too crossed borders and tested limits.[3] Derrida's first impulse, when the invitation arrived from Jean Piel at *Critique* in early 1963, was to write about Levinas, but he decided to delay this project, fearing it would require more time and energy than he could devote that spring.[4] Nonetheless, it is clear from the work that Derrida composed between the time he read *Totality and Infinity* and published on it that at this crucial moment when the concept of difference was first brewing, when the trace first emerged in his thought, Levinas was a key node of influence and an indispensable foil to the formulation of Derrida's conception of writing.

In 1963, at the same time that Derrida was auditing Levinas's courses, just before the publication of "Violence and Metaphysics," Derrida sent Levinas his earlier articles. He appended a note in which he explained that he realized that what he had to say in these "dead leaves' . . . is sometimes linked in another way, with what I ventured in the text you will soon read in the *R[evue] de M[étaphysique]*," that is to say, in "Violence and Metaphysics," forthcoming in that journal.[5] I argue in this chapter that the essays written between Derrida's first encounter with *Totality and Infinity* and his formulation of "Violence and Metaphysics" can be read as an interlocking set of arguments motivated by and responding to Levinas. This is not to suggest that the essays "Force and Signification" and "Edmond Jabès and the Question of the Book" are not concerned with their stated topics—Jean Rousset's structuralism and Edmond Jabès's poetry—but only that these readings included Levinas as something like an intended audience, an ideal reader to which Derrida addressed his remarks.

It was in and through this conversation that Derrida began to formulate his own position with and against Levinas on the question of literature and religion and to follow Levinas in orienting these questions toward a political intervention, which began for both with a rethinking of the liberal concept of freedom. My argument here has two components. The first is to provide a reading of the early essays in *Writing and Difference*. I will show the centrality of the concept of literary writing to "Violence and Metaphysics" by developing an interpretation that integrates "Violence and Metaphysics" with "Edmond Jabès and the Question of the Book" and "Force and Signification." The second is to consider more precisely the importance of

Judaism to this reading. While Derrida clearly treats *Totality and Infinity* as Levinas's central work, it is important to remember that when he finally wrote "Violence and Metaphysics" he had read also *Difficile liberté,* and, while it is rarely cited in the essay, its presence is instrumental to the political claims undergirding Derrida's philosophical position and instrumental as well to Derrida's development of a politics for which literature is central. If Levinas's rewriting of freedom is founded on Jewish sources, Derrida will make no secret of the fact that his is founded on literature.

REWRITING THEOLOGY

It is striking to think of the title of "Violence et métaphysique" and even of the collection *L'ecriture et la différence* as themselves a gloss on Levinas's work. While the linking of two concepts by *et* was not an uncommon formulation for Derrida's essays, Derrida often used it to provide an alternative reading of linked concepts in response to another thinker as a replacement for a dichotomy in that thinker's work that Derrida wanted to supplement. In each case the formulation played on the homophone between *est* and *et,* thus calling into question the possibility that one *could* establish a stable dichotomy, insisting on the mutual dependence of the terms and their inextricability.[6] If Levinas paired totality and infinity together to suggest the latter as the break with the former, Derrida paired violence and metaphysics together to suggest that the break from both was impossible. In *Writing and Difference* we have the first steps on an alternative route, one that claims to overcome totality not through the recourse to infinity but merely by exploiting the play of difference already present within the conceptual and linguistic framework of the metaphysical tradition.

Recognizing the centrality of *Totality and Infinity* to Derrida's project in *Writing and Difference* allows us to conceptualize it as, from the beginning, a project about the relationship between religion and literature by way of the intermediary of philosophy. There is nothing in itself fundamentally new about seeing religion as a component of Derrida's thought going back to his earliest works. But the debates over that question have primarily concerned the role of apophatic language in Derrida's conceptualization of difference.[7] The most recent foray into this question, however, takes a different tack, by considering Derrida's exposure to and writings on Christian existentialism. Given the evidence that Edward Baring's *The Young Derrida and French Philosophy* brings to bear on this issue from readings of Derrida's student papers, it is clear that Derrida was, at the very least, interested in the capacity of appeals to transcendence to serve a role in the critique of reason.

Baring goes back to Derrida's 1949 essays, written at the Lycée Louis Le Grand when he was only nineteen, and finds a thinker already looking to discern the boundaries of philosophy and to transcend its margins. The young Derrida found in Christian existentialism "a surpassing that would also be a return to an existence enriched and purified by reflection."[8] Baring also shows that Derrida was preoccupied by the concept of the secret and the form of fidelity to secrecy manifest in artistic creation. Already in 1949 Derrida had written that art "restitutes the secret in attributing it a sense." Baring traces this religious fascination through Derrida's years at École normale supérieure, finding in his 1954 thesis on Husserl, later published as *The Problem of Genesis in Husserl's Philosophy,* a Marcellian preoccupation with mystery.[9]

By the time of Derrida's thesis, all that remained of Marcel, however, was a sense of philosophy's aporias. Specifically Derrida was concerned in the thesis to expose the tensions inherent in Husserl's project to ground the sciences, the fact that "the supposed *a priori* possibility of re-actualization," that is, of reconstituting the genesis of a science, geometry for example, "will always suppose a constituted tradition in some form or other" (*PG* 262, 164). At the heart of this work was a preoccupation with origins, with the impossibility of their purity or their persistent contamination. "A law of differential contamination imposes its logic from one end of the book to the other," Derrida wrote in his 1990 preface to its publication (*PG* vii, xv). For Derrida the retrospective question in 1990 was how and why this concern about contamination so insistently imposed itself on him from the point of the thesis forward. But Baring, looking backward from the thesis, sees the remnant of the opposition between problem and mystery in Marcel, an opposition that Marcel defines in *Être et Avoir* as the difference between a problem as "something which I meet, which I find complete before me, but which I can therefore lay siege to and reduce" and a mystery as "something in which I myself am involved, and can therefore only be thought of as 'a sphere where the distinction between what is in me and what is before me loses its meaning and its initial validity.'"[10] A problem can be solved, but a mystery can only be degraded into a problem. This distinction, however, is only useful to Derrida insofar as he is concerned to show the sites in modern philosophy where its recourse to self-grounding falls back on presuppositions that the project itself is supposed to call into question. Marcel's notion of mystery could be similarly critiqued. His definition of mystery already involves a set of theological assumptions. Furthermore it demands an ethical stance. "The recognition of a mystery," Marcel writes, "is an essentially positive act of mind, 'the supremely positive act in virtue of which all positivity may perhaps be strictly defined.'"[11] Derrida's work is very distant from such claims. In *The Problem of Genesis* there is no evidence of Derrida's counseling such a position or resituating philosophy's problems of grounding within a theological context. In fact the closest he comes to *advocating* anything is perhaps in the very act of closing the thesis, which ends not with a conclusion but with a quotation from Husserl that appeared in *Deucalion* in 1950 in Walter Biemel's introduction to "La philosophie comme prise de conscience de l'humanité." The quote with which Derrida closes *The Problem of Genesis* is itself about repetition, and it is this very act of repetition that, I would argue, Derrida comes to advocate here and in the essays collected in *Writing and Difference*. The citation is from a conversation Husserl had with his sister on his deathbed, and it begins, "I did not know it would be so hard to die," and concludes, "Just when I am getting to the end and when everything is finished for me, I know that I must start everything again from the beginning" (*PG* 283, 178). Opening and closing with a quotation is a technique that Derrida came to repeat on multiple occasions in his work and is an expression of the task of repetition as he articulates it in "Ellipsis," the final chapter of *Writing and Difference*, where he ties repetition to what he calls "a negative atheology . . . it still pronounces the absence of a center, when it is play that should be affirmed. But is not the desire for a center, as a function of play itself, the indestructible itself? And in the repetition or return of play, how could the phantom of the center not call to us?" (*ED* 432–33; *WD* 297). Repetition is thus articulated as an activity in relation to a theological tradition, to a metaphysics of presence, moreover, in which theology is itself complicit. By the time Derrida published *Writing and Difference,* he had placed this concept of repetition at the center of his project and adopted it as an explicit strategy of destabilization. But the theological paradigm had found a new locus.

Derrida's engagement with Levinas's work provided the ideal testing ground for this new strategy. For in Levinas the question of religion's capacity to break the hegemony of reason is intertwined with the force of Judaism as disruption to the Christian West. Through his reading of Levinas, Derrida had the chance to rethink this question in relation to his own identity and all of his ambivalences toward it. Derrida's reading of Levinas in "Violence and Metaphysics" insists on the claim for Judaism in Levinas's work, even though Levinas himself went to efforts in *Totality and Infinity* to describe religion in generic terms. By reading Levinas's Jewish writings and philosophical texts together, so that Levinas's claims for what he names in *Totality and Infinity* "Religion" or "Revelation" are mapped onto a description of Judaism as the carrier of the truth of these concepts in the essays collected in *Difficult Freedom,* Derrida rightly identified the fact that Levinas set up a confrontation between cultures. Mobilizing this dynamic, Derrida sometimes described his own project in terms that apply to both Levinas and himself while at the same time opposing the possibility that Judaism or even "religion," in the more neutral terminology of *Totality and Infinity,* offers a means to resist philosophy. In an interview with Richard Kearney, Derrida described his relationship to the philosophical tradition with the very terms he uses to characterize Levinas in "Violence and Metaphysics": "While I consider it essential to think through this copulative synthesis of Greek and Jew, I consider my own thought neither Greek nor Jewish. I often feel that the questions I attempt to formulate on the outskirts of the Greek philosophical tradition have as their 'other' the model of the Jew that is the Jew-as-other. And yet the paradox is that I never actually invoked the Jewish tradition in any 'rooted' or direct manner. Though I was born a Jew, I do not work or think within a living Jewish tradition."[12] This description of his own enterprise privileges a reference to Levinas's and treats the figure of the Jew as one means of negotiating "the outskirts," the margins of philosophy. But Derrida suggests here both an alliance and a differentiation from Levinas. For both thinkers Judaism was a means to formulate the site of the border, but they disagreed on how to harness its force.

"OLD BROKEN TABLETS AROUND ME
AND ALSO NEW HALF TABLETS"

"Force et signification," "Edmond Jabès et la question du livre," and "Violence et métaphysique" may not seem to have much in common at first glance. Each deals with its own genre: "Force and Signification" with literary criticism, "Edmond Jabès and the Question of the Book" with poetry, and "Violence and Metaphysics" with the work of a phenomenologist. In fact, the variety itself is striking for a philosopher who had previously published only on the phenomenological tradition. In these essays Derrida was already resisting disciplinary boundaries by writing, over the course of a year, a philosophical critique of structuralist literary criticism, a work of literary criticism on a little-known Egyptian Jewish poet, and a study of a phenomenologist bookmarked by literary citations.[13] When the first two are read, however, with the knowledge that Derrida was at the same time wrestling with and formulating his response to Levinas in the third, their interrelation becomes evident.

In *Totality and Infinity* Levinas attempts to show that metaphysics is troubled by that which exceeds presence, that ethics is first philosophy, prohibiting the totalizing grasp of knowledge. In "Force and Signification" Derrida stages an analogous intervention when he argues that the structuralist approach to literature rests on an unrecuperable foundation, one that troubles its claims to treat meaning as fully accessible. Rousset had previously written a critically successful study of seventeenth-century literature in which he expanded the term *baroque* to apply to literary texts as well as the visual arts. *Forme and Signification* was Rousset's first foray into a more formal style of analysis. Like Derrida's work, Rousset's book sought to provide an analysis of literature that frees it from suppositions about authorial intention. For Rousset this was a means to finally deliver the work up to the critic's gaze. In his study, Derrida situates Rousset's move within the structuralist paradigm and argues that it is constituent of that project. For Derrida, structuralism is defined by its effort to elevate the form of the work by freeing it from historicism and analysis of authorial intention and thus to offer it up to the gaze in its spatialized completion, reproducing in the form of the panorama the deepest mechanism of the work, not what appears on the page, but the work's internal system, its functional dynamics.

Like Levinas's *Totality and Infinity,* Derrida's essay poses the question, "But what does this opening [into totality] hide, not by virtue of what it leaves aside and out of sight, but by virtue of its very power to illuminate? One continually asks oneself this question in reading Jean Rousset's fine book," Derrida contends (*ED* 14; *WD* 6). But the question itself would only be an obvious one within a particular line of philosophical questioning. It is a question that already reveals a conversation that far exceeds the matter of Rousset's structuralist readings and exposes the fact that the essay is an occasion to engage in a conversation about what it means to think that which cannot come to presence.

Derrida poses his question as though it were the obvious one. In fact, it seems a strange one to pose to a work of literary criticism. Is it not a sign of success that the critic has achieved such an illuminating account of a text, one which cracks its code, offering a schema that can illuminate how its elements contribute to its meaning? Derrida criticizes Rousset for having done too good a job in exposing the morphology of his object. This would be an odd charge unless the target of Derrida's essay were not structuralism, but the very aim of criticism in general to illuminate the meaning of a work.

At moments, Derrida employs a Heideggerian lens, borrowing the language of concealing and revealing that characterizes Heidegger's analysis of being in texts such as "The Onto-theological Constitution of Metaphysics." Derrida's conception of historicity in the essay is also clearly dependent on Heidegger. But Derrida quotes Heidegger directly in a passage that aligns Heidegger's own treatment of poetry with Rousset and ultimately with Platonism insofar as both seek a path toward truth that maintains the structure of revelation. He quotes Heidegger's "Letter on Humanism," in which Heidegger seeks out a conception of language beyond the signifying task, such that language would be "the clearing-concealing advent of being itself."[14] This is a reading of Heidegger that aligns Derrida with Levinas, for whom Heidegger is the end of a long tradition that prioritizes illumination.[15] As we saw in the last chapter, in Levinas's essay on Heidegger and Blanchot, "The Poet's Vision," published in 1956, Levinas explicitly draws a contrast between the two: where Heidegger's conception of poetry seeks the luminosity of truth, Blanchot characterizes literature as "foreign to the World and the worlds-behind-the-worlds."

Derrida even invokes Blanchot in the opening of the essay as the one who "reminds us, with the *insistence* of profundity," that literature is a departure from the world, the evocation of absence (*ED* 17; *WD* 8). In "Force and Signification" Derrida thus establishes his project in such a way that it parallels the aims of *Totality and Infinity* and assumes along with Levinas that the very question of taking into account what is hidden by the illuminating function is itself the relevant question worth asking.

But he comes at the question in a way that puts him at odds with Levinas. The essay takes an avowedly Nietzschean stance in its choice of topic: force. It recuperates the language of Apollo and Dionysus from *The Birth of Tragedy* and closes with a citation from *Thus Spoke Zarathustra*. Levinas was no fan of Nietzsche: he describes Nietzsche as a philosopher of cruelty in *Difficile liberté* and uses Nietzsche's description of poetry in *Totality and Infinity* only to condemn the whole genre as the beguilement of rhythm (*DF* 186; *DL* 279; *TI* 222, 203). This is a fact of which Derrida was only too aware. As Derrida points out in a footnote in "Violence and Metaphysics," to which we will return, Levinas "recommends the good usage of prose which breaks Dionysiac charm or violence, and forbids poetic rapture" (*ED* 124; *WD* 312). Derrida's entire project in "Force and Signification" could be read as a rehabilition of the Dionysian. His opening move is to charge structuralism with having favored the Apollonian dynamic of literature to the exclusion of the Dionysian with a lapse of attention given to force (*ED* 11; *WD* 4). It is clear that for Levinas the site of what is hidden, that which he seeks to recuperate in *Totality and Infinity*, is not the Dionysian.

If all that were at stake for Derrida were this recuperation, then any debate between Levinas and Derrida would simply return us to the debate we already tracked in the previous chapter between Bataille and Levinas, in which Bataille credits Levinas with exposing the site of existence without existents and then charges him with banishing aesthetics out of fear that this dark site could not be adequately distinguished from ethics. But "Force and Signification" already sets Derrida's project apart from such a move.[16] As he writes explicitly:

> Our intention here is not . . . to oppose duration to space, quality to quantity, force to form, the depth of meaning or value to the surface of figures. Quite to the contrary. To counter this simple alternative, to counter the simple

choice of one of the terms or one of the series against the other, we maintain
that it is necessary to seek new concepts and new models, an *economy* escaping this system of metaphysical oppostions. This economy would not be an
energetics of pure, shapeless force. The differences examined *simultaneously*
would be differences of site and differences of force. If we appear to oppose
one series to the other, it is because within the classical system we wish to
make apparent the noncritical privilege naively granted to the other series
by a certain structuralism. Our discourse irreducibly belongs to the system
of metaphysical oppositions. The break with this structure of belonging can
be announced only through a *certain* organization, a certain *strategic* arrangement which, within the field of metaphysical opposition, uses the strengths
of the field to turn its own stratagems against it, producing a force of dislocation that spreads itself throughout the entire system, fissuring it in every
direction and thoroughly *delimiting* it.

(*ED* 34; *WD* 19–20)

This paragraph marks an early articulation of the method that Derrida will
later, with some hesitation, call deconstruction. He produces a critique that
could be taken as a mere rehearsal of the familiar act of choosing one side
of a binary against the other. He claims, though, to resist this move and
to exceed it. Thus the second prong of his own attack on structuralism is
inaugurated. The first is to claim that structuralism overlooks force or at
least that it will be remembered as such. The second is to claim that there is
in fact no way to bring force to light: "To say that force is the origin of the
phenomenon is to say nothing. By its very articulation, force becomes a phenomenon . . . Force is the other of language without which language would
not be what it is" (*ED* 45; *WD* 26–27).

In this second move, the parallel with *Totality and Infinity* comes to a
halt. Now, instead of establishing an argument that mirrors Levinas's, he
rehearses the argument he will make in "Violence and Metaphysics." In
"Force and Signification" the object is force: "One would seek in vain a
concept in phenomenology which would permit the conceptualization of
intensity or force" (*ED* 46; *WD* 27). But the point applies to any object of
knowledge supposed to be outside of the domain of knowledge or illumination. Derrida applies it also to Levinas. "As soon as one attempts to think
Infinity as a positive plenitude . . . the other becomes unthinkable, impossible, unutterable. . . . The other cannot be what it is, infinitely other except

in finitude and mortality.... It is such as soon as it comes into language" (*ED* 169; *WD* 114–15). But where Derrida places force outside of light, Levinas associates the illumination of knowledge itself with force. As he puts it in the essay "Ethics and Spirit," "Violence is applied to the thing. . . . Knowledge seizes hold of its object. It possesses it" (*DL* 23; *DF* 8). Thus Derrida charges Levinas with committing the very violence he condemns by translating the relation to the other, which Levinas presents as allergic to light, into philosophical discourse. Levinas must be, Derrida writes, "resigned to betraying his own intentions in his philosophical discourse" (*ED* 224; *WD* 151). Thus the argument in "Violence and Metaphysics" is parallel but also reversed. In "Force and Signification" Derrida claims that philosophical discourse cannot bring force to light without reducing it to a phenomenon. In "Violence and Metaphysics" Derrida claims that insofar as Levinas, following Hegel, associates the activity of meaning making with seizure, he is necessarily complicit in that activity through his own discourse. But of course Derrida also says the same about himself: "Our discourse irreducibly belongs to the system of metaphysical oppositions" (*ED* 34; *WD* 20). Thus Levinas's failure is inevitable, as is Derrida's. The question then becomes how to remain attentive to that which cannot be brought to light without betraying it in language?

This is the approach that Derrida outlines in "Force and Signification," as a "strategic arrangement which, within the field of metaphysical opposition, uses the strengths of the field to turn its own stratagems against it, producing a force of dislocation that spreads itself throughout the entire system, fissuring it in every direction and thoroughly delimiting it" (*ED* 34; *WD* 20). Even as he critiques Levinas for failing at his stated aims, he ironically credits Levinas with performing, however unwittingly, the exact procedure that he lays out for himself in "Force and Signification."

Derrida claims that, in the metaphoric process of attempting to express exteriority, Levinas in fact shows us another path, a path that finds its route not by announcing an outside but by retracing philosophical discourse itself. Like a pencil rubbing revealing the veins of a leaf merely by applying pressure on an overlaid piece of paper, the repetition of philosophical discourse in Levinas's own attempt to write something new discloses "by philosophy's own light that philosophy's surface is severely cracked, and that what was taken for its solidity is its rigidity" (*ED* 134; *WD* 90). In this passage Derrida seems almost to give Levinas credit for Derrida's own method, except, of course, that Levinas had done it unwittingly. For Derrida argues that it is by reading Levinas's use of metaphor that Derrida discerns this operation. Derrida indicates in the opening to "Violence and Metaphysics" how and why *Totality and Infinity* had made such an impact on him. Or as he puts it, using a metaphor that would become stock for him later on, "the thought of Emmanuel Levinas would make us tremble."[17] For it "makes us dream" of "an incredible [*inouïes*] process of dismantling and disposession" (*ED* 122; *WD* 82).[18] That is to say it promises a way out of the Greek idiom of being even as it fails in this promise. To say that it makes us dream of such a process returns us to the primary trope of "Force and Signification": the relation of the Apollonian and the Dionysian and Nietzsche's solicitation to "dream on."[19] The thrust is both to register the promise and to indicate its dependence on illumination. Thus Derrida says of Levinas's alterity what he says of force. It "is worked by difference" (*ED* 47; *WD* 29). But this is what Levinas fails to register. For Levinas promises to break with totality through only one avenue: the ethical relation "as the only one capable of opening the space of transcendence and liberating metaphysics" (*ED* 123; *WD* 83). "Violence and Metaphysics" indicates how this route fails while at the same time suggesting that, in so arguing, Levinas misses the fact that he had himself already found an alternative route revealed at times by his own language. In the footnote mentioned earlier in which Derrida draws attention to Levinas's suspicion of poetry, Derrida continues: Levinas "forbids poetic rapture, but to no avail in *Totality and Infinity* the use of metaphor, remaining admirable and most often—if not always—beyond rhetorical abuse, shelters within its pathos the most decisive moments of the discourse" (*ED* 124; *WD* 312). Derrida describes Levinas's work as more artwork then treatise, but Derrida also claims it is this aspect of *Totality and Infinity* that serves as its asset. This is not an argument he develops in relation to Levinas in "Violence and Metaphysics" itself, but he will seventeen years later in "En ce moment même dans cette ouvrage me voici." He had already worked out the principle in "Force and Signification."

In "Force and Signification" the issue of metaphor is central. Derrida himself makes the point that his strategy of describing what cannot come to light mirrors apophatic discourse.[20] One might be tempted to say that Derrida's interest in metaphor here already points in that direction: "Metaphor in general, the passage from one existent to another, or from one signified meaning to another, authorized by the initial *submission* of Being to the existent, the *analogical* displacement of Being, is the essential weight which anchors discourse in metaphysics, irremediably repressing discourse into its metaphysical state" (*ED* 45; *WD* 27). It is tempting to read him here as arguing for language's incapacity to capture that which it describes, a falling short that prompts a proliferation of discourse. But at stake is the fact that these metaphors, under which there is no ground, play and replay the metaphor of the fall itself, the fall into metaphor, which is itself a metaphor, or, as Derrida puts it, it "deserves its quotation marks" (*ED* 45; *WD* 27). It is by tracking these metaphors that we discover our dependence on them and that they reveal the West as a network of such oppositions, infinitely displaceable.

But Levinas makes a key move in this history by himself displacing the site of exteriority onto the other. Derrida endorses this shift, but one of Derrida's main points in "Violence and Metaphysics" is to show that Levinas is *nonetheless* dependent on the heliotropic metaphor. He reproduces the forms of Greek metaphoricity even as he claims to escape them. Now this could be taken as a naive repetition of an age-old dynamic, or the very *repetition*, the act of repeating the tradition, could provide the key. I signaled at the outset that I wanted to read "Force and Signification" as addressed to Levinas, or to argue at least that Levinas appears as one possible ideal reader. The most important evidence for that claim arises in its final pages, where Derrida invokes Zarathustra and the image of "tables brisées" (*ED* 48; *WD* 29). This is an image, we will see, that reappears in the essay on Jabès.

But it is not only the invocation of the tablets of the law that leads me to believe that Levinas is invoked in these final pages; it also the fact that Derrida in this passage endorses Levinas's shift of exteriority's site, but not in the way that Levinas articulates it. Where Levinas argues that transcendence is only accessible through the ethical relation, Derrida argues that the escape from totality is only accessible in and through the very play of metaphor that Levinas engaged in but disavowed, that is to say, through writing.

> Writing is the outlet as the descent of meaning outside itself within itself: metaphor for the other [*autrui*]-in-view-of-the-other [*autrui*]-here-below, metaphor as the possibility of-an-other here-below, metaphor as metaphysics

which must hide itself if one want that the other [*l'autre*] to appear. Digging [*Creusement*] in the other [*l'autre*] toward the other [*l'autre*] where the same seeks its vein and the true gold of its phenomenon. Submission where it can always be lost. . . . For the fraternal other [*l'autre*] is not first in the peace of that which one calls intersubjectivity, but in the work and the peril of inter-rogation: he is not first in the peace of the response where two affirmations *espouse* each other but he is called in the night by the hollowing out or inscription [*travaille en creux*] of interrogation. Writing is the moment of this original valley of the other in being. The moment of depth also as forfeit. Instance and insistance of inscription [*du grave*].

(ED 49; WD 29)

Part of what is at stake in this complex passage is the very fact that it is embedded in a reading of Nieztsche's *Zarathustra*, the section entitled "Old and New Tablets," in which Nietzsche's Zarathustra's declares what would seem to be the antithesis of a Levinasian philosophy, "This is what my great love of the farthest demands: *do not spare your neighbor!* Human being is something that must be overcome."[21] And yet what Derrida does in the conclusion of "Force and Signification" is intertwine a reading of this chapter of *Zarathustra* with a response to Levinas in order to indicate and dramatize a thinking of alterity that ties it indeed to *autrui*, to the other person, but in and through writing. What is emphasized thus in Zarathustra's legacy is not the overcoming of Christianity, the announcement of the overman, but rather Nietzsche's use of equivocity, his emphasis on it as a means of pointing to the metaphoricity of the discourse. Derrida quotes from the opening of Nietzsche's chapter, "the hour of my going down [*Niederganges*], going under [*Unterganges*]: for I want to return to mankind once more" (*ED* 49; *WD* 29).[22] Derrida emphasizes that the verb for descent is maintained in duplicity: both *Niederganges* and *Unterganges*, and that this is tied to the act of reading and interpreting. Which is it? Is Zarathustra going down or a going under? The answer can only be determined by his reception. Either way, the descent is itself a form of submission, the giving of oneself over to the future, to being read. "It will be necessary to descend, to work, to bend, in order to engrave and carry the new Tables to the valleys, in order to read them and have them read," Derrida writes, interpreting Nietzsche. "Writing is the outlet as the descent of meaning" (*ED* 49; *WD* 29).

It is not insignificant, of course, that Zarathustra is already a rewriting of the Moses story itself, a revision of the trope of the religious prophet. And it is this rewriting and Derrida's own reinterpretation of it that Derrida puts forward here as a model of intersubjectivity. He furthermore introduces the terminology of interrogation, writing of the "work and peril of interroga-tion" (*ED* 49; *WD* 29).

Here Heidegger, for whom the human being is the being for which being is a question, seems again to be subtly invoked. Derrida thus outlines a modality of questioning itself, one in which the play of metaphor, inextricable to the articulation of being, is multiplied in and through writing and reading—the form of risk and chance, the form of submission to the other that fissures totality in and through its very dissemination.

In 1963, the same year in which Derrida was writing and thinking with Levinas, he gave a course entitled, "L'ironie, le doute, et la question," in which he considered irony and doubt as the two dominant modes of questioning.[23] Heidegger was at the center of this endeavor, which examined a series of thinkers—Socrates, Kierkegaard, Descartes—as following different methods of questioning, but so was Levinas, if only implicitly, as Derrida sought through these studies to consider text as a site of intersubjectivity.

When "Force and Signification" is read as one in a three-pronged response to Levinas's *Totality and Infinity*, it can be rethought as a presentation placing Derrida's aims in line with Levinas, joining them both to a community of those who, along with Heidegger and Nietzsche, ask after what is hidden in the very act of bringing to light. But the essay claims further that the route to excavating such a site fails, whether that alterity is force or the face of the other. At the same time, it reclaims the mantle of Levinas's endeavor by insisting on a different route if not to exteriority then at least to intersubjectivity and thus to a break with totality.

In "Violence and Metaphysics" Derrida recognized that what is at stake in *Totality and Infinity* is the project of rethinking eschatology, rethinking it not as a moment external to time but as one that could be inserted into time: "it is but a question of designating a space or a hollow (*creux*) within naked experience where this eschatology can be understood and where it must resonate. This hollow space (*creux*) is not an opening among others. It is opening itself, the opening of opening, that which can be enclosed within no category or totality, that is everything within experience which can no longer be described by traditional concepts and which resists every philosopheme" (*ED* 124; *WD* 83).

Even in using the same language of carving or hollowing out (*creuser*) to describe both Levinas and Derrida's projects, Derrida aligns himself with Levinas. Eschatology is thus rethought through an alternative metaphor, not through *la croix* but through *le creux*.[24] In this endeavor they share as well the conviction that "the infinitely other cannot be bound by a concept, cannot be thought on the basis of a horizon" (*ED* 141; *WD* 95). Levinas nonetheless committed himself to articulating what cannot be conceptualized, and doing so within the philosophical idiom. But, Derrida points out, the effect of trying to think the opposite of the concept, which is the very ether of our thought, is itself "stifling [*coup le souffle*]" (*ED* 124; *WD* 83). Levinas did so not by assuming that the darkness could be brought to presence but through the separation between the subject and the other and thus finally through the *trace*. "Not a theoretical interrogation ... but a total question, a distress and denuding, a supplication, a demanding prayer addressed to freedom" (*ED* 142; *WD* 96). And here it seems fair to say that Derrida is not being disingenuous when he says in an interview that between himself and Levinas there were no "philosophical differences."[25]

Except, of course, that for Derrida to employ the same sentence about his own work would imply a very different procedure. For not only is the "trace" for Levinas manifest only in the face-to-face relation, "Levinas calls" the dynamic "religion" (*ED* 142; *WD* 96). What would it mean then for Derrida to employ the religious vocabulary of the eschatological theme— question, supplication, prayer, freedom—and yet submit it to a procedure that altered its function?[26]

POETS AND RABBIS

The function of this repetition is already stated in the epigraph to *Writing and Difference*: "Le tout sans nouveauté qu'un espacement de la lecture." This line from the Mallarme's preface to "Un coup de dés jamais n'abolira le hasard" provides perhaps the most economical formulation of the eschatological theme in Derrida's work, from its beginnings in *Writing and Difference* to his late works, which take eschatology up more explicitly. To return time to philosophical and critical discourse, from which it is so consistently excluded, is one important prong of Derrida's project. As he puts it explicitly in relation to criticism in "Force and Signification,"

> Until it has purposely opened the strategic operation . . . which cannot simply be conceived under the authority of structuralism—criticism will have neither the means nor, more particularly, the motive for renouncing eurythmics, geometry, the privilege given to vision, the Apollonian ecstasy . . . It will not be able to exceed itself to the point of embracing both force and the movement which displaces lines, nor to the point of embracing force as movement, as desire, for itself, and not as the accident or epiphany of lines. To the point of embracing it as writing.
>
> (*ED* 47; *WD* 28)

Structuralism is, he argues, merely symptomatic of the metaphysical desire to freeze meaning, to reduce it to the static image, to possess it. In "Reality and Its Shadow" Levinas accuses art itself of trying to freeze time and thus of a form of idolatry; criticism he praises as its emancipation. For Derrida, it is the "metaphysical intention" manifest in criticism that "always presupposes and appeals to the theological simultaneity of the book, and considers itself deprived of the essential when its simultaneity is not accessible"(*ED* 42; *WD* 24). For Derrida, the very form of the book as "volume" is symptomatic of the desire for simultaneity, even as the text inevitably escapes that closure through its dissemination. Derrida names Stéphane Mallarmé as the great exception to this law, for the very fact that he "unrealized the unity of the Book" by seeking the book as that which differs from itself (*ED* 42; *WD* 25). "I sow, so to speak, this entire double volume here and there ten times," Derrida quotes Mallarmé (*ED* 42; *WD* 25).[27]

The centrality of Mallarmé to Derrida's project is unquestionable. It is a relation to which both Derrida and numerous scholars writing about Derrida have devoted attention.[28] Only a few years later, in 1968, Derrida declared Mallarmé the concluding point in the history of the concept of literature as mimesis that began with Plato. He names him as the one to finally call into question a history of mimesis as the imitation of an original.[29]

Both the epigram to *Writing and Difference* and the prominent citation of Mallarmé in "Force and Signification" indicate that Mallarmé was already central to Derrida's thinking in the early 1960s, but he is otherwise absent from *Writing and Difference*. When Derrida chooses to make the argument more explicitly that the spacing of the text is the site of temporality, to write that "once the circle turns, once the volume rolls itself up, once the book is repeated, its identification with itself gathers an imperceptible difference which permits us efficaciously, rigorously, that is, discreetly, to exit from closure," it is to the poet Edmond Jabès, for whom Mallarmé was a foundational influence, that Derrida turns (*ED* 430; *WD* 295).

In 1963 Jabès was still a little-known poet, a Jewish exile from Egypt who came to Paris in 1957 after the Suez Crisis and worked a day job in advertising to support his family.[30] He wrote poetry mostly on the metro, traveling to and from work.[31] It is not surprising that Derrida found Jabès compelling. A secular Jew, Jabès came to identify with the tradition through the very experience of exile and the trope of the Jews as the people of the book.[32] He too was fascinated by Mallarmé and, indeed, by the theme of the book. He had received no Jewish education and only began to explore Talmud and Kabbalah as sources for his poetry. The rabbis that people his poetry are not ancient sages called upon to provide wisdom to a troubled world; they are figments of his own imagination who make enigmatic statements that touch on mystical themes and reference the name of God, but who never cite proof texts or provide exegetical commentary.

Derrida's essay was a review, written for *Critique* upon the publication of Jabès's second volume of poetry, *The Book of Questions*, the first in a series on the theme of the relationship between the Jew and the book. Derrida's critical attention marked the beginning of an illustrious set of readers for Jabès, with friendships and exchanges between himself and Gabriel Bounoure, Maurice Blanchot, Derrida, and Levinas. Derrida's review was the first in January of 1964; Blanchot's followed in May, and Bounoure's in January of 1965. It was the beginning of Derrida's friendship with the poet, and a network of connections followed for Derrida as well. It was through Jabès that Derrida came into contact with Gabriel Bounoure, and we know from one of Derrida's letters to Levinas that among their first topics of conversation was Jabès, whom they discussed during the period in which Derrida was auditing Levinas's class, but after

Derrida had published his article on Jabès.[33] But it is clear both from the essay, which mentions Levinas, and from the chronology that Derrida's reading of Jabès followed his reading of *Totality and Infinity* and was indeed influenced by it.

Given all these factors, including the timely publication of Jabès's volume, the format of *Critique*, which privileged book reviews as its primary essay form, and the coinciding of its publication with Derrida's reading of Levinas, it is not in itself surprising that Derrida would write about Jabès. Nonetheless, it is striking the role that Jabès plays in *Writing and Difference*. While the first essay on Jabès is elliptical and brief compared to the other contributions to the collection, he is the one figure to whom Derrida returns in composing the volume. "Ellipses," the closing essay, written for the volume's publication, returns to Jabès, thus making his poetry serve as a seal to Derrida's project, to such an extent that Derrida's own signature merges with the pronouncements of Jabès's rabbis at the book's close: "'*Tomorrow is the shadow and reflexibility of our hands.' Reb Derissa*" (*ED* 436; *WD* 300). Furthermore, these essays on Jabès did more than merely introduce the poet to *Critique*'s readership. They develop a number of claims made in "Force and Signification," many of which would also get worked out in "Violence and Metaphysics." They can thus be read as another strand in a conversation that evolved between Levinas and Derrida concerning the means by which to think about the relationship between presence and absence and the capacity of writing to reveal difference without making claims for a hidden ground or a transcendent beyond.

Neither of the two Jabès essays in *Writing and Difference* is constructed as a straightforward analysis; nor do they function according to the deconstructive logic that Derrida had already developed in "Force and Signification." Rather, they follow from the proposal articulated in "Force and Signification" that criticism itself participate in writing, in a relation to its object that foregoes the production of its object's meaning as graspable form or thesis. In fact, both essays, the latter dedicated to Bounoure, proceed without any clear line of argument. They function almost like a *melitzah,* the medieval Hebrew literary form of weaving together biblical and rabbinic citations in a different context and thus providing them with a new meaning and set of associations. The citations are not biblical; they are from Jabès's poetry, and Derrida's comments are interspersed in between, but the comments themselves often feel merely like bridges or frames allowing him to connect to another citation.

Derrida later called such a strategy countersignature, borrowing from the term's legal definition as a secondary signature that authenticates the primary signature. It inscribes a promise, but also something of a threat: "a 'yes' to the other's 'yes,' a sort of blessing and (ring of) alliance. Not infringing this law but the possibility of betrayal is part of respect for the law. . . . It is impossible that the 'counter' of the vis-à-vis proximity, iterability or affirmation should not be encroached on by the 'counter' of destructive opposition."[34] Part of this threat follows from the relation between the countersignature and the promissory note. A signature or endorsement carries with it a promise for the future, but the inscription itself is also a giving oneself over to the future, a "trusting to a 'perhaps' or an 'as if' where performative mastery fails."[35] The grafting onto another is a submission to the other work, but also a submission to future readings to which the signature commits but from which the signature relinquishes control. Derrida enacted this most clearly with the final citations in the two essays on Jabès, both of which close with a signature. Signed "Reb Rida," and "Reb Derissa," the play on Derrida's name makes this citation itself a perjury, a betrayal, a displacement of the original by his own signature, but also a repetition and a fold (*ride*), which simultaneously endorses and displaces Jabès's project (*ED* 116; *WD* 78 and *ED* 436; *WD* 300).

At the same time, these essays serve Derrida as an opportunity to articulate a new set of critical practices. They include some of the volume's strongest declarative statements concerning the nature of his own project. "Writing is thus originally hermetic and secondary," he writes in a gloss on Exodus 32:14 and 33:17, highlighting already the difference between the two sets of Mosaic tablets and the very mark of historicity itself (*ED* 102; *WD* 67). He credits Jabès with the accomplishment of that which he denies to both Rousset and Levinas. Jabès conveys both the necessity and the impossibility of bringing what is allergic to light into illumination: "*Le livre des questions* is simultaneously the interminable song of absence and a book on the book. Absence attempts to produce itself in the book and is lost in being pronounced; it knows itself as disappearing and lost, and to this extent it remains inaccessible and impenetrable" (*ED* 105; *WD* 69). And in "Ellipses," written three years later for *Writing and Difference's* publication, he articulates clearly for the first time what he later describes as the relation between religion and literature. Here it is developed as two approaches to the book. The project of the book is always already the writing of the origin, which retraces it, "tracking down the signs of its disappearance" (*ED* 430; *WD* 295). But in so doing it is already supplement: "a trace which replaces a presence which has never been present" (*ED* 430; *WD* 295). Nonetheless, one can approach its supplementary form in one of two ways. One can try to protect the book, keep it "sheltered from play, irreplaceable, withdrawn from metaphor and metonymy" (*ED* 431; *WD* 296) or one can cultivate its repetition, its redoubling. "The return to the book is then the abandoning of the book." In "Edmond Jabès and the Question of the Book" (*ED* 430; *WD* 295) Derrida referred to these two approaches as the difference between the poet and the rabbi: "The necessity of commentary, like poetic necessity, is the very form of exiled speech. In the beginning is hermeneutics. But the *shared* necessity of exegesis, the interpretive imperative, is interpreted differently by the rabbi and the poet. The difference between the horizon of the original text and exegetical writing makes the difference between the rabbi and the poet irreducible" (*ED* 102; *WD* 67). For Derrida, Judaism and its relations to the book are emblematic of a more universal structure. In "Structure, Sign, and Play," written for a conference at Johns Hopkins in 1966 and included in *Writing and Difference*, the same dichotomy is famously reproduced as that between mourning and play. One key topic of the first essay on Jabès is the position of Jew as emblem, suffering allegory, oscillating between Pauline trope and the exemplary nation. The theme of Jewish exemplarity pervades all Derrida's writing on the Jewish question, even if it represents only one tangent in his larger philosophical and critical project. What *Writing and Difference* reveals is that, from the beginning, in Derrida's first articulations of his new method and project, the Jewish question was already in play.

By choosing Jabès as the poet through whom he would first articulate literature's capacity to repeat and liberate religious themes from their submission to an inaccessible origin, Derrida was able to use Judaism, and particularly Levinas's relation to the tradition, as the site to articulate the dichotomy between religion and literature. Read together, "Violence and Metaphysics" and "Edmond Jabès and the Question of the Book" provide two forms for working out that structure of exemplarity, two forms for working out the dichotomy between poet and rabbi. Considered historically, Jabès and Levinas represented two different means of navigating the effort to salvage Judaism in the postwar context, cultivating anew the locus of broken tablets and indeed the possibility of Judaism's survival.

BETWEEN HEBRAISM AND HELLENISM

The ordering of the essays in *Writing and Difference* is chronological, but there is furthermore a way in which "Edmond Jabès and the Question of the Book" and "Violence and Metaphysics" speak to one another. They are linked by a series of motifs, some of which emerged already in "Force and Signification": the motif of the broken tablets, the community of the question and the dream. Within the essay "Violence and Metaphysics," Derrida enacts a conversation between the two by citing Jabès in key spaces. Derrida closes "Edmond Jabès and the Question of the Book" with the theme of survival. Literature is here described as a means of survival: "Life negates itself in literature only so that it may *survive* [my emphasis] better. In order to be better [*Pour mieux être*]" (*ED* 116; *WD* 78).[36] This is the first articulation in Derrida's corpus of literature as legacy; the claims of "Literature in Secret" is already telegraphed here. Then the term *survivre* repeats again as a noun in the following line: "Les livres sont toujours des livres de *vie*. . . . ou de *survie*" (*ED* 116; *WD* 78). In this context the term is clearly tied to the question of Jewish existence and persistence, an explicit theme for both Levinas and Jabès. In the final lines this survival is articulated in theological terms. How can the "interrogation of God" survive? (*ED* 116; *WD* 78)[37] Literature, he concludes, would be the "dreamlike displacement" (*le déplacement somnabulique*) of this question (*ED* 116; *WD* 78).

"Violence and Metaphysics" then opens with the reiteration of many of these themes: Right away there is the issue of survival, this time philosophy's: "beyond the death or dying nature, of philosophy, perhaps even because of it, thought still has a future" (*ED* 115; *WD* 79).

Once again the form of the question is presented as a means of survival. As a community of the question, philosophy survives. One way to phrase Derrida's challenge to Levinas is whether Levinas's own philosophy can in fact tolerate the ambiguity of the question. But this challenge is itself posed in and through literature, with Jabès and then with Joyce. The first part of the essay, which Derrida published separately in *Revue de Metaphysique et des Morals*, concludes with the question, could Levinas subscribe to the "infinitely ambiguous sentence from the *Book of Questions* . . . 'All faces are His; this is why He has no face"? (*ED* 160; *WD* 109).[38] And the second part of the essay closes with another question, "And what is the legitimacy, what is the meaning of the *copula* in this proposition from perhaps the most Hegelian of novelists: 'Jewgreek is greekjew. Extremes meet.'?" It is against these literary models of survival that Derrida measured Levinas's own (*ED* 228; *WD* 153).[39]

At issue, of course, is not only philosophy's survival but Judaism's, if in fact they can be definitively differentiated. Derrida is cautious about introducing this question too hastily. It shows up in the epigram from Matthew Arnold's *Culture and Anarchy*, "Hebraism and Hellenism—between these two points of influence moves our world," but is not announced until the essay's conclusion. In the meantime, Derrida focuses on the various tropes employed in *Totality and Infinity*. These range from exteriority to messianic eschatology and the face. Judaism finally appears in the conclusion as that which Levinas has not fully admitted but which Derrida hypothesizes as nonetheless present in Levinas's philosophical work:

> But if one calls this experience of the infinitely other Judaism (which is only a hypothesis for us) one must reflect upon the necessity in which this experience finds itself, the injunction by which it is ordered to occur as logos, and to reawaken the Greek in the autistic syntax of his own dream. . . . Such a [Greek philosophical] site cannot offer *occasional* hospitality to a thought that would remain foreign to it. And still less may the Greek absent himself having loaned his house and his language. . . . Greece is not neutral, provisional territory, beyond borders.
>
> (*ED* 226; *WD* 152)

The question in this essay is a variation on the theme from "Edmond Jabès and the Question of the Book." It is a question of whether this other thought, Judaism, can survive philosophy: can it appear in and through philosophical discourse and, if so, can it succeed in calling into question the grounds of the tradition in which it emerged while borrowing its idiom?

Derrida treats the possibility that this site of exteriority should be called Judaism as a hypothesis, but he quotes from *Difficile liberté* in the service of the claim. Levinas was explicit in the 1963 collection both about the necessity of building the cultural and educational infrastructure that can ensure Jewish survival and about Judaism's significance as philosophy's opposing force. In the 1963 essay from which Derrida quotes at the conclusion of "Violence and Metaphysics," "Pièces d'identité," Levinas explores the strategies by which Judaism could both maintain its integrity and serve as a prophetic voice for the West. The essay opens: "The very fact of questioning one's Jewish identity means it is already lost. But it is still the way to hold onto it, otherwise we would be avoiding interrogation. Between this already and this still, the limit is drawn, like a tightrope on which the Judaism of western Jews is ventured and risked" (*DL* 85; *DF* 50).[40]

In this essay Levinas outlines an approach that involves translating Judaism into the language of philosophy, identifying its universalism so that one day one might even "speak against the civilization in which the University lives and by which it lives" (*DL* 87; *DF* 52). He counsels returning to the Jewish canonical sources themselves, Judaism's old books, to find the "embers which lie under the ashes, like the words of the sages according to Rabbi Eliezer. The flame thus traverses history without burning in it" (*DL* 89; *DF* 53).[41]

Derrida's hypothesis is that Levinas's *Totality and Infinity* is indeed such a project, a project that Levinas believes to be a translation, harnessed to resist the tradition of the idiom in which it speaks. With this claim Derrida also links Levinas's project to Rosenzweig's *Star of Redemption*, about which Levinas famously said in the preface to *Totality and Infinity* that it was "a work too often present in this book to be cited" (*TI* 14, 28). Derrida cites that line as well in his own footnote, but he is not explicit about where and how he sees the relationship at work.[42]

As we saw already in the first chapter, it is characteristic of Derrida that he does not cite the passages for "Pièces d'identité" that best corroborate his argument, but rather treats quotations often like proof texts to which the reader needs to return to discern the argument. Thus, in "Violence and Metaphysics," he cites Levinas: "If one has to philosophize, one has to philosophize" and "One could not possibly reject the Scriptures without knowing how to read them, nor say philology without philology"—all without disclosing the theme of Levinas's essay "Pièces d'identité" (*ED* 226; *WD* 152). Perhaps an even more crucial omission is of the fact that Levinas stakes his claim for this Jewish project against hypocrisy: "The only criteria on which we can base the rational examination that is required are those of the maximum degree of universality and the minimum degree of hypocrisy" (*DL* 88; *DF* 52). Derrida takes up the theme of hypocrisy in the penultimate paragraph of "Violence and Metaphysics": "Are we Jews? Are we Greeks? We live in the difference between the Jew and the Greek, which is perhaps the unity of what is called history. We live in and of that difference, that is, in *hypocrisy*, about which Levinas so profoundly says that it is 'not only a base contingent defect of man, but the underlying rending of a world attached to both philosophers and prophets'" (*ED* 227; *WD* 153). Derrida is responding not only to *Totality and Infinity* but also to *Difficult Freedom*, to the possibility that the cultural and political project that Levinas outlines in *Difficile liberté* could be anything *but* a form of hypocrisy or, at the very least, a doubling, manifesting a tension and indeed thus an engagement in history, understood by Derrida as the very appearance of difference, or diachrony, rather than "a flame that traverses History without burning in it" (*DL* 89; *DF* 53).

In "Jabès and the Question of Writing," Derrida writes, "But the Jew's identification with himself does not exist." This is another way of saying that Judaism carries within it the structure of dissimulation. "The Jew is split and split, and split first of all between the two dimensions of the letter: allegory and literality. His history would be but one empirical history among others if he established or nationalized himself within difference and literality. He would have no history at all if he let himself be attenuated within the algebra of an abstract universalism" (*ED* 112; *WD* 75).

For Derrida, Levinas's attempted evasion of this split is a missed opportunity, his failure not only to affirm it but moreover to exploit it. For Derrida, the impossibility of self-identification, the fact that one can never rediscover a univocal voice, can never evade time: this primary difference itself is indeed not *merely* "a base contingent defect of man"; it is the structure of contingency itself; it is time (*WD* 153; *ED* 227).[43] But it is also freedom and it is exactly what writing exemplifies.

Fairly early on in the essay, Derrida is explicit about the stakes of such a freedom as a potential response to Levinas's project. Addressing Levinas's preference for the living voice, Derrida asks, "could [one] invert all of Levinas's statements on this point?"

By showing, for example, that writing can assist itself, for it has *time* and freedom, escaping better than speech from empirical urgencies. Derrida asks whether, by neutralizing the demands of empirical

> economy, writing's essence is more "metaphysical" (in Levinas's sense) than speech? That the writer absents himself better, that is, expresses himself better as other, addresses himself to the other more effectively than the man of speech? And that, in depriving himself of the *enjoyments* and effects of his signs, the writer more effectively renounces violence? It is true that he perhaps intends only to multiply his signs to infinity.... The thematic of the *trace* ... should lead to a certain rehabilitation of writing.
>
> (*ED* 150–51; *WD* 102)

Here Derrida knows himself to be very close to Maurice Blanchot, who in 1961 had already addressed Levinas's work in the essay "Connaissance de l'inconnu." Like Derrida's essay on Rousset and "Violence and Metaphysics," Blanchot's essay is concerned with the question of how "to discover the obscure without exposing it to view."[44] And while Blanchot does not consider at any length Levinas's aversion to writing, except to note his aversion to poetry, Blanchot's own conception of writing is already at stake in the description that Derrida gives of Levinas's project in "Violence and Metaphysics." As Blanchot writes in "Literature and the Right to Death" (1949), "In writing, he [the writer] has put himself to the test as nothingness at work, and after having written, he puts his work to the test as something in the act of disappearing."[45]

In the years in which he composed the essays collected in *Writing and Difference*, Derrida was working out a concept of writing that distinguished him from Blanchot. One can see the traces of that work in the revisions Derrida made to this passage between its original publication and its inclusion in the volume *Writing and Difference*. In the later version he adds, "It is true that he perhaps intends only to multiply his signs to infinity, thus forgetting—at very least—the other, the infinitely other as death, and thus practicing writing as *deferral* and as an *economy of death*" (*ED* 150–51; *WD* 102). The notion of the "economy of death," borrowing from Derrida's 1967 essay on Bataille published in the same volume, functions in such a way that Derrida could counter Levinas's own treatment of economy in the Hegelian sense, as a circulation within the same, with a concept of economy as expenditure without return. The emphasis on deferral followed from Derrida's engagement with Freud in 1966. These terms establish a vocabulary unique to Derrida and become the mainstays of his critical readings.

Even without the imprint of these later influences, it is already evident in 1964 that Derrida wanted to suggest a model of *liberté* that, like Levinas's, would derive from the structure of the trace, but with different ramifications.

DIFFICULT AND DIFFERENT FREEDOMS

Derrida's endeavor to think a concept of freedom that draws from the movement of writing and is cultivated in literature provides one of the key lines of continuity in his work. In the next chapter we will consider its political development in Derrida's later works. But it is already nascent in the early essays of *Writing and Difference*. The word *liberté* appears fourteen times in "Violence and Metaphysics" alone. In "Force and Signification" Derrida was already concerned to think the freedom of writing in such a way that it is differentiated from the creative will (*ED* 23; *WD* 12).[46] And in "Edmond Jabès and the Question of the Book" he describes the letter's freedom as tied to its absence (*ED* 108; *WD* 72).

In Levinas's work he confronted a very different notion of freedom, one that departs from a liberal tradition founding freedom on autonomy. The project of rethinking the concept of freedom is central to *Totality and Infinity*, but freedom appears primarily here as the object of critique, and, insofar as *Totality and Infinity* can be read as a political theory, it replaces the primacy given to freedom in liberalism with the concept of justice. Yet, in choosing to title his book of essays on Judaism *Difficile Liberté*, Levinas returns this concept to the center of his project.

In *Totality and Infinity* freedom is first introduced as constitutive of ontology, when ontology is conceived as "the comprehension of beings," and defined *as* "the identification of the same, not allowing itself to be alienated by the other" (*TI* 32, 42). Levinas then tracks the role that freedom has played in philosophy, considering in each case how ontology confirms a view of freedom as "egology" (*TI* 35, 44). But even as the model is comprehension and thus philosophical, the ramifications, Levinas argues, following Hegel, are political. Insofar as ontology is first philosophy, it is a "philosophy of power. It issues in the State and in the non-violence of the totality" (*TI* 37, 46). In so far as this nonviolence is a consequence of the reduction of the other to the same, it is tyranny.

For the philosophical tradition, *conflicts* between the same and the other are resolved theoretically, whereby the other is reduced to the same, or, concretely, by the community of the state, where, beneath autonomous power, though it be intelligible, the I rediscovers war in the tyrannical oppression it undergoes from the totality (*TI* 38, 47).

The path toward an alternative conception of freedom arrives out of a rethinking of what constitutes first philosophy, a reversal of the relation between the same and the other, such that the relation with the Other would found the very movement of comprehension. Once it is recognized that "thinking the Other" is not, in fact, thinking an object, that it is an encounter with transcendence that resists comprehension, then ethics must be resituated as first philosophy and freedom as the movement of comprehension is put into question. As Levinas puts it: "To welcome the Other is to put in question my freedom" (*TI* 84, 85). Justice conditions freedom. But Levinas is not *only* critiquing freedom. For this conditioning reveals a metaphysics other than ontology, provides a glimpse of a thinking "older" than the Greek. "*Creation ex nihilo* breaks with system, posits a being outside of every system, that is, there where its freedom is possible" (*TI* 108, 104). Levinas's project can be read thus as one that refounds philosophy on religion. Following in Rosenzweig's footsteps, religion is reconceived from the separation that creation initiates, thus founding philosophy on a metaphysics of pluralism. This pluralism is not discovered through the movement of comprehension, but in the face-to-face relation where the separation of beings is revealed as ethics. Thus the ensuing conception of freedom is thought not then in terms of autonomy and power but as *freedom from* the same, as the movement toward exteriority.

Levinas's rethought concept is here conceived as a break from politics. Rather than revealing new political structures, it provides a glimpse of a space of peace outside politics. But this does not divest it of political ramifications. The very critique or "investiture" of freedom marks and alters

politics (*TI* 83, 84). In *Totality and Infinity* this is confirmed as the prioritization of justice *over* autonomy. In *Otherwise Than Being* Levinas goes a
bit further. There justice is reconfigured *as* politics, as the necessity of adjudication, and the state. Yet Levinas imagines a politics in which even the
state would be leveraged on his alternative conception of freedom, a state
inspired by the face-to-face relation even when that face to face gives way
to problems (*AE* 245–49; *OTB* 159–61). But this description encompasses
only a few pages and offers little in terms of directive.

Many years after their first encounter, in his eulogizing homage to
Levinas, Derrida argued that Levinas's work offers no plan or program
for the transition from ethics to politics and thus could be thought as an
incitement to "think law and politics otherwise" (*AEL* 45–46, 20–21).[47]
Derrida's development of an alternative conception of freedom can indeed
be read, going all the way back to 1963, as a response to that incitement.
And, even as he made the move to outline a "prophetic politics" only in
Otherwise Than Being and in essays from that period, Levinas had long been
thinking concretely about the political implications of conceiving freedom
otherwise. Why else would he have titled his book of essays on Judaism *Difficile liberté?*[48] In his philosophical works, Levinas universalized from Jewish
emblems to conceive philosophical paradigms that only gestured toward
the political, but in his Jewish writings politics is never far from the surface,
for the very project of conceiving of Judaism's place in the postwar world
is inevitably political. Derrida could not have failed to see this in his first
encounter with the 1963 version of the book.

In its first instantiation, *Difficile liberté* was a collection of occasional
essays Levinas had written between 1950 and 1963 on the topic that Levinas
very broadly treated as a "bearing witness to a Judaism that has been passed
down" and "finding oneself a Jew in the wake of the Nazi massacres."[49]
Levinas later revised the collection and republished it in 1976. One effect
of this revision is the omission of some of Levinas's political interventions.
The later volume omits, for example, an entire section entitled "Le Grand
Jeu" that contemplates the new realities of the cold war as well as essays that
navigate Levinas's changing relationship to the Zionist project. It would not
be surprising for Derrida to have seen some hypocrisy evident in the negotiations present here. Levinas wanted to hold onto the view he formulated
in the 1930s of Judaism standing outside and thus judging history, while, at

the same time, his own frustration with the weakness of a diasporic Judaism that had been diluted by generations of assimilation and decimated by the war led him to embrace the vitality he saw in Zionism.

In "Judaïsme privé," for example, which Levinas excluded from the 1976 edition, Levinas responds to a prompt in the journal *Évidences* on the spiritual state of contemporary Judaism. Levinas argues that anti-Semitism is the event that returned Judaism to the plane of history. "The scapegoat, le bouc émissaire, c'était tout de meme un role historique."[50] This return to history marked the end of a confessional Judaism, a Judaism confined to the inner life and the family, a Judaism that found its confirmation, and thus the site of its disappearance, in the flourishing of nineteenth-century European liberalism. In the face of the crisis of this tradition, Judaism had to announce its presence on the plane of objective spirit," Levinas writes. "For this," he continues, "neither the opinions of Jewish intellectuals nor the reform of the administrative structure of the community would suffice, only perhaps, the existence of the state of Israel could serve this function."[51]

"And of what relevance the infidelities to Judaism's great teaching, for which the state itself could eventually be rendered culpable, and what importance the injury rendered to our fine European sensibility by the violence of its young reality. Its reality alone counts. Today at least Israel constitutes the form by which underground Judaism makes its exit toward history."[52]

Here the survival of Judaism, Levinas argues, depends on the state of Israel. Its survival necessitated a return to the land. "Heidegger, Gagarin, and Us" appears in the same volume, an essay Derrida refers to in a note of "Violence and Metaphysics" as one of Levinas's more "violent" articles, thus noting, of course, the tension between Levinas's denouncement of violence and his own rhetoric. Here Judaism is described as the negation of enrootedness, as "free with regard to place . . . the Bible knows only a Holy Land, a fabulous place that spews forth the unjust" (*DL* 350; *DF* 233). No doubt the evident tension between Levinas's definition of Judaism and the demands of historical reality fueled what might appear as hypocrisy in his texts. Taken as a collection of occasional essays, *Difficult Freedom* can be read as a series of negotiations with a range of political contexts. In the preface alone, Levinas makes reference to multiple dynamics that followed from the complexities of the postwar moment. Directly or indirectly, he refers to life after Hitler, the realities of colonialism and postcolonialism, and the complexities of

Jewish-Christian relations, given both the long history of Christian super-sessionism and the fact that many French Jews were sheltered by Christians during the war. The glaring omission of the preface is the fact of Israel, which is nonetheless present in many of the essays.

Also evident, despite these complexities, is the strategy of framing Judaism as a teaching that has something very old to offer in the face of very new conflicts. The last paragraph of the preface in particular makes oblique reference to the cold war conflict between Marxist materialism and a liberal concept of freedom founded in autonomy; for Judaism, Levinas suggests, "The Other's hunger—be it of the flesh, or of bread—is sacred; only the hunger of the third party limits its rights; there is no bad materialism other than our own. This first inequality perhaps defines Judaism. A difficult con-dition. An inversion of the apparent order" (*DL* 10; *DF* xiv).

Judaism is thus set in opposition to the two prominent ideologies of the 1950s, the liberal language of rights is retained but inverted, and the inver-sion itself speaks to the Marxist claim that calls for an overturning of the base and superstructure of capitalist culture. Judasim, Levinas suggests, sup-plies its own spiritual revolution, one that puts the hunger of the other at the foundation of culture. Judaism would thus be the model for what Levinas in his title refers to as *Difficile liberté*.

One can imagine that Derrida saw in Levinas's essays from the 1950s a political intervention analogous to Mounier's personalism, an impulse to reinsert religion into the postwar political tug-of-war, an intervention in a political scene in which everyone agreed that American capitalism was on the opposing side, but alignment with Marxist concerns had to be negoti-ated without concession to its dogma.

This is not to say that Levinas proposed Judaism as a complete politi-cal ideology, one that could compete with theories of liberal democracy or Marxism, rather to suggest that he saw the answer to this conflict not in another ideology but in a supplement to liberalism that would itself reorient the classic relationship between reason and religion in the West after John Locke. In *Totality and Infinity* this relation is framed in generic terms as the relation between "politics" and "religion": "Politics tends toward reciprocal recognition, that is, toward equality; it ensures happiness. And political law accomplishes and sanctions the struggle for recognition. Religion is desire and not struggle for recognition. It is the surplus possible in a society of equals, that of glorious humility, responsibility, and sacrifice, which are the condition for equality itself" (*TI* 58, 64).[53]

Here the Lockean model, which relegates any element of religion not in accordance with reason to the realm of opinion, thus treating religion as a kind of political supplement, is replaced with the language of "surplus." And the Hegelian struggle for recognition is deemed inadequate to the phenomenon of religion, which does not conform to its law. Religion is reframed as condition and interruption of reason.

This is particularly clear in the 1960 essay "Religion and Tolerance." In it Levinas takes on the model of toleration that emerged out of the Enlightenment, one that subordinates religion to the realm of private confession, a model, he suggests, that does not sustain "the imperishable aspect of religion" (*DL* 261; *DF* 173). Clearly the survival of Judaism is at stake. The assumption that public religion and toleration are in tension "does not adequately account for Judaism, he argues. "That tolerance can itself be inherent without religion losing its exclusivity—this is perhaps the meaning of Judaism: It is a religion of tolerance" (*DL* 261; *DF* 173).

But Jacques Derrida's exposure to Judaism did not corroborate this assessment. Especially as he grew older, Derrida repeatedly told the story of his expulsion from the Lycée Bar Aknoun in El Bair during World War II and his subsequent inscription into the Jewish community at the Lycée Maïmonide. As he put, it in an interview with Élisabeth Roudinesco,

> It was there, I believe, that I began to recognize—if not to contract—this ill, this malaise, this ill-being that, throughout my life, rendered me inapt for "communitarian" experience, incapable of enjoying any kind of membership in any group. . . . I could not tolerate being "integrated" into this Jewish school, this homogeneous milieu that reproduced and in a certain way countersigned—in a reactive and vaguely specular fashion, at once forced (by the outside threat) and compulsive—the terrible violence that had been done to it.[54]

It was an experience that subsequently inflected his philosophical positions. The theme of inscription pervades not only writings that address the theme of Judaism, such as *Circumfession, Schibboleth,* and *Mal d'archive,* but also the very experience of being a speaking subject, as in *Monolingualism of the Other*, in which Derrida borrows Levinas's trademark terms—*hostage, passion, irreplaceability*—to describe his "exemplary" experience of being a "speaking subject."[55]

In 1963 Derrida was still recovering from another experience of conflicted inscription, his military service between 1957 and 1959 in Algeria for the French army. While he served in a civil post as a teacher at a school for the children of military personnel, it was a period in which the experience of conflicting allegiances was no doubt acute. In 1962, when the Évian agreements were signed, Derrida's whole family left Algeria for France with no sense of when or if they would be able to return.[56]

Derrida was of another generation than Levinas and from a different Jewish cultural context. He thus had a different experience during the war, as well as after, one that gave him the liberty to reflect on his Jewish identity from a certain distance, the room even to play with the logic of the "marrano": "*As if* the one who disavowed the most, and who appeared to betray the dogmas of belonging . . . represented the last demand, the hyperbolic request of the very thing he appears to betray by perjuring himself." Derrida called himself "the least and the last of the Jews" (AA 20; AO 13). [57]

But in 1963, when Derrida first read *Difficile liberté* he was among those to whom it was addressed. For Levinas was not first and foremost speaking to those who, like him, underwent the Nazi persecution and lived to describe it. Instead he was speaking as an educator and addressing that generation of Jews for whom the burden of living after the Shoah implied a new kind of responsibility. Levinas had written these essays as the director of the École normale israélite orientale, a school whose original mission was to train North African Jews to become schoolteachers at Alliance Israélite Universelle schools in North Africa. Under Levinas's leadership, and given the new historical realities, it shifted its focus in the 1950s and early 1960s as North African Jews sought to immigrate to France rather than to return to their home countries. Instead of providing a means to make North African Jews more cosmopolitan, it became, through Levinas's urging, a Jewish secondary school with an emphasis on reinvigorating Jewish education in order to ensure the future of the tradition. "The existence of Jews who wish to remain Jews—even apart from belonging to the State of Israel—depends on Jewish education," Levinas wrote in "Reflections on Jewish Education," an essay that appeared originally in

Les Cahiers de l'Alliance Israélite Universelle in 1951 (*DL* 394; *DF* 265). He counseled renewed emphasis on Hebrew study, not in order to learn about a dead past but to teach the next generation to speak from that tradition *to* the modern world. "It is finally time to allow Rabbi Akiba and Rabbi Tarphon to speak if we want to be Jews, that is to say, to reclaim them for ourselves" (*DL* 399; *DF* 268). He lamented the renewed exodus of Jews away from Judaism, "attracted by assimilation . . . forgetting the vows of fidelity which we survivors formulated after the liberation."[58] He spoke of the seductions of the modern world and criticized those who failed to learn the language of Jewish canon. He championed the superiority of its wisdom, lambasting those Jews, like Simone Weil, who failed to see in Judaism the resources for righteous ethical and political thinking. And, of course, he pitted religion against literature. "We distrust theater, the petrification of our faces, the figure that our person weds. We distrust poetry, which stresses and bewitches our gestures, all that which in our lucid lives plays us despite ourselves," he wrote in an essay on Paul Claudel (*DL* 188; *DF* 121). Art and literature are described as magic, play, idolatry, as the transformation of life into death, and religion was defined as "life at the extreme point of life" (*DL* 52; *DF* 27). Judaism is represented again and again as religion's truest instantiation.

RETURNING TO THE FOLD

Imagine Derrida reading this collection of essays in 1963, when he was preparing to write his essay on Levinas. He confronted in *Difficilé liberté* a renewed call to inscription, the claim that it was his obligation to reinvest in the Jewish tradition, the conviction that the path to rethinking philosophy lay in religion. The latter is a position he had already confronted, but in the form of Christian theology. Here it was reconfigured in the language of the tradition that he had already spent his adolescence resisting.

He also saw the consequences of that call in the position that Levinas was just beginning to form around Zionism, a project that conjoined nationalism and universalism in such a way that Israel was framed as the potential instantiation of a prophetic politics. Already in 1951, in the essay "The State of Israel and the Religion of Israel," Levinas argued that Israel's hope lay in its capacity to instantiate that possibility: "The subordination of the state to its social promises articulates the significance of the resurrection of Israel as, in ancient times, the execution of justice justified one's presence on the land" (*DL* 327; *DF* 218) This was its hope and, he argued, its only possibility, "it will be religious or it will not be at all" (*DL* 328; *DF* 219). Levinas's political interventions for years to come articulated the tension between prophetic religion and state as Israel's promise. But this was not framed only in terms of an expectation but also as the concrete manifestation of Judaism's exemplarity, thus the reason that Israel's existence was not only a concern for Jews but for all peoples.

In 1980, in a volume of the *Annals of International Studies* devoted to the theme "Religions and Revolution," Levinas wrote that the establishment of the state of Israel was the accomplishment of Judaism's prophetic impulse, the actualization of Judaism's essential stance toward social justice. Can Judaism be called a religion, he asked? "Is this not a nation whose destiny would reveal its true nature in the state of Israel? But this political existence: hasn't it still a prophetic inspiration? Can one feel Jewish in Israel without the consciousness of participating in an exceptional order and of accomplishing a universal plan?"[59]

Between these years, even as the gap grew between the promise of Israel and its actual political manifestation, the ideal itself lost its power as challenge and was reabsorbed into the state's concrete reality. It was no longer a question primarily of using the ideal to counter reality but of treating this ideal as the state's *idea*, that is to say, its form and meaning and thus the grounds upon which the current state, whatever its policies or actions, could still be defended.

We cannot know for certain whether Derrida in 1964 could foresee the path that Levinas's politics would take. But it was less than two years later that he went with Levinas to the Colloque des intellectuels juifs de langue française, where Levinas made the joke to him with which I opened chapter 1. The incident thus occurred after the publication of "Violence and Metaphysics" but before its appearance in *Writing and Difference*.

At this meeting Levinas gave one of his signature Talmud readings. The reading was Sotah 34b–35a and the theme was "Israel in the eyes of the nations." Levinas spoke thus on the commentary to Numbers, chapter 13, the story of the spies returning from Canaan and reporting that the land kills or devours its inhabitants.

For Levinas, the Talmudic passage provides an opportunity to compare two divergent ways of inhabiting a land. On the one side there is the way of the Canaanites, who "take human faces for grasshoppers" (*QLT* 145; *NTR* 68). On the other side are the Israelites, who enter the land in order to establish a just society and who thus, of course, have doubts about usurping the land—moral doubts that stem from their respect for the rights of its current inhabitants. "What we call the Torah provides norms for human justice. And it is in the name of this universal justice and not in the name of some national justice or other that the Israelites lay claim to the land of Israel.... Moreover, those who are about to conquer a country the way heaven is conquered, those who ascend, are already beyond ... beautiful tears. They not only commit themselves to justice but also apply it rigorously to themselves" (*QLT* 141, 147; *NTR* 66, 68). Levinas does not deny the brutality of politics or that the Israeli conquest of Palestinian land involved the violation of the rights of others. But he suggests that Israel provides, at the very least, the best hope for what he had named "difficult freedom," the best hope for a standard of human justice that one applies more rigorously to oneself than to others.

Surely the Colloque des intellectuels juifs de langue française, and indeed Levinas's intervention there, must have looked to Derrida like one instantiation of a project for Jewish survival, an experiment to rethink the relationship between religion and philosophy and to conceive of freedom in new terms. But Derrida himself had already embarked on a project to rethink freedom, one that exploited the structure of exemplarity quite differently. Is it a coincidence then, that he closed the 1967 volume with a second essay devoted to Edmond Jabès?

In Levinas's 1965 reading of the Talmud he returns to the canon, and indeed to the Torah, to Numbers, chapter 13, in order to find the resources to interpret the relationship between the contemporary state of Israel and its great books. The books would inspire a prophetic state, he insists. In his essay on Jabès's *Le Retour au livre*, Derrida writes, "The book has lived on this lure: to have given us to believe that passion, having originally been impassioned by *something*, could in the end be appeased by the return of that something. Lure of the origin, the end, the line, the ring, the volume, the center" (*ED* 430; *WD* 295).

Where Levinas, in "Pièces d'identité," returned to real rabbis and insisted that their word was a flame that "traverses history without burning in it," Jabès had written poetry, the end of the trilogy that closes *The Book of Questions* (*DL* 89, *DF* 53). He too staged a return, but thematized through the theme of *retour*, not the rekindling of a tradition but what it is to live after its ashes. In Jabès's poetry, Derrida found that return is not about recovering a site of origin but of setting something into circulation, a turning again. In the closing essay of *Writing and Difference*, Derrida quotes Jabès citing his imaginary rabbi, Reb Selah: "Where is the center? / In the cinders [Où est le centre? / Sous la cendre]" (*ED* 432; *WD* 297). Derrida acknowledges here the nostalgia that motivated a return to "the mythic book," the same nostalgia that religion lives: "the mythic book, the eve prior to all repetition has lived on the deception that the center was sheltered from play: irreplaceable, withdrawn from metaphor and metonymy" (*ED* 432; *WD* 297). But in Jabès—and ultimately in literature more broadly—he found a model for inhabiting it differently. What he found in Jabès was not the promise of a return to the past, not the recapturing of any flame, but the return understood as repetition and thus as futural. "The circle turns," he writes, and thus "gathers an imperceptible difference" (*ED* 431; *WD* 295). The repetition of the tradition sets it into circulation and also adrift, toward another, any other, who might pick it up to read. Here freedom is no longer autonomy, but neither is it a return to religious heteronomy. Instead, it is conceived as the escape from closure, as exit. "The return of the book is then the abandoning of the book . . . the exit from the identical into the same." But he writes, returning to the parlance of "Violence and Metaphysics," "the other is [already] in the same" (*ED* 431; *WD* 296).

THE PROMISE OF RECEPTION

By the time Derrida wrote "Ellipsis," he had already reappropriated from Levinas the language of trace, and even the project of messianicity, but found another means of articulating these concepts, one that instead of promising transcendence plunges "into the horizontality of a pure surface." He didn't discover in the book's labyrinth a nihilism of pure play, although this has been a frequent charge made against Derrida's work, by Levinas among others (*ED* 434; *WD* 298). Instead he located the passage between ethics and politics, a passage toward the inclusion of the third person. Where is this third person? She is there already in the promise of reception, of readership. As Derrida concludes "Ellipsis" and the volume *Writing and Difference:* It is in "the third party between the hands holding the book, the deferral within the now of writing, the distance between the book and the book, that other hand" (*ED* 436; *WD* 300).

As we'll see in the next chapter, such a claim is more than a poetic statement. It implies a political intervention and, indeed, a claim about the relationship between religion and literature, between ways of relating to the past and means of welcoming the future.

4

TO LOSE ONE'S HEAD

Literature and the Democracy to Come

Dead letters! Does it not sound like dead men?
—Melville, "Bartleby the Scrivener"

No *responsiveness.* Shall we call this death? Death dealt? Death dealing?
I see no reason not to call that life, existence, trace.
And it is not the contrary.
—Derrida, "Passions"

I n 1968 Jacques Derrida accepted an invitation from Johns Hopkins University to teach a seminar on the topic "Literature and Truth." The project of the seminar was to consider how literature has been conceived, constructed, and maintained from Plato on as imitation and thus construed as secondary in order to protect the status of philosophy and, more broadly, science as the province of truth. Derrida developed the argument to show that the representative arts had been subsequently burdened with the task of effacing their position as copy by cultivating the value of originality, thus reproducing the very logic that established their exclusion. But Derrida's purpose was also to show the capacity of literature to call into question the sovereignty of those discourses that defined themselves in and through their own distinction from the imitative act.

In his opening to the second session, in a lecture entitled "Le Parricide," he shared a recent anecdote about his time in America. Through his host at

Johns Hopkins, Derrida had met a physician and scientist who worked at the Pentagon. The scientist, whose job was to measure the progress of American biotechnology against that of the Soviet Union, asked Derrida about his course topic. When Derrida told him the title, the doctor balked. "What does literature have to do with truth?" he demanded, as though the association offended his sensibility.[1] Four years later, in *Dissemination*, the essay collection developed from the course, Derrida provided his rejoinder: "To lose one's head, no longer to know where one's head is, such is perhaps the effect of dissemination" (*D* 17). The doctor's position itself discloses the relationship between sovereignty and knowledge. His job was to protect the superiority of American research, its position as possessor of the truth. This was an act of national defense, one means of securing the nation's sovereign status.

Literature, Derrida argued in the course, had been construed by Plato as a threat to the political order and, in a distinction that Derrida argued has been maintained going forward, excluded from the realm of serious debate. In *The Republic* Plato banishes the poets from the city, but by designating literature as threatening he defines politics by its exclusion, thus establishing a relation of dependency that links the two inextricably. Ironically the dichotomy between politics and literature has been maintained even within the corpus of Derrida scholarship. In the first major work on Derrida and politics in 1996, Richard Beardsworth argues that the prevailing assumption that Derrida's work is apolitical arose from its position within literary studies. Beardsworth thus frames his own work as a "project to shift our political understanding of Derrida's philosophy from literary inscription to a transformation of political modernity."[2] Scholars of Derrida's later work have followed suit, arguing for a turn to the political from "Force of Law" (1989), a turn that for most seems to imply a shift away from literary studies.[3]

And yet Derrida insisted until the end that "the thinking of the political has always been a thinking of différance and the thinking of différance always a thinking *of* the political" (*V* 64; *R* 39). This last statement comes from *Rogues*, Derrida's last major work. *Rogues* itself could be read as a gloss on the line from *Dissemination:* the development of the ramifications of what it means to lose one's head. *Rogues* is Derrida's most explicit meditation on sovereignty as the keystone of the political and his most explicit attempt to think a concept of freedom divorced from self-sovereignty. The first chapter is entitled "La roué libre" (The Free Wheel) and begins "The turn [*le tour*] the turret or tower [*la tour*] the wheel of turns and returns: here is the motivating theme and the Prime Mover, the causes and things around which I will incessantly turn" (*V* 25; *R* 6). In the figure of the turn Derrida locates the confluence of sovereignty, freedom as self-determination, the notion of the unconditioned as the foundation both of reason and the *causa sui,* the first cause or prime mover. At the same time he exposes the manner in which the circular turn of reflexivity and autonomy, of ipseity, is always at the same time also a turning back on one's self, how it functions to undermine itself in a movement that Derrida comes to call quasi-suicide or as autoimmunity.

Derrida's question in the text is how to exploit what might appear to be a weakness in democracy in order to develop a thinking of freedom "that would no longer be the power of the subject, a freedom without autonomy, a heteronomy without servitude" (*V* 210; *R* 152). At stake is not merely theory, but the future of democracy, threatened "by a new violence," by the concentration in so few hands of so much power against dispersed enemies, which justifies itself in and through its own sovereignty. "It is thus no doubt necessary, in the name of reason, to call into question and to limit a logic of nation-state sovereignty," he writes, thus establishing the project as a concrete political intervention, revolutionary one might be tempted to say (*V* 215; *R* 157).

As soon as talk begins about losing one's head and politics, we are not far from the French Revolution. And as much as the act of beheading is taken to be a symbol of political revolution, it might seem to follow that Derrida should be construed as a revolutionary. By that rationale, so would Levinas. For as we began to sketch out in the last chapter, their projects share the endeavor to conceive of a freedom divorced from sovereignty.

And yet neither Derrida nor Levinas could say much for themselves as freedom fighters. In 1968, while Maurice Blanchot threw himself into the student-led ferment, thinking up slogans and anonymously publishing articles in the "semi-clandestine magazine" *Comité,* Derrida participated only marginally and described himself as ambivalent about the whole thing. "I was not against it, but I have always had trouble vibrating in unison," he told an interviewer.[4] Elsewhere he commented that he was wary of the protests' spontaneity.[5] For Levinas, the Six-Day War in June of 1967 was the more significant political moment. To show support for the state under threat, he closed the École normale israéelite orientale and let the students go out into the street.[6] Yet, amidst the fervor of 1968, while teaching at Nanterre, he defended the institution and the authority of the French state and taught through the disruptions insofar as conditions permitted.[7]

Thus to speak of the political implications of either of their projects is not to think in terms of a new order or to align either of them with the Communist Party or the '68 Maoists, although both had certain Marxist sympathies.[8] Rather, it is to speak of their efforts to critique the liberal tradition. Each sought to call into question its foundations and thus to conceive of interventions in its operation that would orient it toward justice.

Our task in this chapter is to show how Derrida established literature as a necessary lever—or should I say guillotine?—in this operation, to show that, for the model of freedom that Derrida works out most explicitly in *Rogues*, literature is a necessary component. In the concluding section of his essay "Passions," he writes: "No democracy without literature; no literature without democracy" (*PA* 65; *OTN* 28). The task of this chapter is to work out the implications of this statement, but also to further establish why and how the political operation that literature represented for Derrida was inextricably bound to its relationship to religion. If religion as Levinas conceived it and literature as Derrida conceived it each replace the autonomous liberal subject with a subject who is first called and thus dependent and heteronomous, why and how is it politically important that Derrida comes to think of literature in *Gift of Death* as a remnant "a link or relay of what is sacrosanct in a society without God"? (*DLM* 208; *GD* 157).

Chapter 3 is primarily an account of how and why Derrida's conception of freedom developed in relationship to his reading of Levinas. This chapter is an account of the political result of that relation and departure. We thus begin with Levinas's efforts to develop a notion of freedom distinct from self-sovereignty subsequent to *Totality and Infinity*. We then follow Derrida's reading of Levinas's later texts and show how they are instrumental to Derrida's own formulation of the category of religion in his most important essay on the topic, "Faith and Knowledge." Once again, we find Derrida articulating a fidelity to Levinas while, at the same time, undercutting Levinas's claims. In the second half of chapter 4, by way of *Gift of Death*, we consider how Levinas was himself representative, for Derrida, of the move among philosophers to privilege theology as a means of upending an Enlightenment model of self-sovereignty. Finally we'll show how the notion of the secret provides Derrida with an alternative to religious mystery, but also points to an alliance between religion and literature. The aim thus is to show how the political dimension of literature, its function for what Derrida calls "democracy to come" proceeds in and through literature's biblical inheritance.

CREATURELY FREEDOM: "WE WILL DO AND WE WILL HEAR!"

As Levinas's work developed after *Totality and Infinity* and into *Otherwise Than Being*, he found consonance between his and Derrida's projects insofar as both exposed, within the philosophical tradition, the relationship between the enlightenment model of the subject and liberal politics, between the construction of a sphere of autonomy and the obsessive concern to guard property and to guard against threat. Aligning his project with Derrida's, in the essay "Wholly Otherwise," Levinas presents the object of their philosophical critique and its political implications. "Leave nothing lying about! Don't lose anything! Keep everything that is yours. The security of the peoples of Europe behind their borders and the walls of their houses, assured of their property (*Eigenheit* that becomes *Eigentum*), is not a sociological condition of metaphysical thought, but the very project of that thought" (*NP* 84; *PN* 58). Both Levinas and Derrida identified a consonance between the subject as ipseity, defined by its identity with itself and the economic and political valence of property. Both sought to invest this tradition with a principle of hospitality, but from that point forward Levinas found Derrida lacking. Derrida's insistence on the power of the Greek to reinstate its claims, Levinas charged, left him spinning on a pessimistic axis, forced again and again to acknowledge that "any attempt to express a lack of presence positively" was still one more way of returning to presence (*NP* 85; *PN* 60). For Levinas, there is no opposition between mourning and play; they amount to the same thing: "a taste for unhappiness" (*NP* 86; *PN* 61). For Levinas, the hope of deconstruction is in the possibility of conceiving "of *the being of the creature* without resorting to the ontic narrative of a divine operation" (*NP* 85; *PN* 60).

Otherwise Than Being thus takes up that path. Like Derrida, Levinas insists that the path to beheading the subject and thus upsetting the role of sovereignty as the cornerstone of European politics is in and through a thinking of the unconditioned. He describes his ethical subject as on "the hither side" of a subject endowed "with political and religious sovereignty or political principality" (*AE* 172; *OTB* 195). The chapter entitled "Substitution" opens with the opposition between a model of the subject predicated on self-certainty and an ethical subject. A subject who possesses itself through knowledge, Levinas contends, through "losing itself and finding itself... as a theme, exposing itself in truth... is never dangerous; it is self-possession, sovereignty, *arkhe*" (*AE* 157; *OTB* 99). In response, Levinas proposes a different formation of the free subject, one that is invested, striated by "what we have called trace" (*AE* 158; *OTB* 100). By the time Levinas wrote this statement, the notion of the trace had already become one of Derrida's primary calling cards. Derrida uses it as well to indicate that self-presence and self-possession are always already disturbed. But for Levinas this trace always leads back to an elsewhere, to the order of creation. This is the space of the unconditioned for Levinas, because the creature always finds itself already abandoned in relation to a cause it can not assume or reappropriate, "an orphan by birth, or an atheist no doubt ignorant of its Creator, for if it knew, it would again be taking up its commencement" (*AE* 165–66; *OTB* 105).

Derrida's impact on Levinas is present in *Otherwise Than Being* as an alternative model. It is evident primarily in Levinas's references to play, of which there are many. In a footnote to the section "Substitution," Levinas returns to the chiasmus, the image central to "Wholly Otherwise" and describes, without naming Derrida, the crossroads of their philosophical choices. "Even if the ego were but a reflection forming an illusion and contenting itself with false semblances, it would have a signification of its own precisely as this possibility of quitting the objective and universal order." It is possible to confirm only play in the face of this conclusion, he concedes, but "to quit the objective order, to go in oneself toward the privation of sacrifice and death... is not something that happens by caprice, but is possible only under the weight of all the responsibilities" (*AE* 191; *OTB* 197).[9]

In making this move, Levinas continues to argue for the prioritization of religion as the corrective to politics. In fact, in *Otherwise Than Being* Levinas shifts the primary locus of religion from prophecy to creation.[10]

While *Otherwise Than Being* is often taken to be a response to Derrida's critique in "Violence and Metaphysics" that Levinas hadn't divested himself enough of the language of ontology, a response to Derrida's claim that "if one does not have to philosophize, one still has to philosophize," it is also a return to an older model within Levinas's own corpus (*ED* 226; *WD* 152).

The model of a freedom from existence rather than in existence is present in Levinas's thinking from the very beginning. He conceives it as liberation "from the enchainment to itself" (*AE* 198; *OTB* 124). Its origins can be traced back to Levinas's 1935 *De l'evasion*. Levinas's first original philosophical work considers the failure of philosophy, culminating in idealism, to overcome the problem of the subject's experience of being riveted to itself. It is first associated with Judaism and with creation in Levinas's 1947 essay "Être Juif," in which Judaism is configured both as an intensification of the experience of being riveted and a resignification of it *as freedom* through the concept of creation. In opposition to a conception of the ego "starting from a freedom in a world without origin," Levinas suggests, in Judaism creation provides a different model of freedom. "In a new sense, then, to be created and to be a son is to be free . . . Jewish existence is thus the fulfillment of the human condition as fact, personhood and freedom" (EJ 263; BJ 210). In the essay "Être Juif" this freedom is configured as a kind of dependence on God, which liberates one from the full responsibility of a pure autonomy. "To exist as a creature is not to be crushed beneath adult responsibility," Levinas wrote in 1947, in a sentence that seems hard to square with his ensuing emphasis on responsibility (EJ 263; BJ 210). But the move that Levinas made between these two texts was to cut off the head of the sovereign. In *Otherwise Than Being*, the creature is abandoned, without a father, "an orphan by birth" (*AE* 165; *OTB* 105). The father is only present as lack, an empty space that disallows self-sovereignty, that is to say, the subject as self-constituting. Consciousness appears as an effort to close the gap. But "the oneself has not issued from its own initiative, as it claims in the plays and figures of consciousness on the way to the unity of an Idea" (*AE 166*; *OTB* 105). This is not resolved in the relation to the other, but it establishes the exposure of the self to the other. "In the exposure to wounds and outrages, in the feeling proper to responsibility, the oneself is provoked as irreplaceable, as devoted to the others, without being able to resign, and thus as incarnated in order to offer itself, to suffer and give" (*AE 166*; *OTB* 105).

Even when Levinas submerges the religious paradigm of this new model, restating it, for example, as a version of Kant's second formulation of the categorical imperative, the connections to the 1947 text "Être Juif" persist.[11] Levinas refers in *Otherwise Than Being*, as in the 1947 work, to "an obedience" that precedes my assent. This model is itself an oblique reference to Exodus 19:17, "Na'aseh v'nishmah" (We will do and we will hear), the classic text describing a Jewish obedience to God that precedes any possibility of adjudication. The term *religion* is mostly effaced from this text, in contrast to *Totality and Infinity* in which it appears a dozen times, but, when it is defined, it is defined as the trace of that command. "Then, the trace of saying, which has never been present, obliges me; the responsibility for the other, never assumed, binds me, a command *never heard is obeyed*. . . . It is the trace of a relationship with illeity that no unity of apperception grasps, ordering me to responsibility. This relationship—or *religion*—exceeding the psychology of faith and the loss of faith it orders me in an anarchic way, without ever becoming or being made into a presence or a disclosure of a principle" (my emphasis; *AE* 261; *OTB* 168).[12]

The function of this command resonates as a disturbance to the self-certainty of philosophy, but it also follows for Levinas that it has political implications. Both Western philosophy and the state, Levinas continues, function to annul the interruption of illeity's trace. The state allies itself with knowledge, with science, with medicine and heals the break up of its own mastery and sovereignty. "The interlocutor that does not yield to logic is threatened with prison or the asylum or undergoes the prestige of the master and the medication of the doctor: violence or reasons of state . . . ensures to the rationalism of logic a universality and to law its subject matter" (*AE* 264; *OTB* 170).

This isn't to say that the trace of these interruptions is not registered. But discourse, what Levinas calls in this volume "the said," can also annul them by talking *about* them and weaving them into culture. "The discourse is ready to say all the ruptures in itself and consume them as silent origin or as eschatology" (*AE* 262; *OTB* 169). In an acknowledgment and acceptance of Derrida's charge in "Violence and Metaphysics," Levinas thus includes his own discourse in the annulling movement of culture. "Are we not at this very moment [*en ce moment même*] in the process of barring the issue that our whole essay attempts, and of encircling our position from all sides?"

Levinas asks, taking up Derrida's critique as question, but also, attempting to interrupt his own discourse (*AE* 262; *OTB* 169). This is the moment that Derrida himself memorialized in the 1980 essay "En ce moment même, me voici" (*P* 149–92, 143–90). Levinas even seems to align himself with Derrida here, speaking of the fecundity of this very process, its capacity to give rise to interpretation by cultivating in itself the unsaid. "Language would exceed the limits of what is thought, by suggesting, letting be understood without ever making understandable, an implication of a meaning distinct from that which comes to signs from the simultaneity of systems or the logical definition of concepts" (*AE* 263; *OTB* 169). In a move almost unprecedented in his early writings, he even includes poetry among such discourses. "This possibility is laid bare in the poetic said, and the interpretation it calls for ad infinitum. It is shown in the prophetic said, scorning its conditions in a sort of levitation. It is by the approach, the-one-for-the-other of saying, related by the said, that the said remains an insurmountable equivocation, where meaning refuses simultaneity, does not enter into being, does not compose a whole" (*AE* 263; *OTB* 170). Levinas compares poetry to prophecy as a discourse that reignites the dimension of the saying, the face to face, by resisting univocal meaning, by demanding that the reader glimpse a lack between what is said and what is meant. But where the poetic only "lays bare" the possibility, the prophetic demonstrates it. Even here literature is subordinated to the religious. More important, the significance of the gap has itself been predetermined by Levinas. He has found a space for poetry, finally, but only by subordinating it to the ethical.

Nowhere is that clearer than in Levinas's essays on Jewish literature written contemporaneously with *Otherwise Than Being*. In essays on Paul Celan (1972) and S. Y. Agnon (1973), Levinas again makes the same point about poetry, but he makes it only with Jewish authors and only by asserting that they exposed the ethical dimension of discourse.[13] In an essay on Agnon, for example, he takes up Agnon's last collection, *Haesh vehaetzim* (The Fire and the Wood) and reads it as a reference to the Akedah but also to the Holocaust. Even as his reading registers the nuance of the collection's final story, "The Sign," it is ultimately itself an affirmation for Levinas not only of the saying and its ethical dimension but of the Jewish people as its witness: "He [Agnon] recognized the unity of Israel, that is, the inevitable binding into a community of those human beings who are dedicated to the other man. . . . He also saw that each one within that community, whatever his or her destiny or death finds a personal meaning through belonging to the whole" (*NP* 25; *PN* 14).

POLITICS, AFTER!

The poetic was thus briefly courted by Levinas, but it was ultimately subordinated to a different project, a political project of affirming the Jewish community as *the* community that politically is able to manifest and maintain a commitment to the interrupting force of the saying. The politics that developed out of these later writings is thus most clearly articulated in Levinas's late essays on Judaism. There the function attributed to religion as it is defined in *Otherwise Than Being* is attributed directly to Judaism. The possibility of a rupture appearing in discourse, in politics, in the mastery of the state is concretized *as* Judaism. "Judaism is a rupture of the natural and historical that are constantly reconstituted and, thus, a Revelation which is always forgotten" (*ADV* 18; *BTV* 4). Jewish observance functions as an expression of allegiance to this interruption, as a means of maintaining what the natural, the historical, and the political cover over. "It is as if the ritual acts prolonged the states of mind expressing and incarnating their internal plenitude, and were to the piety of obedience what the smile is to benevolence, the handshake to friendship and the caress to affection"(*ADV* 21; *BTV* 7). Adherence to the Torah is thus itself a method of protection for that which in Judaism transcends the natural.

The energies that animate Zionism and the state that it produced have in present times come to serve the same function, Levinas goes on to argue. For Levinas this is not merely one means by which Jewish ethics is preserved, it is the primary one. "Only the existence of the State of Israel ensures a similar function [to Torah as safeguard of Jewish memory and ethics] today," Levinas wrote in the first essay of *Beyond the Verse* in 1981 (*ADV* 23; *BTV* 9). Because of the weakness of this interruption, however, because of how easily it can be covered over, Israel is by definition weak. In 1951 Levinas wrote of the state of Israel that it would be religious or it would not be at all (*DL* 328; *DF* 219). Twenty-eight years later, in an essay published in *Les Temps Modernes*, Levinas wrote from an embattled position against a political left that had begun since 1967 to turn its sympathies toward the Palestinians. His telltale irony emerges to mock the prevailing wisdom: "An armed and dominating State, one of the great military powers of Mediterranean basin, against the unarmed Palestinian people whose existence Israel does not recognize! Is that the real state of affairs? In its very real strength, is not Israel also the most fragile, the most vulnerable thing in the world, in the midst of its neighbors, undisputed nations, rich in natural allies, and surrounded by their lands? Lands, lands and lands, as far as the eye can see" (*ADV* 227; *BTV* 193).

Levinas recognizes the tension between what he sees as the state's essence and his action, but he uses it now to defend a commitment to a nation that did not always honor its promise. Its promise, however, is enough to solicit the allegiance. In *Otherwise Than Being* Levinas envisions religion as a force of political interruption, as an obligation that precedes knowledge. But, in modeling that structure on Exodus 19:17, he also inextricably links it to the Jewish canon. In his Jewish writings he makes the connection explicit and sees in the state of Israel the instantiation of the model. But, once instantiated, it seemed that religion's unseating of the mechanisms of power and mastery proper to the state has to be perpetually deferred. In *Totality and Infinity* Levinas describes the voice of the prophet, the eschatological voice as the voice that interrupts history, that refuses to wait, that insists on a justice independent from teleology. In 1979 he writes: "Since 1948 this people has been surrounded by enemies and is still being called into question, yet engaged too in real events, in order to think—and to make and remake—a State which will have to incarnate the prophetic moral code and the idea of peace" (*ADV* 228; *BTV* 194). The promise is real, he maintains, but perhaps its reality will have to wait. He titled the essay "Politics, After," but it is hard to read the essay as anything but an acknowledgment of the fact that politics has to come *before*. His first priority, the world's first priority is, in fact, to protect Israel, to keep it safe from harm, to secure it from threat, to allow the purity of its promise to remain, a flame flickering in the darkness.

POMEGRANATES AND GRENADES
OR AUTOIMMUNITY

One thing all of Derrida's essays and commentaries on Levinas have in common is the charge that Levinas could not keep his word. This was, of course, also Derrida's charge against almost everyone he read. The very method of deconstruction is a means of exposing how texts, arguments, political structures are worked by forces that resist their own claims. In his later essays, from "Faith and Knowledge" (1996) forward, Derrida introduces the concept "autoimmunity." This new terminology emphasizes the way in which that which unworks a system from the inside can also serve to expose it to that which is other. Derrida defines autoimmunity as that dynamic by which an organism in trying to protect itself against itself destroys its own self-protection. While such vulnerability has been traditionally construed as a weakness, Derrida argues in these later works, it could also serve as a form of hospitality and could provide the means of transition between ethics and politics. Particularly in relation to Levinas, he argues that this dynamic within Levinas's own texts could serve the aims of Levinas's project. This claim, if not the term *autoimmunity,* is already evident in "Violence and Metaphysics," when he argues for the possibility of a lesser violence. By "En ce moment même me voici" (1980) Derrida speaks of purity and contamination. "Now to make us (without doing anything) receive otherwise the otherwise, he [Levinas] has been unable to do otherwise than negotiate with the risk; in the same language, the language of the same, one must always receive badly, wrongly this otherwise-said. Even before the fault, the risk contaminates every proposition" (*P* 165, 145). What Levinas attempts to establish in his discourse in *Otherwise Than Being* is a means of "letting be understood without ever making understandable, an implication of a meaning distinct from that which comes to signs" (*AE* 263; *OTB* 169). His prose thus seems to be animated by a principle of hospitality. But this hospitality involves the risk, Derrida points out, of contamination, of it being understood otherwise. In taking that risk, Levinas also courts another. He might lose the argument that what is exposed in the disjunction between the sign and its meaning *is* transcendence—that the gap between the two points back to ethics. As I argue in chapter 1, Derrida demonstrates this risk in his own essay through the play he performs on Levinas's name. By transforming Levinas's initials E. L. into Elle, Derrida introduces the feminine, one of the principles toward which he felt Levinas was inhospitable. Moreover, by centering his own essay around passages in which Levinas inserts himself into *Otherwise Than Being*, by speaking of the here and now, Derrida is able to show that Levinas's own attempts to control the interruption of discourse calls attention to the very movement of iteration by which presence is effaced through repetition. As this becomes a kind of practice that Levinas cultivates in the text, Levinas troubles the distinction between "use and mention" such that it is unclear, as repetition, whether the interruption is not already the citation of the earlier interruption, thus producing a series within the text. "This is a series," Derrida argues, "where the text composes and compromises with its own (if this may still be said) tear" (*P* 173, 157).

In illustrating Levinas's incapacity to keep or guard his word, Derrida is not *exactly* critiquing Levinas. For the impossibility of protecting against the risk *is*, Derrida insists, exactly what opens Levinas's texts *to* the ethical, construed by Derrida as the principle of hospitality. "Language must be allowed this freedom to betray so that it can surrender to its essence, which is ethical" (*P* 174, 158). For Derrida this exposure is inevitable, and it is, as we've seen, tied to the relinquishing of one's text to the other, to that risk. But what marks the difference between discourses, between religion and literature, is a matter of thinking through the stakes of tradition. It is a matter of how one relates to the fact of legacy. Does one continually shore up the essence of the said, insist against history on the purity of the message? Or does one relinquish control and welcome the drift?

In *Otherwise Than Being* Levinas draws a distinction between what he considers to be discourses of mastery—science and medicine—and those he considered to be disruptive: the prophetic and the poetic. In "Faith and Knowledge" Derrida troubles this dichotomy. He returned to the language of purity and contamination in order to argue that, in their efforts to protect themselves against contamination, science and religion are on the same side. "Can a discourse on religion be dissociated from a discourse on salvation: which is to say, on the holy, the sacred, the safe and sound, the unscathed, the immune?" (*FS* 9; FK 42). And science, ironically, would be similarly animated in its very attempt to show itself free of belief, to establish itself as pure, sovereign in its capacity to found itself in truth.

At the very same time, both, Derrida argues, are equally discourses of the pledge or the promise, each requires the other to establish itself as credible, or trustworthy. "Religion and reason develop in tandem, drawing from this common resource: the testimonial pledge of every performative. . . . *Either* it addresses the absolute other as such, with an address that it understood, heard, respected faithfully and responsibily; *or* it retorts, retaliates, compensates and *indemnifies itself* in the war of resentment and of reactivity" (*FS* 45; FK 66). As Derrida's story at Hopkins in 1968 reveals, in trying to declare himself uncontaminated by literature, the doctor responded as though threatened and, indeed, retorted, retaliated, and tried to indemnify himself.

Now, in writing about *religion* in "Faith and Knowledge," Derrida speaks broadly of the term as it had developed in the Latinate world. He emphasizes its Latin origin and its implication in that world's colonizing and universalizing tendencies. *Religion* is thus a term tied to Christianity but applicable beyond it, especially insofar as other traditions now bear the mark both of its influence and their attempt to thwart it. The term supersedes, for Derrida, any strict reference to Levinas and his specific use of it. It addresses a contemporary political landscape that is the result of certain kinds of globalization and thus the spreading of the Latinate concept of religion. It is also a means to engage with other philosophers who take up the theme of religion as a philosophical category, most clearly Kant and Bergson, whose arguments are themselves referenced in the article's subtitle: "the two sources of 'Religion' at the limits of reason alone." Levinas is cited sparingly throughout, but most importantly at the end of the essay, where he is credited with providing an alternative dichotomy for the splitting of religion's sources. Instead of faith and indemnity, the two sources Derrida associates with the Latinate version of religion, Levinas distinguishes between the sacred and the holy. In distinguishing these two, Derrida points the reader toward Levinas's second volume of Talmudic readings, *Du sacré au Saint*, a collection including readings from the years 1969 to 1975. In so doing Derrida also references another cultural resource, the Hebraic, as providing the notion of holiness distinct from sacrality. But this turn complicates the dichotomy that Derrida has already established in the essay between indemnification and faith.

In the Talmudic reading "Désacralisation et Déseensorcellement" in which Levinas draws the distinction, he describes Judaism as providing the world with a conception of religion as the fiduciary, or the movement toward the other person. This for Levinas is manifest in the term *kiddush,* which means separate. As a principle of separation, Levinas distinguishes holiness from the sacred. "The sacred is in fact the half light in which the sorcery the Jewish tradition abhors flourishes" (*DSS* 89; *NTR* 141). Holiness [*Kadosh*], on the other hand, is separation, or purity, "the essence without admixture, or that toward which Judaism aspires" (*DSS* 89; *NTR* 141). This principle of purity and separation is intrinsically tied in Judaism, to the priestly purity codes and dietary law. Mapping Levinas's claims onto his own at the very end of the text, Derrida thus complicates the very dichotomy the essay has already established, especially as Derrida wants to affirm in the essay "the ether of the address and the relation to the utterly other" over and against indemnification (*FS* 98; *FK* 99). In Levinas the avenue toward the other is *through* purification. By the end of the reading, Levinas has argued for a conception of *sainteté,* his translation of kiddush, as presence to the world, as a principle of disenchantment. It repels sacrality, understood as that which would distract and tempt one beyond the concerns of the world, whether toward artifice, illusion, or mystification. In his preface to the volume, Levinas addresses what he saw as a contemporary fascination for the mythical, premodern world, the vogue of Lévi-Strauss, religion as the possibility of reenchanting the universe. His purpose is to argue for a different religious principle at the heart of Judaism, one that emerges *through* disenchantment.

Derrida seems to have ascribed to the possibility of such a disenchantment with his own notions of chora and messianicity. These principles are invoked in the first part of the essay, as "messianicity without messianism" and "as a desert in the desert" (*FS* 16, 32, 35; *FK* 47, 57, 59).[14] Messianicity is defined as "the opening to the future or to the coming of the other as the advent of justice, but without horizon of expectation and without prophetic prefiguration," a stripping down of religion to a principle of pure faith (*FS* 30; *FK* 56). When Derrida uses Levinas's model of disenchantment, rather than a "secularization or laicization, concepts," Derrida says, "that are too Christian," to describe a principle for the philosophy of religion, he appears to be allying the notion of disenchantment with his own project as well (*FS* 98; FK 99).

But the function of the reference is not in fact to allow for a simple symmetry between their projects, but ultimately as a move to set in motion an autoimmune function *through* the analogy itself. For Levinas's argument in the Talmudic lecture "Desacralization and Disenchantment" follows exactly the logic of indemnification, the attempt to draw lines between one's discourse and another, to protect it from external threat. Thus, in aligning the two, Derrida's move to retain from religion what he calls the "*salut* of greeting or salutation of the other," over and against the "*salut* of salvation," would *seem* to be caught up in its own process of indemnification, its own move to protect faith from the sacred (*V* 15; *R* xvi). But in fact this is exactly the point. Derrida uses Levinas to reveal an autoimmune function in Derrida's text. Levinas's has not served Derrida, then, as a way out of a conundrum, but as a means of exposing that Derrida's own arguments too are subject to an autoimmune unworking, to a function that betrays their principles.

At the end of the essay, he affirms that there cannot be only *one* source to religion: There is no faith without the movement of indemnification, no sanctity without the sacred:

> There would be faith and religion, faith or religion, because *there are at least two*. Because there are, for the best and for the worst, division and iterability of the source. This supplement introduces the incalculable at the heart of the calculable. (Levinas: "It is this being two <*être à deux*> that is human, that is spiritual.") But the more than One <*plus d'Un*> is at once more than two. There is no alliance of two, unless it is to signify in effect the pure madness of pure faith. The worst violence. The more than One is this n + One which introduces the order of faith or of trust in the address of the other, but also the mechanical, machine-like division (testimonial affirmation and reactivity, "yes, yes," etc., answering machine and the possibility of *radical evil*: perjury, lies, remote-control murder, ordered at a distance even when it rapes and kills with bare hands).
>
> (*FS* 99; FK 100)

Coming only a paragraph after Levinas is presented as providing a model, the reference here once again reveals the ironic dimension to the relationship Derrida established between their thinking. Levinas is treated as an authority, but in a move that undercuts his claims. Levinas appears here as a source, but now for the principle that being is first and foremost plurality, that there is always more than one. As Levinas himself put it in the conclusion to *Totality and Infinity*: "The social relation engenders this surplus of the Good over being, multiplicity over the One" (*TI* 325, 292). Only one paragraph after Derrida aligns himself with Levinas in "Faith and Knowledge," the reference serves as a rejoinder against the very argument of *Du sacré au saint*. Derrida is here affirming the principle of plurality as applicable to religion. He is thus calling attention to Levinas's desire to identify Judaism's essence *only* with sanctification. And Derrida goes further; he returns to the language of "Violence and Metaphysics," to the claim that Levinas cannot break with history, cannot break with the realm of light and meaning in announcing the transcendent, cannot do so without risking the "worst violence, the violence of primitive and prelogical silence" (*FS* 99; FK 100). There is always already representation, repetition, reactivity.

Against a model of religion, as Levinas has defined it, against a model of Judaism as the force of sanctity that bans sorcery by pain of death, by stoning—as Rabbi Akiva affirms, citing Exodus 22:18 with Exodus 19:13 in the Gemara that Levinas read for his Talmudic reading in "Desacralization and Disenchantment"—Derrida invokes a different image: "the Spanish Marrano who would have lost—in truth—dispersed, multiplied—everything up to and including the memory of his unique secret. Emblem of a still life: an opened pomegranate [*grenade*], one Passover evening, on a tray" (*FS* 100; FK 100).

The word *grenade* appears once before in "Faith and Knowledge," as the subtitle between the thirty-seventh and thirty-eighth paragraphs. A term that in French could mean either "grenade" or a "pomegranate," as a subtitle the word is decontextualized, and thus it is not clear whether Derrida is referencing fruit or weapons. It returns in paragraph 51, the penultimate paragraph of the essay, to do its damage. Both Sam Weber, the essay's translator, and Michael Naas have offered explanations of the function of the line within Derrida's essay.[15] Clearly it has many. It tempts us to read it as an autobiographical insertion, thus reminding us once again of another way of being Jewish, one that differs from Levinas's. The custom of including the pomegranate on the seder plate is a custom particular to North African and Sephardic Jews on Rosh Hashanah (not Passover). But we should keep in mind it is placed there precisely *not* as an autobiographical confession. It is introduced as a part of an analogy: "Ontotheology en*crypts* faith and destines it to the condition of a sort of Spanish Marrano who would have lost—in truth, dispersed, multiplied—everything up to and including the memory of his unique secret. Emblem of a still life: an opened pomegranate [*grenade*], one Passover evening, on a tray" (*FS* 100; FK 100).

The ambiguity of the reference is itself in striking contrast to Levinas's own invocation of his biography as a key to his philosophy. Both editions of Levinas's *Difficile liberté* conclude with what he calls a *signature*. Levinas provides a kind of curriculum vitae in order to situate his work. Derrida, in contrast, introduces the reference to the Marrano to complicate the relation between his autobiography and his writings. As a literary turn so often does, it tempts us to decode it, to map the references, as Naas and Weber have done, to consider how it links Derrida to both the Jewish and the Greek, how it works as a reference to Persephone, how it functions as Jewish symbol (according to Jewish tradition, pomegranates contain 613 seeds thus symbolizing the 613 commandments contained in the Torah), how the term itself in its ambiguity—both weapon and fruit—belies its function as religious symbol. It seems to serve here as an emblem for the secret. But ultimately this is a secret that cannot be revealed. It can only proliferate in meaning.

The final paragraph of the essay leaves behind one more tantalizing clue. Derrida ends the essay with a reference to *Genet à Chatila*, which he says he had been reading at the time that he gave the first version of "Faith and Knowledge" in Capri at a conference organized with Gianni Vattimo on religion. The reference dates the text to a singular moment, but also encrypts it. This is what a date does, Derrida theorized elsewhere: "This date will have signed or sealed the unique, the unrepeatable, but to do so, it must have given itself to be read in a form sufficiently coded, readable and decipherable for the indecipherable *to appear*" (*S* 37, 18). It also forms what Celan theorized as a meridian, a linkage between two dates that does not sacrifice the singularity of either, but links them—a line connecting two unrepeatable moments. For Celan this is the way a poem speaks, not by disclosing the moment of its composition to a reader, but by ciphering it and yet, nonetheless, opening itself up to interpretation.[16] Between Derrida's reading of Genet and "one Passover evening," Derrida creates a meridian and also invokes two sources. We know nothing about either event—the meaning of neither has been disclosed—but the essay itself provides the connection Celan theorizes as an "act of freedom, a step."[17] It is the possibility of an encounter, the traverse between two poles, two singular events. It does not collapse their difference but connects them.

Derrida tells us that while at Capri he was reading Genet's essays on his time with Palestinian refugees at the camp of Shatila. We do not know what Derrida thought of the book, only that he says the essays "deserve to be remembered here, in so many languages, the actors and the victims, and the eves and the consequences, all the landscapes and all the spectres" (*FS* 100; FK 101).

One of those specters is Levinas's infamous remarks following the massacres in 1982 at Sabra and Shatila in an interview with Alain Finkelkraut and Solomon Malka. Levinas speaks of the third person and what happens when the third intervenes in the ethical face-to-face relation. When asked whether, for the Israeli, "the other isn't above all the Palestinian?" he replies:

> My definition of the other is completely different. The other is the neighbor, who is not necessarily kin, but who can be. And in that sense, if you're for the other, you're the neighbor. But if your neighbor attacks another neighbor or treats him unjustly, what can you do? Then alterity takes on another character, in alterity we can find an enemy, or at least we are faced with the problem of knowing who is right and who is wrong, who is just and who is unjust. There are people who are wrong.[18]

Levinas's response has been critiqued by Judith Butler and Howard Caygill, among others.[19] But it is perfectly representative of Levinas's philosophical model, for Levinas merely lays out the difficulty of the transition between ethics and politics and the need for adjudication that intervenes with the third.

This dynamic and all its difficulties is the theme in particular of Derrida's eulogy for Levinas, "Adieu to Emmanuel Levinas" and "A Word of Welcome," both written soon after "Faith and Knowledge" and published together as *Adieu to Emmanuel Levinas*. In these two essays dedicated to Levinas, Derrida insists that the transition between ethics and politics must be thought, but also that it must be thought *in and through* Levinas's own writings. And Derrida claims to do exactly that, but through themes and with terminology that Levinas did not explicitly take up—through the notion of *oath* and *perjury*. Derrida insists that his own thinking on this topic arose out of fidelity to Levinas's texts, "though Levinas never puts it in these terms" (A 54, 33). "Henceforth, in the operation of justice one can no longer distinguish between fidelity to oath and the perjury of false witness, and even before this, between betrayal and betrayal, always more than one betrayal," Derrida writes, using a political vocabulary that pervaded his writings in the late 1990s and early 2000s—though rarely associated with Levinas—as he came to think the relationship between religion, literature, and politics (A 54, 33).

In the closing of his interview with Finkielkraut and Malka, Levinas spoke of a Zionism that would be much more than nationalism. He spoke of its "genuine messianic element." He went as far as saying "one is closer to the Messiah in Israel than here." He then described Zionism's essence as "conformity with the heritage of our scriptures. . . . It is not only our thought we must defend and protect, it's our souls and that which upholds our souls: our books! . . . The supreme threat: that our books should be in jeopardy."[20]

Much of what Derrida has to say in *Adieu to Emmanuel Levinas* reads as a response to these statements, which are replicated in various formulations in *Beyond the Verse*, from which Derrida quotes liberally in *Adieu*. Derrida defines his own messianicity in *Adieu* as a fidelity to Levinas as well and argues that it was Levinas who announced the possibility of an "a priori messianicity." He describes his own duty to Levinas's principle as that which "would lead me to dissociate, with all the consequences that might follow, a structural messianicity, an irrecusable and threatening promise, an eschatology without teleology from every determinate messianism" (*AEL* 203–4, 118–19).

But what of Derrida's fidelity to those Jewish books that Levinas had insisted must be protected?

In the closing of "Faith and Knowledge," Derrida—faithful to the principle that there cannot be just one—raises the names of two figures to whom he owed fidelity. He could not close merely with a reference to Levinas, but brings in a figure whose very presence in proximity to Levinas would seem to unwork any claim of alliance between Derrida and Levinas. This is not the first time Genet functions this way for Derrida. Genet already appears alongside Derrida's paraphrasing of Hegel's description of Judaism in "The Spirit of Christianity and Its Fate" in *Glas* some twenty years earlier. And it is Genet that Derrida credits with having revealed to him the role of literature as "betrayal of truth." In the 2004 essay "Countersignature" Derrida explicitly worked out the ambiguity between fidelity and betrayal that he had only briefly mentioned in *Adieu:*

> Perjury—or betrayal, if you prefer—is lodged like a double band at the very heart of the countersignature. That is the betrayal of truth as truth of betrayal. That is also, however terrifying it may seem, faithfulness. One must faithfully recognize it and be as faithful as possible to faithfulness.... But in order for my countersignature, that is, this law that comes before any literary theory, before any critical methodology, before any concept of exegesis or hermeneutics or criticism or commentary ... to attest both to knowledge [*conaissance*] ... and to recognition [*re-conaissance*] ... it must both respect the absolute, absolutely irreducible, untranslatable idiom of the other *and* inscribe in my own "yes" at the moment I recognize the other's singularity, the work of the other.[21]

Derrida's *grenade* at the close of "Faith and Knowledge" is no doubt a double gesture, a double affirmation of both mentors, a meridian, a line of connection, formed between the two, a site where Jews and Palestinians could be brought together, where Jewish symbols become terrorist symbols, where the 613 commandments explode, or, are like seeds, disseminated in an afterlife for which one must cede control.[22] Like Levinas, Derrida too affirms his fidelity to the book, but only as a betrayal.[23]

THE SECRET OF THE BOOK

We've established thus far that Levinas's politics developed from the conviction that Judaism's great books bear witness to the truth of ethics and that the tradition that bears witness to that truth needs to be protected. Protecting that tradition, for Levinas, meant affirming Zionism as if not always the instantiation of those principles than at least the site of their promise. Thus even if ethics was for Levinas the source for a notion of freedom that uproots the sovereignty of the self, it had to be protected in and through the sovereign state of Israel.

For Derrida, the principle of dissemination calls into question the possibility that the singular event of ethics could ever be something to which one could bear witness. For Levinas, "Judaism's great books" are themselves a metonym for the tradition, the site in which the truth of the face-to-face relation could be rediscovered, while for Derrida "the book" is the figure for the inevitable disruption between the singular and the universal. It *also* has to be politically protected, but *as* literature, as "the right to say anything," which Derrida saw as intrinsic to "the democracy to come."

In multiple essays Derrida developed his thinking on the disruption between the singular and the universal through what he named "the secret." Derrida uses the term to describe the remainder that does not translate or transfer into language and representation from the singular or the absolute: "the condition of any bond, detached, and which itself cannot bind."[24] Even when he does not name it as such, the dynamic of the secret is already in play in any discussion of trace. Already in *Of Grammatology* all its crucial dynamics are at work. The trace is defined as "self-occultation": "When the other announces itself as such, it presents itself in the dissimulation of itself. . . . The presentation of the other as such, that is to say the dissimulation of its 'as such,' has always already begun and no structure of the entity escapes it" (*DG* 69; *OG* 47). Presentation is always already tied to duplicity, to the production of an image or text that can be put into circulation. In presenting itself, the other thus hides itself.

When Derrida refers to the secret instead of the trace, however, he uses the term often to emphasize the "'theological' moment in its movement" and the desire concomitant with that moment or movement.[25] As Derrida put it in *Sauf le nom*, "The Secret is not a reserve of potential knowing, a potential manifestion . . . [it is] Passion of, for the place." It is tied as well to the power of passage, inheritance, tradition, generated by the alliance of desire and nonmanifestation, to the dynamics of keeping or entrusting "the secret with the very strict limits of those who hear/understand it *right*" (*SLN* 62–63; *OTN* 59).

Religion would thus refer to a certain relation to the secret, one involving protection, entrusting, and the maintaining of the secret as secret. But because the secret is itself nontransferable, because it cannot pass into representation, it has always already been betrayed. Religion designates a certain means of relating to that betrayal, whether through the promise of disclosure—a promise always deferred—or through the perpetuation of a discourse, such as negative theology, that calls attention to its own inadequacy.

In *Gift of Death* Derrida argues that this definition of religion does not require dogma or even God at its center, rather it is a matter of a certain logic "that has no need of *the event of a revelation or the revelation of an event.* It needs to think the possibility of such an event but not the event itself" (*DLM* 74; *GD* 50). By this definition, Derrida is able to group together a whole set of thinkers bound by their relation to the secret: Lévinas, Heidegger, Marion, Patočka, Kierkegaard, and "even a certain Kant and Hegel" (*DLM* 75; *GD* 50)

It is a definition in some ways consonant with Levinas's own formulation of religion in *Totality and Infinity*. Manifest in the face to face, religion is that which cannot be totalized, that which is "refractory to categories" (*TI* 30, 40) But for Derrida religion implies a form of relating to the secret that continues to perpetuate the promise of its disclosure even when it does not attempt to determine its content. That promise itself leads to certain strategies for dealing with and perpetuating the desire concomitant with the secret, strategies that themselves have clear consequences, often political, which, Derrida writes, made him "tremble" (*DLM* 79; *GD* 54). Through this promise, he argues, one he recognizes in all three Abrahamic traditions, the religions of the book resort to the function of economy, even as the secret, as the singular, would seem to be that which disrupts economy. The economy or function of exchange is put in place through the introduction of a different form of secrecy, that of being seen, or being called, by the one who "sees in secret," Derrida quotes Kierkegaard quoting Matthew. Secrecy here takes on a new form: the simultaneous denunciation of self-interest, calculation, retribution and the inevitable wager of an infinite return. It is a truth that can only be witnessed with one's life and through the logic of sacrifice, an act that foregoes the calculation of consequence, but for the cause of deliverance. It is also the beginning of esotericism. Kierkegaard closed *Fear and Trembling*: "But there is no one who could understand Abraham. And yet what did he achieve? He remained true to his love. But anyone who loves God needs no tears, no admiration; he forgets the suffering in the love. Indeed so completely has he forgotten it that there would not be the slightest trace of his suffering left if God himself did not remember it, *for he sees in secret* and recognizes distress and counts the tears and forgets nothing."[26] Kierkegaard claims here to be denouncing calculation, the promise of return, but, at the same time, the reference to Matthew 6:4 speaks only to those who can read it as a reference already and who know as well that in 6:19 Jesus calls his followers to relinquish the treasures of the seen world for the treasures of the unseen. But this wager, which simultaneously interrupts the economy of exchange and amplifies it, is already present in the telling of the Akedah, in Abraham's sacrifice of Isaac, in the language of test (*nisa*). In the story, God demands faith in the One, even when there is always already another, in this case the son, whom Abraham loved. As Derrida puts it in *Mal d'archive*, "As soon as there is One, there is murder, wounding, traumatism" (*MA* 124; *AF* 78).

It might seem that those thinkers who ascribe to the secret without dogma would escape the political consequences tied to dogma—that of claiming to determine the secret as truth and perpetuating it, thus needing to distinguish the false from the true. But Derrida argues in *Gift of Death* that the problem emerges as soon one tries to determine the singular, to distinguish between types of alterity, to encode it in discourse. Both Kierkegaard and Levinas fail then in opposing religion and ethics insofar as they both try to distinguish the alterity of God from the alterity of the other. "Neither one nor the other can assure himself of a concept of the ethical and of the religious that is of consequence; and consequently they are especially unable to determine the limit between these two orders" (*DLM* 117; *GD* 84).

But what they also share in common is that for each the singular is identified as a threat to the universal. At least, thus, in both the incalculable is registered in the horror of the choice that Abraham makes. The Enlightenment attempt to overcome the violence of religious distinction creates the further problem of effacing the groundlessness of its ethical/political concepts.

> In the axiomatics of private, public or international law, in the conduct of internal politics, diplomacy and war, is a lexicon concerning responsibility that can be said to hover vaguely about a concept that is nowhere to be found. . . . It amounts to a disavowal whose resources, as one knows, are inexhaustible. One simply keeps on denying the aporia and antinomy, tirelessly, and one treats as nihilist, relativist, even poststructuralist, or worse still deconstructionist, all those who remain concerned in the face of such a good conscience.
>
> (*DLM* 118; *GD* 85)

Derrida would seem to be allied on some level then with the attempts by those thinkers invested in religion's return insofar as he was invested in exposing the secret at the heart of the subject. It is in this alliance that we can also see how and where Derrida and Levinas's political concerns map onto one another, for the affirmation of the secret calls into question the political and philosophical subject as a pure self-consciousness, as transparency and as self-grounding. Politics demands that "the manifest is given priority over the secret . . . no irreducible secret can be legally justified," as Derrida put it in *Gift of Death* (*DLM* 91; *GD* 64).

The first chapter of *Gift of Death* considers recent efforts to recover the secret by way of a reading of Jan Patočka's *Heretical Essays in the Philosophy of History*. Derrida paraphrases Patočka, "To inherit this politics of Greco-Platonic provenance is to neglect, repress or exclude from itself every essential possibility of secrecy and every link between responsibility and the keeping of a secret; everything that allows responsibility to be dedicated to a secret" (*DLM* 54; *GD* 34). This is a sentence that could have come from Levinas. Levinas's own investment in Judaism can be read as an attempt to recover what had been neglected or repressed. But, as Derrida points out in *Gift of Death*, in his weaving together of analyses of Patočhka, Levinas, Heidegger, and Kierkegaard, Levinas is not alone here. He is part of a tradition of those who want to recover what modernity has repressed. Derrida is among them. But the problem with the secret is that it cannot be shared, cannot be passed on. "It is a passion that, sworn to secrecy, cannot be transmitted from generation to generation. In this sense it has no history." And yet, in a certain sense, it can and it is. "A secret can be transmitted, but in transmitting a secret as secret that remains secret, has one transmitted at all? Does it amount to history, to a story?" (*DLM* 113; *GD* 80).

The difference between religion and the modern institution of literature can be rendered as a difference between how one relates to this paradox: that the secret cannot be transmitted and yet it is transmitted. It is not that literature is truer to the secret than religion, that it guards it better, but rather that, in betraying it, it copies and counterfeits religion's betrayal, but in so doing it also announces itself *as* copy. This, Derrida argues, can in fact *be* a way of guarding the secret.

"I WOULD PREFER NOT TO . . . "

In 1991–1992 Derrida gave a seminar on the secret and responsibility in which he read, among others, Poe, Henry James, and Melville. One year later, but six years before he wrote "Literature in Secret," Derrida first worked out the dynamics of the relation between religion, literature, and politics in the essay "Passions" (1993). He then renders his argument in more programmatic terms in "Literature in Secret," later appended to *Gift of Death*, and published in French as *Donner la mort*. As the title implies, "Passions" is an essay about the parody or repetition of a religious narrative. The modern institution of literature, Derrida then writes in the essay "Literature in Secret," is an exposure that "descralizes" or "secularizes" the Scriptures, holy or sacred scriptures; it "repeats the sacrifice . . . stripping it bare, delivering and exposing it to the world" (*DLM* 203; *GD* 154).

The two essays share many of the same themes, particularly the assertion that there is no democracy without literature. Even the title "Passions" ties it with *Donner la Mort*, as the phrase itself is an idiom for suicide. "Passions" can be read furthermore as participating in the function of a biblical exposure that characterizes literature, in its parody of "The Last Supper," a replay that places Derrida in the position of Christ with his twelve apostles.[27] The essay was written for the compilation *Derrida: A Critical Reader*, and "Passions" was Derrida's contribution to a volume that included eleven other essays by scholars on Derrida. Although there was no conference, no meal, no gathering, Derrida imagines the ritual, and its ritualistic dissection by a scholar, in the essay's opening paragraphs. As every ritual is by definition already a repetition, Derrida was interested in replaying this repetition. As the body and body of work on which his commentators fed, he set himself up as a sacrifice to be served up.

But this repetition of the "Passion" narrative already indexes a literary work, "Bartleby the Scrivener," and another sacrifice, Bartleby's. For, in *Gift of Death,* Derrida reads Melville's "Bartleby" as a replay of the Passion narrative. "Bartleby's 'I would prefer not to,'" Derrida writes, "is also a sacrificial passion that would lead him to death, a death given by the law, by a society that doesn't even know why it acts the way it does" (*DLM* 107; *GD* 75).

Insofar as Derrida poses in "Passions" as a Christ figure, it is by means of the paradigm he already presents in his reading of "Bartleby." The comparison of himself to Christ in relation to his respondents sets up exactly the ironic relation to the story that he sees literature playing out in relation to the biblical covenant. "This is no Last Supper [*Cène*], and the ironic friendship which brings us together consists in knowing this, while peering with a 'squinty eye' toward this cannibalism in mourning" (P 46, OTN 19). This play acting of the "last supper," which Derrida oversignifies in the essay, daring us to make use of it, takes on another layer of meaning when read through Derrida's comment about Bartleby in "Gift of Death."

Read with Melville's story, Derrida's performance, his nonresponse, so attentive to the politics of politesse, reads like a reenactment and repetition of Bartleby's "I prefer not to." Like Bartleby, Derrida subjected himself to the infinite misinterpretation of others, without ever relinquishing the fundamental privacy that more than anything characterizes Bartleby as a literary figure and characterizes literature itself.

This refusal to relinquish does not concern a withholding, however, even as it solicits that effect. There is no dimension of depth, a dimension that religion would continue to maintain, but rather, as Derrida defined literature in "Passions," "a chance of saying everything without touching upon the secret. When all hypotheses are permitted, groundless and ad infinitum, about the meaning of the text, or the final intentions of an author, whose person is no more represented than nonrepresented by a character or by a narrator" (*P* 66; *OTN* 29).

By reading himself as the literary parody of Christ, Derrida plays the role of Bartleby whom Derrida has already described as modern literature's Christ figure. The theme thus articulated is the secret, but not the secret as it remains within the paradigm of the religious ritual, a paradigm in which the theological dynamic of the trace remains intact, where it retains its promise of delivery, of presence disclosed, but the secret as it is replayed, and replaced in literature, as Derrida described it later in "La Littérature au secret," as "the place of all these secrets without secrecy, all these crypts without depth, with no other basis than the abyss of the call or address, without any law other than the secret of the event called work" (*DLM* 206; *GD* 157).

Derrida first makes the claim in "Passions" for a relationship between literature and "democracy to come."[28] The connection itself seems straightforward, reducible even to freedom of speech: "The possibility of literature, the legitimation that a society gives to it, all that goes together—politically—with the unlimited right to ask any question, to suspect all dogmatism, to analyze every proposition, even those of the ethics or politics of responsibility" (*P* 65; *OTN* 28). While Levinas is not evoked in the essay itself, what is present is the very issue of how to move from an ethics of responsibility to a politics of responsibility. This transition, as is evident in *Gift of Death* and earlier works, is intimately tied to Derrida's negotiations with Levinas. The story of Bartleby provides a literary representation of this impossible transition.

On one level, the story seems to repay a reading as a kind of Levinasian parable. The narrator, the attorney who hires Bartleby as a copyist, first engages him because of his docile and sedate temperament, seeing him as an implement to be harnessed both for the narrator's own needs and as a balance to his other seemingly unpredictable but completely explicable copyists. The narrator puts Bartleby in his office, but separates him with a screen so as to be able to call him for a task yet not to have to see him. This mechanism conveniently shields the narrator from having to endure a face-to-face encounter with Bartleby. What is striking in the story is the way in which Bartleby's secrecy, and increasing use of the phrase "I prefer not to" in response to the narrator's requests, alters the prescribed relation between the narrator and his employee. As Bartleby resists the narrator's efforts to implement, explain, or understand him, his efforts to plumb his psyche, Bartleby's humanity emerges as an obstacle to his instrumentalization. In the face of it, the narrator is overcome with a melancholy unlike any he has ever experienced, "a fraternal melancholy," he calls it.[29] Finally, the narrator's masterly intentions are reversed to the point that he finds himself inviting Bartleby to come and live with him. The responsibility that follows from the narrator's recognition of Bartleby's humanity is such that no gesture can dispense with it; he is beholden to Bartleby even beyond Bartleby's own death.

At the same time that the story exemplifies the ethical relation, it also evokes a great deal about the presumptions of democratic society, which depends on the accountable, transparent, responsive subject.

Bartleby's disruption of the world around him requires no force, no argument. It all takes place within the boundaries of politesse. But the effects of his secrecy, his elusiveness, his nonresponsiveness are nonetheless transformative. The little society that he inhabits, governed by the story's narrator, the attorney, ceases to function as a consequence of Bartleby's elusive unresponsiveness. Its rules don't work. Its order doesn't function. It must be literally reconstituted in a new location to try to guard itself against the effect of Bartleby's foreignness, even as all Bartleby can be said to have done is "nothing."[30] At one point Bartleby's passivity is so ironically effective that the narrator describes himself as "thunderstruck" by it like "a man who, pipe in mouth, was killed one cloudless afternoon long ago in Virginia, by a summer lightning; at his own warm open window . . . and remained leaning out there upon the dreamy afternoon, till some one touched him, when he fell."[31] In this image Bartleby is the bolt of lightning and the narrator its passive target.

The story, at the same time that it narrates a kind of conversion on the part of the narrator in the face of what he recognizes as Bartleby's "humanity," a humanity that reveals itself not in rationality or understanding, but in strangeness and unresponsiveness, also discloses the expectations that accompany democracy insofar as it "links," in Derrida's words in "Passions," "to the concept of a subject that is calculable, accountable, imputable and responsible, a subject having-to-respond, having-to-tell" (*P* 67; *OTN* 29). It discloses these expectations by sending an invader into that world, a human being in all his foreignness.

As "Bartleby" illustrates, democracy assumes that it cannot handle this opacity. It deals with it by sending its representative to the tombs, to poorhouses and insane asylums—a point that Levinas himself made in *Otherwise*

Than Being (*AE* 264; *OTB* 170). But, as the story itself reveals, democracy also never operates without its subjects' opacity. At one point in the story, the narrator is guessing about Bartleby, whether or not he has budged from the office, convincing himself that he must have; it would be irrational and impossible that he would not have. At this point the narrator hears a passerby say, "I'll take odds that he doesn't."[32] For a moment the narrator thinks the passerby is talking about Bartleby and then realizes that in fact it is Election Day. For the narrator, the fact of Bartleby is impossible in the face of the law, a code that supposedly assures us that we can calculate the Other's next move, his every move. The narrator is right that his world—our world—could not operate without such calculation, but it is also endemic to democracy that the incalculable stymie its process.

For Derrida, the structural inclusion of its own defeat, the autoimmunity built into the concept of democracy, is what necessitates our understanding it as something that cannot be actualized, except as a kind of promissory note. But this is also what makes literature inseparable from it. Bartleby functions for Derrida on two levels: it is a parable about democracy's failure, but it is also itself an intervention into democracy through literature's relation to the secret.

The author of any literary work, particularly one presented as fiction, is always himself functioning like Bartleby insofar as the relation between what is said and the author as source is never transparent. Despite every attempt at an interpretation, the reader cannot plumb its depths, and the author has retained the right to say anything. But this right is also the right to nonresponse. "Just where there can be no question of responding, of being able to or having to respond. This nonresponse is more original and more secret than the modalities of power and duty because it is fundamentally heterogeneous to them" (*P* 66; *OTN* 29).

We find here announced thus another means of intervening into the political scene. One that, like the return of religion, calls into question "the calculable, accountable, imputable . . . having to respond, having to tell the truth, having to testify according to the sworn word, having to reveal the secret" subject (*P* 66–67; *OTN* 29). This approach, like Patočka's and Levinas's, calls the West to account for a repression, but relates to that repression differently, because it doesn't leverage it on a truth or a source to which it provides access.

Derrida makes a similar point in his essay on Kafka, "Préjugés: devant la loi" (1985) in relation to Freud's totemic meal. Freud's account is a myth, an attempt to account for the force of law by providing a myth of origin. Derrida reads Kafka's "Before the Law" as a reimagining of this same scene, but one that replaces myth with fiction. It imagines the conundrum of the law and the relation between its force and its source. But it is a work of fiction. It dramatizes and performs the conundrum of law, but also that of fiction. The difference between the two parallels the difference between literature and religion, where myth within the context of a religious tradition holds out the promise of disclosure (in this sense psychoanalysis would function like a modern religion), literature *dramatizes* that promise, but without retaining the promise of truth as its secret. "The inaccessible incites from its place of hiding," Derrida writes, describing the relation between the law and history. "To enter into relations with the law which says 'you must' and 'you must not' is to act as if it had no history or at any rate as if it no longer depended on its historical presentation. At the same time it is to let oneself be enticed, provoked, and hailed by the history of this non-history. It is to let oneself be tempted by the impossible: a theory of the origin of the law, and therefore its non-origin" (DLL 110; BTL 192). Thinking the relation between religion and literature means thinking the possibility of relating to this paradox, but without reinstating the structure of myth. In "Passions" the contrast between the two is made only obliquely, but it is the premise of the essay, and already evident in the very notion of an "oblique offering," the essay's subtitle: literature is a sacrifice without martyrdom, as Derrida puts it in the essay's final line. In this sense it is a parody of sacrifice, but, at the same time, it reveals something about the lure of the secret that the religious ritual has obscured. "Can one ever finish with obliqueness?" Derrida asks (*P* 68; *OTN* 30). Is obliqueness perhaps the truth of the secret, one that escapes the very logic of disclosure? "The secret, if there is one, is not hidden at the corner of an angle, it does not lay itself open to a double view or a squinting gaze. It cannot be seen, quite simply. No more than a word. As soon as there are words . . . as soon as there is a trace. Or, if you prefer, one can only deny it" (*P* 68; *OTN* 30). The effacement of singularity is present as soon as there are words. Whether or not the words themselves attest to the effacement or if they "make out that there is something [or someone] there when there is not . . . one can cite it as an impregnable resource. One can try in this way to secure for oneself a phantasmatic power over others. That happens ever day. But this very simulacrum still bears witness to a possibility which exceeds it" (*P* 70; *OTN* 30). One could say that these possibilities refer to both religion and literature. Literature's "passion without martyrdom," this offering up of the body of a text without holding anything in reserve, offering it up to endless reading and dissemination, a sacrifice that will proliferate, multiplying, as Derrida writes at the conclusion of "Literature in Secret," quoting Genesis 22:16, "like the stars of the heavens," this refers to the textual dimension of both religion and literature. But there is a difference between whether this dynamic is welcomed or denied (*DLM* 209; *GD* 158).

MORE THAN ONE

"Literature in Secret," appended to *Donner la mort* in 1999, meditates on the difference between religion and literature through the phrase "pardon for not meaning to say." In the opening chapter, we briefly considered the role of this phrase and its function as an iteration of the relationship between religion and literature, but, more important, as a means of articulating the relationship that Derrida saw himself playing in relation to Levinas as well. Derrida's use of irony in relationship to Levinas, I argue in chapter 1, is itself a method of communicating this "pardon for not meaning to say." Derrida faults Levinas, from the beginning in "Violence and Metaphysics," for the constitutive failure of his philosophy to remain faithful to the singularity of the face to face. At the same time, he sought both in his relation to Levinas and his portrayal of him to articulate his own loyalty to Levinas by formulating a method that accounted for the constituent betrayal in representation of the face-to-face. By cultivating, through the use of irony, the instability of the sign, Derrida thus guarded the secret of his own singular relationship to Levinas by revealing language's failure to do anything but betray it.

We return here to consider how this dynamic, which Derrida theorizes in "La Littérature au secret," as the relation between literature and religion *as* a "pardon for not meaning to say," can function politically and can produce a conception of freedom explicitly divorced from sovereignty.

Let us begin with the question, what would it mean for literature to say pardon?

Derrida is clear in "Literature in Secret," as he had been elsewhere, that to speak of a text as "literature" is not to speak of a quality intrinsic to it. A text becomes literature insofar as it functions like the phrase itself, "pardon for not meaning to say." The moment one is no longer sure of the signatory, addressee, or referent, when a text is released from the ruse of the secret, from the promise of it hiding something—something in particular—it has become literary. It is thus a convention, which doesn't even require pseudonymous authorship, even if that would be one way to secure its status.

"Literature would begin wherever one no longer knows who writes and signs the narrative of the call—and of the 'Here I am' between the absolute Father and Son" (*DLM* 179; *GD* 134). In this Derrida says it inherits its notion of the pardon from the Abrahamic tradition. Like Noah's rainbow, a message from the sky, a meteorite, the pardon in the tradition is already one that is only genuine insofar as it arrives out of nowhere, subject to no contract, with no expectation. With literature this dynamic is repeated through the quality of the text *as* meteor, but by sustaining itself "up in the air," its coming from nowhere, the "secretless secret" (*DLM* 177; *GD* 133). Ironically, it is by absolutely suspending the singularity of the covenant, of the identity of its participants, that literature says pardon. Literature thus takes its notion of pardon from the Abrahamic tradition, but in performing and exposing the dynamics of secrecy itself it thus potentially reveals the participation of those religious texts in the same dynamic.

In "Literature in Secret" and "Before the Law" Derrida uses Kafka to illustrate how this could be done, how Kafka's own texts repeat and replay the dynamics of mystery and power of religious texts and in the process expose the workings of religious and legal discourse such that they too appear to play according to the same dynamics as literature and yet they do this without unmasking the story, without reducing or deflating their power, without exposing it as "différance." "What is delayed is not this or that experience, the access to some enjoyment or to some supreme good, the possession or penetration of something or somebody. What is deferred forever till death is entry into the law itself, which is nothing other than that which dictates the delay" (DLL 122; BTL 205)

In Kafka's parable "Before the Law," the logic of the promise is retained structurally, but without any content and with no effect but deferral and the passage of time. In all of Kafka's texts, but perhaps most iconically in "Before the Law," "the text guards itself" as text (DLL 128; BTL 211). When the doorkeeper shuts the door, the text ends. "This 'I' of the doorkeeper is also that of the text or of the law, announcing the identity with itself of a bequeathed corpus, of a heritage that pronounces non-identity with itself" (DLL 129; BTL 211). In so doing the story is itself also a parable about textuality. It is a story that describes not only the dynamic between the man from the country and the doorkeeper but also the relation of the reader to the text. Just as the man from the country stays fixated at the door, so we remain fixated, waiting for the meaning of the parable to be disclosed. It provokes us thus into interpretation, but it also functions as a mirror to show us that the meaning will not be disclosed, the door will not open.

Kafka's parable is thus one example of how literature can teach us to read differently, and to relate to power differently, to behead the sovereign without claiming to overcome its effects. "Literality is not a natural essence, an intrinsic property of the text," Derrida insists, but rather an intentionality and a functioning: the suspension of a naïveté in regards to the text's thetic properties.[33] The lure of the secret remains but as the principle of dissemination. At the same time, however, deferral is also the source of a freedom that undermines sovereignty. Derrida developed the notion of "democracy to come" to mobilize the power of that annulment, to inaugurate a form of freedom inherent to democracy that is not synonymous with autonomy.[34] As he puts it in *Rogues*, "If every send-off [*renvoi*] is differ*antial,* and if the trace is a synonym for this send-off, then there is always some trace of democracy; indeed every trace is a trace of democracy. Of democracy there could only be but a trace" (*V* 64; *R* 39). But this involves more than a mere description. It involves a set of practices—the deformation or, as Derrida will also call it, the "salutation" of our very conception of reason. Somehow we must behead the king that reigns within our very conception of what we think it means to think. This involves mobilizing the literary structures within reason itself, finding its fictions and making them function as such.

Central to this operation is a rethinking of the site of the unconditioned. There is perhaps no more important construct in the history of philosophy than this "unconditioned." It is also the theological concept par excellence—the unmoved mover, the *causa sui,* but it is *retained* as the foundation of the autonomous subject, in Kant as the necessity of reason to be based on something other than the calculable and the claim that philosophy can provide and locate that site. In Kant this is the space of autonomy as freedom, the spontaneous power of will in its freedom, the site of a *causa sui* within reason itself. But in reading Kant, in "Before the Law" and later in *Rogues,* Derrida seeks to show that the categorical imperative can never detach the claims of reason's autonomy from fiction, from the *als ob* of the regulative ideals and even from the *als ob* that distinguishes the maxim of practical reason itself. The reasonable being acts as if he were legislator: "Act *as if* your maxims were to serve at the same time as a universal law."[35] Derrida uses the term fiction repeatedly in reference particularly to the Kantian postulates to argue that it is "as if" all of the "modal, rhetorical, logical or phenomenological trajectories of the 'as,' 'as such' and 'as if' converged on and confronted one another . . . so as to provoke or defy this architectonic desire, this unifying and appropriating order of reason" (*V* 171; *R* 121). He recalls an image from Kant's First Critique to suggest that all this fiction, which is necessary for the foundation of reason, may in fact run it aground. The passage in the First Critique is one of Kant's most literary moments, one in which he seems to give free reign to his poetic impulse. It is a striking moment at the opening of chapter 3 of book 2 of the transcendental analytic: "On the ground of the distinction of all objects in general into *phenomena* and *noumena.*" Here Kant describes reason as a "mariner" beset by fog banks and "rapidly melting icebergs" pretending "to be new lands."[36] There is quite clearly already in play the danger of reason running aground. Thus Derrida reintroduces the metaphor so as to exploit the question of ground and expose the possibility that the issue for reason is not so much locating a ground but choosing between *running aground,* the moment when a ship is accidentally immobilized, and *grounding,* the desperate attempt of a ship captain to maintain intentionality, autonomy in the moment of the encounter. The question at stake, is in fact the very question of the role of fiction in philosophy—the *als ob.* Might fiction or poetry play another role in philosophy, one in which running aground is no longer reason's menace but its chance? Derrida asks this question quite clearly, even if he doesn't link it explicitly at first to literature. Is there a chance, he writes, "To think or to grant the thought of the unconditional event to a reason that is other than we have just spoken about, namely the classical reason of what presents itself or announces its presentation according to *eidos*, the *idea,* the ideal, the regulative Idea or something that amounts to the same, the telos" (*V* 188; *R* 135). Derrida's task is thus to reorient the site of the unconditioned from foundation to the unforeseeable event, from the ground to the encounter with the iceberg. It is a matter of giving up ground and replacing it with the crisis of running aground.

This shift does not do away with the concept of the unconditioned, but it replaces it into a dynamic of futurity, into a strategy of cultivating the literary dynamic in any utterance, its meteoric quality. One means of cultivating this shift for Derrida was through a parody of the form of the oath or the maxim. The formulation of maxims, is, in Kant, the means to secure the freedom of the subject as autonomy, and the oath is the means to secure the transparency of the subject, her responsibility before the law. As we've already shown in our discussion of the relation between the singular and the universal, such utterances are all already duplicitous insofar as the passage into their formulation splits the subject, so that the speaking "I" is never identical to the "I "for whom she speaks. The choice then becomes one of trying to veil this duplicity—these speech acts are formulaic for a reason: to guard against their deformation, to protect and maintain their transparency—or of cultivating it. To cultivate their literary quality would thus mean to highlight the fact that the movement of difference, of time, that is to say repetition, will always alter them. This serves as a practice for Derrida, his own revolutionary act, which he performs consistently in his essays. Thus the phrase "Pardon for not meaning to say," which serves as the maxim/oath/phrase of "Literature in secret" is, on the one hand, axiomatic of that procedure and, at the same time, one more phrase through which indeterminacy is sown. In the opening to *Rogues*, Derrida offers up "Oui, il y a de l'amitié a penser" (*V* 23; *R* 4). But here he is explicit about thinking this phrase through as *le serment* (the oath; *V* 23; *R* 4). The orthographic proximity of this term to *le serpent*, Derrida insists, is no coincidence. The oath too can become a symbol for evil or *le serpent*. These terms are so close, they are separated in the dictionary only by the terms *sermon, séropositif,* and *serpe* (indicating conveniently the proximity between religion, autoimmunity, and the cut). It is a wordplay that emphasizes the fact that deconstruction is always already political and announces Derrida's contemporary project as a rereading of the threat (*le serpent*) as the promise (*le serment*). "Menace and promise at the same time," he writes, already reversing the significance, such that the oath would be flagged as a threat insofar as it attempts to stave off difference and the serpent would be flagged as a sign of promise, insofar as it opens to the future. "Menace and chance not to be missed," he continues, "for it is not certain that the snake is simply, as a reading of Genesis would tempt us to believe, a figure of malice, along the axis of evil" (*axis of evil* is in English, to remind us that he is already talking about politics). Then follows the line "Only a certain poetics can deform [*détourner*] a dominant inter-pretation—of the Bible or of some other canonical text" (*V* 23; *R* 5).

What we have then in Derrida's texts written between the early 1980s and his death is a series of meditations on the relation between religion and politics, between literature and politics, and between religion and literature. All three intersections establish an alliance between religion and literature insofar as they mobilize "the secret" toward uncovering the repressed ele-ment of subjectivity. Political liberalism represses this secret at the heart of the subject in formulating its model of subjectivity and its relation to reason and freedom. Calling attention to this lapse allows Derrida to argue for lit-erature's political function. At the same time, these relations imply a set of procedures, which Derrida uses in his own essays and identifies in the texts of others, procedures that could mobilize both the relationship between religion and literature and their differences to relate to the secret otherwise. This involves highlighting the subject *of* literature as that subject which exposes the autoimmunity of democracy as a system founded in *both* the principles of responsibility and freedom, principles whose conflict them-selves incite an autoimmune reaction. Derrida's procedure thus involves calling attention to, dramatizing and exaggerating the element of perjury in every claim to make a vow or a promise, complicating the assumption of agency within his own essays, revealing the spaces of fiction within philo-sophical arguments, and exposing the literary dynamics within the Abra-hamic religious canon. These techniques and interventions are themselves scattered through Derrida's essays, and the thinking of their political poten-tial can be traced back at least as far Derrida's course at Johns Hopkins if not further. But there is only one site in which Derrida provides something like a formulaic presentation of what the effect of these relationships could be on a thinking of democracy *as* "Democracy to come." This appears in the final pages of "Literature in Secret" in a form itself mimicking a last will and testament. In its very form it refers to a covenant and, as the repetition of such a document, already participates in the dynamic that Derrida has established between literature and religion or law. This would seem to be Derrida's own attempt at a fictionalization of the law.

At the same time, this "document," inserted at the close of *Gift of Death,* can be read as a response to Patočka's *Heretical Essays,* to its task of returning to its place the role of mystery, the importance of its history in constituting the European political subject.[37] But it is, more broadly, a response to a whole group of philosophers, perhaps to that very community of thinkers that Derrida addresses in the opening of "Violence and Metaphysics," the community of the question, invested in uncovering the "tradition's origin" in summoning it forth. This lineage includes Heidegger and Levinas. Patočka's role would be to articulate the logic of return in Christian terms. But it also implicates those thinkers who have returned as well to a Schmittian political theology as a regrounding of sovereignty in the tradition of a Christian God. One aim of the address would be to redraw the lines of debate in such a way that Kierkegaard, Levinas, Schmitt, and Patočka would all appear on the same side, as those reinvesting politics with its theological dimension. To all those whose thought supposes the necessity of a *return* to the site of theological mystery as either ground of politics or exception to it, Derrida proposed a different model, that of a theological inheritance *as* literature.[38] Instead, however, of a model of politics grounded in a theological notion of sovereignty or a model of religion in which a pure aporia is maintained between the demands of the universal and faith, or a model of religion as messianic interruption of the political, Derrida proposes literature as inheriting from all these traditions, but in a form that divests itself of authority, originality, exclusivity, or primacy. He formulates a series of principles that repeats the relation drawn between religion and the public sphere, but with the crucial difference that literature plays its role in relation to the political "with no other basis than the abyss of the call or address, without any law other than the singularity of the event called *the work*" (*V* 206; *GD* 157).

The first principle outlined is that of "freedom of speech," which Derrida broaches already in "Passions": "Literature (in the strict sense, as modern Western institution) implies *in principle* the right to say everything and to hide everything which makes it inseparable from a democracy to come"

(*V* 205; *R* 156) This principle, stated as the first of his principles, shows how literature mobilizes the autoimmune function of democracy. Insofar as democracy depends on the transparency of the subject, it threatens the freedom that democracy supposedly guarantees and protects. Insofar as the city is itself supposed to be grounded in truth, literature would seem to be a threat, but it is a freedom that in principle democracy would be instituted in order to protect.

The second principle refers to literature as exempt from responsibility and yet at the same time overdetermined in its responsibility for its effect of multiplying reference: "*Whereas* the presumed fictive structure of every work exonerates its signatory from responsibility, before political or civil law, for its sense and referent . . . while at the same time increasing in inverse proportion, to infinity, responsibility for the singular event constituted by every work" (*DLM* 206; *GD* 156). This principle would seem to speak to literature's capacity to interrupt the political, the space of universal law. If for Kierkegaard the knight of faith is one for whom the universal law is suspended, literature—in this sense, Kierkegaard too through his own use of pseudonymity would count as literary—rewrites this act in a different register, through its exemption from responsibility before the law for its "sense and referent." Literature's perjury can be read politically as resistance to the logic of the oath that grounds responsibility in a democracy and that always includes implicitly or explicitly the demand to tell the truth. At the same time, this perjury protects the singularity of the event "constituted by every work," insofar as it testifies to the perjury inherent in any act of testimony (*DLM* 206; *GD* 156). This also correlates with what Derrida elsewhere referred to as the dating of the text, its encryption. Literature thus negotiates the very divide narrated in *Fear and Trembling*, but in a passion *without* sacrifice.[39] Politically thus it functions to reveal the aporia between the universality of the law and the singularity of responsibility.

The third principle refers to literature's capacity to suspend law. "*Whereas* the secrets or effects of secrecy encrypted in such a literary event do not have to answer or correspond to any sense of reality in the world and appeal for a suspension of such. It relates literature to religion's claim to the miraculous and thus to the space of the exception, or a sovereignty that supersedes the law" (*DLM* 206; *GD* 156). This suspension correlates with what Benjamin referred to as "divine violence" "or sovereign violence" in his "Critique of

Violence," "defined not by miracles performed directly by God, but by the expiating moment within them, that strikes without bloodshed, and finally by the absence of all lawmaking."[40] In "Force of Law" Derrida writes clearly and critically of Benjamin's attempt to hold this "Judaic" form of violence apart and separate from mythological violence. In a critique that would certainly apply to any attempt to reclaim a tradition of political theology, or even any return to religion in the wake of the Holocaust, Derrida writes in the essay on Benjamin of the way in which arguments for an expiatory force that could annul the law "resemble too closely the point of specular fascination and vertigo, the very thing against which one must act and think, do and speak" (FOL 298). While Derrida's target here is Benjamin, Levinas is also in the background. Earlier in "Force of Law" Derrida speaks of Levinas's invocation of the other's "infinite right," which itself would annul the law (FOL 250). No doubt the charge made against Benjamin is meant to apply to Levinas as well. Literature would relate to this expiating power, but in a fashion devoid of violence, as "an appeal for a suspension of such (not for suspending reference but for suspending, or placing within parentheses or quotation marks the *thesis* or arrest the placing or stopping of determinate sense or real referent . . .)" (DLM 206; GD 157). Literature would thus, like the miracle, provide relief from the factical, from the tyranny of its law. It relates thus to a theological discourse of forgiveness, to the appeal to the supernatural, but without any invocation of authority. This last point is Derrida's next principle: literature "is the place of all secrets without secrecy." It relates to the secret, but without transcendence, invoking a crypt "without depth" founded in a singularity that requires no theological reference for its power (DLM 206; GD 157).

The two final principles refer to the dynamic explored in "Before the Law" and thus the capacity of literature to expose the function of power in religion and law: the supposition of an agency or authority behind the scenes and the fact that this authority is itself bestowed "according to context and convention," and yet in literature exposure of this agency does not annul the secret but perpetuates it (DLM 208; GD 157). In "Before the Law" Derrida refers to the relation between author and institution as a "splitting of the line," which creates a kind of mise en abyme that upholds its authority. In Kafka's parable itself this line is represented by the difference between the doorkeeper and the man before the door. This difference engenders them both as subjects and subject to the law. This structure is replicated by the modern institution of literature, which perpetuates itself in and through its guardians: "critics, academics, literary theorists, writers, and philosophers. They all have to appeal to a law and appear before it, at once to watch over it and be watched by it." It is this convention that allows literature to *play the law:* it can "under certain determined conditions . . . exercise the legislative power of linguistic performativity to sidestep existing laws from which, however, it derives protection and receives its conditions of emergence" (DLL 134; BTL 216).

The upshot of this subservience is that literature will never be revolutionary. But this perhaps is also its virtue. For it does not replace the sovereignty of the autonomous subject with a new lord. Its political function thus would be to reveal the *fiction* of sovereignty, of the exceptional one.

This dynamic that operates within the Abrahamic traditions, even as it is not explicitly theorized by them as such, is, according to Derrida, already evident in the biblical text and is revealed by the Abrahamic story itself, insofar as it must safeguard God's singularity. But communicating it involves a promise and an iteration, an *explicit* reference to dissemination. Derrida thus closes *Gift of Death* and the essay "Literature in Secret" with God's pact with Abraham and with its aporia—for God to remain unique and unified, for secrecy itself to remain intact, he must mean to say nothing; but for his oath to retain the structure of the promise, it must indeed invest in the future, in multiplicity and in dissemination. "At this instant, and on the basis of this instant alone, autonomy and heteronomy no longer add up to but One, yes, more than One [*ne font plus qu'Un, oui, plus qu'Un*]" (*DLM* 209; *GD* 158). We could understand this as an endorsement of the fact that tradition itself always multiplies, that Abraham's seed will be like the stars of the heaven. But it is more than that, as it serves as the culmination of Derrida's own contract, the contract he forges between religion and literature; it is also an investment in the procedures that would insert this principle into the political scene.

If this action is not revolutionary, it is perhaps because the sovereign is never simply one to begin with. It is because one does not *have to* cut off the sovereign's head, if he doesn't have *one*.

5

LITERATURE AND THE POLITICAL-THEOLOGICAL REMAINS

The response no longer belongs to me—that is all
I want to tell you, my friend the reader.
—Derrida, *Politics of Friendship*

THE THEOLOGICAL IMAGINARY

Claude Lefort's essay "Permanence of the Theologico-Political?" in answering the question as to why political philosophers in the modern era make recourse to theological language, suggests that democracy makes possible the identifiable sphere of the political as such through the very appearance of an empty place of sovereignty. As Lefort puts it, "The formula 'power belongs to no one' can also be translated into the formula 'power belongs to none of us.'"[1] This itself generates the need for a symbolic register, a vacuum into which the religious enters, not necessarily as the guarantor of power itself but as a marker of an empty spot. "Its efficacy is no longer symbolic but imaginary . . . ultimately, it is an expression of the unavoidable—and no doubt ontological—difficulty democracy has in reading its own story."[2]

One could make a similar argument about "the turn to religion" in post-modernity. The severed head, the king's remains, the trace of God, these have proven to be symbols too powerful and enticing to remain securely in the past.[3] Philosophers of religion and theologians have reminded us for decades now that even those modern thinkers—Descartes, Kant, Fichte—who sought to ground the autonomous subject in and through the pure light of reason were forced to rely on a theological remainder. Critiques of the Enlightenment model of the subject gave rise to an empty space in the very concern to think of a subject without self-sovereignty, and, indeed, the language of religion has functioned as the marker of that absence. Furthermore, recourse to a language of transcendence has served as one means of countering the technological, data-driven description of human life. What has also become clear is that these two returns of religion—in discourse on the subject and on the political sphere—are inseparable. As Derrrida argues in *Rogues,* the question of sovereignty is at the heart of both.[4]

As with political theology, such claims can have both a normative and descriptive function. And yet scholarly debate within the fields of theology and philosophy of religion concerning the turn to religion has revolved around two options: embracing the theological trace in either a strong or a weak form. The former is the track radical orthodoxy takes, reading postmodern critiques of Enlightenment as providing an articulation of the problem of modernity, for which the Christian tradition in its conception of transcendence provides a solution.[5] In response, others argue that the resources of religion can equally promote liberalism through an embrace of the groundlessness that religious terminology and concepts disclose.[6] The opposition itself seems to assume that there *are* only two choices, that if we acknowledge the persistence of a theological remainder then we should cultivate it in one form or another.[7] What has ensued is a battle over theological idioms, following the assumption, as Hent de Vries puts it in *Minimal Theologies,* "that the invocation of religion, its concept no less than its historical manifestations, better enables one to highlight the most pressing questions of ethics and politics and give these concepts a renewed urgency."[8] Alternately, Simon Critchley, in *The Faith of the Faithless,* argues that "If political life is to arrest a slide into demotivated cynicism, then it would seem to require a motivating and authorizing faith . . . which might be capable of forming solidarity in a locality, a site, a region."[9] For both theorists, literature appears as a referent: Wallace Stevens is cited, Paul Celan discussed, yet only in the service of philosophical and theological claims. But, if Lefort is right, there is another story to tell, one in which literature can help us to consider the very difficulty we have in telling our story without those theological placeholders, one in which their status as imaginary may come to bear.[10]

While it is largely conceded that literature too can function to counter an immanentist, rationalist conception of the subject, complicating what it means to consider the complexity of intention and action, its potential role as political supplement has yet to be sufficiently treated.[11] But, as we saw in the last chapter, in the final pages of "Literature in Secret" Derrida provides us with something like a blueprint, a series of principles, all of which consider whether and how literature takes up the Abrahamic legacy and thus how it might impact the political sphere. While Derrida never developed these principles—perhaps he had only begun to think them—I have argued in the preceding chapters that their genesis can be traced all the way back to Derrida's earliest encounters with Levinas and that the very terms of the debate were already set by the demands of the postwar context and the exigency of thinking civilization anew. I have shown that Derrida's own reading of Levinas, his further ironizing of Levinas's rhetorical strategies, his disclosure of Levinas's dependence on literary modes of speech and his alternative conception of "difficult freedom" reveal a path forward for living with our theological remainders in and through the theorizing of literature. In chapter 4 I connected this strategy to Derrida's larger argument for literature's relation to politics through its ties to religion.

Here I want to put this argument in conversation with current debates over our theological dependencies in order to argue that the project of thinking literature as a religious legacy provides us with a means to accept our religious inheritance, but to use it in such a way that literature can be theorized as the neccessary "imaginary" supplement to the democratic context. Literature can show us the opacity of the subject but without the necessity of invoking transcendence. When we replace Christ with Bartleby, secrecy appears as an inviolable privacy one maintained in and through an exposure to the other. In Derrida's theorizing of literature, secrecy is transformed from a model invoking depth, interiority, and the possibility of revelation into a site of nonresponse that, nonetheless, "keeps our passion aroused" (*P* 63; *OTN* 31).

LITERATURE AND THE MODERN WORLD

In arguing for this model, we need to consider again what it means to think literature as a religious legacy in the West. This is not to exclude other sources or to restrict the category to a very narrow slice of history. Certainly, non-Abrahamic cultures have national literatures, and literature as a cultural form stretches back as far as Homer in the West and the Vedas in the East. But the force of the argument in favor of thinking literature as a biblical legacy arises from the consideration of how the very act of reading changes in and through the process of European secularization. Treating literature as biblical legacy refers us to a mode of reading that only came about insofar as a politically secular space was cleared in the Christian West and that space generated a different relation to text and a new social-political function for acts of reading and writing.[12] It commences only with the destabilization of a relation between church and state. For Derrida, who wanted to think about the European context, and European function, it is "within a tradition that cannot not be inherited from the Bible" (*DLM* 177; *GD* 132). As for the privileging of Europe itself, it is here only that we begin the conversation, with the full knowledge that, as Derrida points out in *Monolingualism of the Other*, the very words *culture* and *colony* have the same Latin root (*cul* or *col*) (*MLO* 68, 39). Speaking as an inheritor of this tradition does not mean promoting the supremacy of Europe but accepting the fact of being determined by a language not one's own.[13] Accepting the legacy of Europe implies the obligation to engage critically with the history of European cultural dominance but also the recognition that, insofar as we are determined by it, we cannot fully speak from a place outside it. This reading does not, however, prohibit one from thinking the relation between religion and literature in a more global context, but at least presumes that the category of literature in its global context has itself been marked by European colonialism.

Recent debates about the category of "world literature" seek to further consider the genesis of literature's function both as a means of creating a "world republic of letters" and as a tool of nation building. Construed in either way, it is clear that the modern function of literature as cultural capital, received and consumed as the embodiment of freedom, is a European invention and export.[14] What these conversations clarify is that literature, *as* a modern institution, should be recognized as inextricably political. But insofar as its modern function ties it both to the project of colonialism and to the emergence of a secular political subject—thus also to the birth of liberalism—one might assume that it would serve as a supporting player for these political ideologies. As Pascale Casanova argues, the cultural capital of Paris, as literary world capital in the nineteenth century "'the international bank of foreign exchange and commerce' in literature" arose from its position as site of the Revolution.[15] But, as I argue in chapter 4, its political implications emerge out of its potential to serve as a site of resistance to Enlightenment theories of political subjectivity. At the same time, as an *institution*, literature is supported by the university and various academies and prize commissions. Sometimes invisible in its reach and increasingly transnational, literature reproduces a certain system of class and valuation, one not entirely monetary, but nonetheless elite. As Casanova puts it, quoting Valery Larbaud, "'There exists an aristocracy open to all, but which has never been very numerous, an invisible, dispersed aristocracy.'" It functions like a priestly class "to recognize, or to consecrate, all those whom it designates as great writers."[16]

NEW POLITICAL THEOLOGIES

I do not wish to deny the persistence of gatekeepers in the literary world, but I do want to argue that the function of authority is radically different when the gatekeepers are arbiters of taste rather than arbiters of truth.[17] Recent interventions in political theology have sometimes sought to collapse the differences between the secular and the religious in order to find new uses for theological and religious sources, to argue for their continued relevance, and to read ourselves as modern subjects back into the traditions out of which our thinking arises.

In the case of Derrida's legacy, the shift to consider him within the field of philosophy of religion has emerged as literature departments themselves decided that the heyday of French theory lay in the past, but, as a consequence, the contribution of his own theorizing of literature to debates over the persistence of religious concepts in contemporary political and philosophical debates has not been sufficiently considered.

One contemporary thinker who successfully treats the political implications for Derrida's own analyses of literature is Judith Butler in her now classic *Gender Trouble*. There she takes Derrida's analysis of Kafka's "Before the
Law" as a starting point for thinking the role of performativity in the politics
of gender identity.[18] In her more recent work, however, Butler herself turns
to Judaism as her political resource. She begins from the fact that the suturing of Israel with Judaism has become so secure that the two terms are often
treated as synonymous. For this reason, she sees it as important to derive
from Judaism's resources the tools to develop a critique of state violence.[19]

At first, she acknowledges, Levinas seemed like her leading candidate. "I
expected at first to be able to derive the strongest Jewish statement of ethical
obligation to the other from Levinas."[20] She finds in Levinas the claim that
"contact with alterity animates the ethical scene," exactly the kind of 'minimal theology' which, she argues, we must bring into play once we accept,
following Talal Asad, Saba Mahmood, and Charles Taylor, that there can be
no secular sphere uninflected by religion. Her response is thus to locate Jewish sources for a Jewish diasporic politics.[21] According to Butler, this makes
Levinas crucial, because he "gave us a conception of ethical relations that
make us ethically responsive to those who exceed our immediate sphere of
belonging."[22] But Butler discovers in Levinas's own statements about Zionism, and indeed about the Palestinian other, a conflict with this teaching as
she identifies it. "He was, of course the one who implied in an interview that
the Palestinian had no face" (23). For Butler this tension only obligates her
to use Levinas against himself.

As I have illustrated in the preceding chapters, despite early ambivalence,
Levinas's position on Israel was no mere lapse in judgment but rather grew
out of his philosophy or at least out of the commitment that his philosophy
was itself a recovery of the meaning of ancient Jewish sources. The tradition
that produced this ethical teaching had to be protected. Does this mean
that Levinas's sources cannot be used against him? Butler finds warrant for
her move to do so in Derrida, in fact, in what she refers to as Derrida's idea of
"dissemination." But in this move she re-Judaizes Derrida and refers to this
principle as itself "messianic," calling up readings of Derrida that relate his
philosophy to the Lurianic kabbalistic notion of the *shevirat hakelim,* the
breaking of the vessels and the scattering of the sparks. There is no doubt
that both claims *can* be made: Levinas's philosophy can be mobilized against

his politics and Derrida *can* be read as a postmodern kabbalist. Derrida's conception of dissemination makes both compelling options. But the impetus for such recoveries seems to derive from the conclusion that, if secularity is a ruse, we had better cultivate our theological resources.

And yet in Butler's work, within this very argument, is also a submerged plea for literature. For Butler also uses Derrida's notion of dissemination to develop a model of translation, understood as the recasting "of the problem of religious meaning for us within a different set of terms" (17). She speaks of it as a way of thinking our religious remains, as a navigating of the ruins, "sparking the past on occasion" (17). And it is finally in Mahmoud Darwish's poetry that she finds her most potent political source, particularly in the poem "Edward Said: A Contrapuntal Reading," where, as in Kafka's "Letter to My Father," a dialogue proceeds through a ventriloquized voice. Said's is invoked, but after his death, thus as a fictionalized specter. The poem solicits his presence as a way of signaling his absence, as a legacy whose force comes not only from what he says but from the fact that the poem is already about his loss, the fact that he is no longer there, yet the poem speaks and has a future.

Near the close of the book, Butler asks, with Darwish, "what can poetry say in a time of catastrophe?" and also "what does the saying of poetry do to open up a future beyond catastrophe?" (221). Butler's book thus itself makes clear the task at hand, even as she does not always differentiate between her sources and *how* they speak, between Levinas and Darwish and the sources from which they build the authority of their texts. She writes in a note, "the heretical moment or possibility is constitutive of religion itself" (227). Butler herself is clearly interested in blurring the difference between her resources, in thinking translation as itself religious, suggesting that lines cannot be drawn between the two modes of dissemination.

One of the tasks of this work has been to theorize the difference between religion and literature, to consider how a source for political theory is different when its appeal to the future is not in the hands of one who claims to speak for the tradition but is rather available for anyone to pick up a text and read. Butler insists that the Jewishness she seeks is "noncommunitarian," and that the sources for such a Judaism can be derived from thinking both with and against the tradition, putting it in conversation with different traditions. But, as I've argued elsewhere, this claim also requires the move to call its own exercises in community inscription into question.[23]

Other recent efforts in political theology have been expressly oriented against Jewish communitarianism by way of the figure of Paul. Alain Badiou in his 1997 volume only began the trend. Additionally Badiou's rehabilitation of Paul was also accompanied by a series of books in which he wrote specific tirades against Jews.[24] While we cannot hold Paul accountable for Badiou's attacks, we can recognize that Badiou mobilized Paul because his invocation sets in motion a supersessionist logic. Badiou goes as far as calling Paul the first authentic Jew, the first to say "in the name of all others that there is no law separating them. He is the one who takes it upon himself to break the divisive law and devote humanity to the universal." The outcome for Badiou is that real Jews are only "virtual Jews."[25] He has announced the coming of the new Israel. More recently he has argued for the legitimacy of contemporary anti-Jewish sentiment inasmuch as it originates in criticism of Israel.[26] Rather then trying to disentangle the two, he suggests that the Jewish establishment has itself so tightly woven the two together and so successfully silenced internal critique that anti-Zionists could not be faulted for treating Judaism and Zionism as synonymous.

In Badiou and in the popular rhetoric that echoes his sentiments, one sees some of the more inflammatory consequences of reinvoking religious paradigms as interventions in contemporary politics. While the militancy of his claims makes them particularly noteworthy, his use of Paul is not anomalous. If we accept with David Nirenberg that the history of critical thought has largely been produced by thinking about Judaism, then it should come as no surprise that, when the architect of the distinction between the spirit and the letter is invoked as a tool for contemporary universalist discourse, the Jew would concomitantly resurface as a figure of particularism.[27] By exploiting that product, Badiou has done us the service of exposing some of the inherent dangers of reanimating theological symbols for political purposes.

But the return to Paul has also been championed by many others with different aims: to rethink messianism (Jacob Taubes, Giorgio Agamben), as a form of faith (Simon Critchley), and as a foundation of new materialism (Ward Blanton), with more or less attention to the explosive potential of their rehabilitation. In some cases, one finds the acknowledgment that our religious resources "are all the more 'with' us the more we abandon them to operate as unthought, undertheorized comparative potentials."[28] Their unearthing thus is viewed as a kind cultural talk therapy, a controlled release of pressure, following Freud's hydrolic model.

While I would be the first to laud such work as necessary and important, these accounts are often accompanied by the explicitly normative claim that these figures should be rehabilitated because of a contemporary exigency.[29] The argument for their currency tends to follow from arguments for historical recovery going back to Heidegger and Benjamin. The claim is that through Paul we find the right constellation for our moment, that the invocation of Paul provides us with "a conception of the present as the 'time of the now.'"[30] No doubt in the excitement of this flash of discovery, in the return of new forms of Christian or Jewish politics, one tends to forget that in unearthing the theological traces of secular modernity the sediment burying them must be dug up too. It may thus find its own constellating forces, create its own chemical reactions, and reignite conflicts that have been long buried.[31]

In drawing attention to these strategies of recovery, I don't want to suggest a philosophy of forgetfulness or of presentism, but rather to claim that Derrida's argument for the relationship of religion to literature suggests another means of relating to the fact of our religious legacies.

COUNTERFEIT COINS

In analyzing the relationship between Patočka, Levinas, and Heidegger in *Gift of Death*, I made the claim in chapter 4 that Derrida implicates himself when he speaks of discourses of a "philosophical type" that propose "a nondogmatic doublet of dogma, a philosophical and metaphysical doublet, in any case a *thinking* that 'repeats' the *possibility* of religion without religion" (*DLM* 75; *GD* 50). The lineage that Derrida draws out in the chapters on Patočka in *Gift of Death* would suggest that the discipline of philosophy of religion, from its inception forward, has been caught up in this endeavor of both ridding "religion" of its dogma and attachment to the theological event, while at the same time identifying a religious logic at the center of the philosophical endeavor.

This claim immediately precedes the chapter of *Gift of Death* in which Derrida offers an alternative lineage of secrecy and its role in European politics, one that proceeds not according to Patočka's narrative—from mystery cults through Plato to a concept of Christian responsibility that depends on the one who sees me in secret—but rather one that commences with Abraham and Isaac, through Kierkegaard's reinterpretation of the binding of Isaac and the Gospel of Matthew to Baudelaire's "L'école paienne." This alternative narrative of secrecy and its relation to responsibility produces an account of a theological logic, but its culmination is not in philosophy of religion but rather in literature. As we discussed in the previous chapter, Derrida argues that secrecy's tie to responsibility stems not from the holding back of some particular content, but from the very fact of singularity and the necessary encryption of that singularity in any account or dissemination of the secret. The tomb will not be dug up, the secret will not be produced, but from a site of nondisclosure the secret will proliferate its effects.[32] Out of this dynamic, Derrida argues, religion and literature are both generated, as is the very site of secrecy as Patočka has defined it. But in Derrida's version, which proceeds through Kierkegaard and Matthew, the site of the one who sees in secret is an aftereffect of the Abrahamic moment. It is generated in and through the appearance of God *as* "the one who sees . . . [and] will pay back your salary and on an infinitely greater scale" (*DLM* 146; *GD* 107). This hyperbolic logic deals with the inaccessibility of the singular, the impossibility of recovery and return, by deferring it into the future so that the future itself is figured as the site of an exponential return. By keeping the secret, by his willingness to sacrifice Isaac, Abraham becomes the recipient of a new promise, the promise of an incalculable reward: that his seed will be "as the stars of the heavens and as the sand . . . upon the sea shore."[33] The advent of Christianity then repeats and amplifies the relation, the assumption that God can become in and through his invisibility the guarantor of credit. "Christianity's relation to itself, its self-affirmation or self-presentation, its being-*self* is constituted in the hyperbole of this market, in the visibility of the invisible heart," Derrida writes, describing Christianity as a kind of announcement of its secret *as* a hyperbolic logic (*DLM* 149; *GD* 109). This very announcement, he continues, essentially secures the return of a certain political-theological logic, a colonializing mechanism within Christianity itself such that "there could not then be an 'external' critique of Christianity that was not the extension of an internal *possibility* and that did not reveal the still intact *powers* of an unforeseeable future, of an event or *worldwide* advent of Christianity. . . . Every demystifying of Christianity submits again and again [*se plie et replie*] to justifying a proto-Christianity to come" (*DLM* 149; *GD* 109). Simply put, the logic of Christianity makes critique Christian.

This account would make philosophy of religion the rightful heir of Christianity, a kind of hyper-Christianity, which in the work of demystification continues and replicates the tradition. Derrida is not the only one to say something resembling this claim. Among others, Friedrich Schleiermacher spoke about the fundamental relation between Christianity and reformation in *On Religion: Speeches to Its Cultured Despisers,* Nietzsche argued for the tie between modern philosophy and Christianity in *On the Genealogy of Morals* and *Twilight of the Idols,* and Jean-Luc Nancy similarly argues for Christianity's persistence in *Dis-Enclosure.* The reclamations of Paul furthermore illustrate this logic insofar as their governing assumption is that the concept of advent itself requires the rehabilitation of Paul. Can Derrida repeat it here without implicating himself in the logic he identifies as a "nondogmatic doublet of dogma"? (*DLM* 75; *GD* 50). Can he announce a new heir, one that might function differently?

In telling this story, Derrida provides a narrative of the West and of responsibility that depends upon the Abrahamic form of the secret and the promise. He accepts that by virtue of this narrative every critique of Judaism or of Christianity is itself implicated in the tradition and perpetuates it. But with literature he also suggests an alternative, another means of inhabiting Christianity's hyperbolic logic, of accepting its wager and indeed announcing it, another heir, but one that relates to its legacy differently, even as it would seem to arise in and through the perpetuation of the Abrahamic promise.

"Each time *the* son is lost and saved *by* the father, by *the* father alone. A story of men," Derrida writes.

> In the fold of this Abrahamic or Ibrahimic moment, folded back by the Gospel between the two other "religions of the book" in the recess [*repli*] of this fathomless secret, there would be announced the *possibility* of the fiction nicknamed literature: its *possibility* rather than the event of its *institution,* its structural accommodation but by no means yet what readies and in*states* it [*la* met en État] or confers upon it the status it derives from that name, which is a modern sequence barely a few centuries old.
>
> (*DLM* 150; *GD* 110)

In Christianity, Derrida suggests, we find already a repetition, a fold of the Abrahamic.[34] But in the image of the fold we find not only repetition but an attempt *through* repetition to return to the point of origin, to make good on the relation between the past and the future. The Gospel thus would exemplify that economy itself: by spreading the news, by proliferating the secret, the son can be saved by the father. The source can redeem. Literature would be announced in this possibility *as* the announcement of the secret—its announcement, but not its disclosure. This telling does not disenable the economy, but it does present it as such. Literature's possibility is thus endemic to Christianity itself, Derrida argues, in the repetition of the Abrahamic and in a concept of tradition that, through proliferation, promises a connection to the source.[35] But Derrida distinguishes here between its possibility and its "instantiation." He conceives literature as a modern institution that entails public reception and the obscuring of the signature—a lack of transparency between author and text.

The relationship between religion and the possibility of literature is generated not by way of critique but in the maintenance of a secret that proliferates the secret's effects. Like religion, literature cultivates desire for disclosure, but the effect is the proliferation of interpretation, the encryption of the secret and its dissemination.

In Derrida's reading of Kierkegaard, he indicates Kierkegaard's own relation to the political-theological dynamic as itself a fold, a repetition that both implicates him in its proliferation and asks forgiveness for it.[36] But Derrida uses Baudelaire as well to reveal a strategy he refers to as a "suicidal and homicidal literature" that operates through the production and proliferation of the counterfeit, which is itself an exposure to the other and a self-sacrifice at the same time that it is also its opposite.

Derrida quotes a pamphlet of Baudelaire's entitled *The Pagan School* (1852), in which Baudelaire takes up a "Christian Critique" in the sense that he employs a hyperbolic logic to criticize contemporary neoclassicism as pagan, but ups the ante to the point of ventriloquizing an iconoclasm. "I understand the rage of iconoclasts and Moslems against images." Baudelaire writes, "The danger is so great that I excuse the suppression of the object." He then tells a story of "an artist" who, in receiving a false coin, said that he would "Keep it for some poor person" (*DLM* 152; *GD* 112).[37] The story functions, on the one hand, as a critique of hypocrisy, of those who seek to profit from the outward show of goodness without actually giving, except of course that the artist has announced what he's doing. But at the moment Baudelaire tells the story he implicates himself as a hypocrite. For the announcement of critique appears to be a show, an outward display, a demonstration that calls attention to itself.

But then Baudelaire is also the author of the prose poem "La fausee monaie" (1864), about which Derrida writes extensively in *Given Time*.[38] "L'École païenne" which is presented as an essay, thus as nonfiction, predates the later story by twelve years, but their relation to each other draws Baudelaire's reader, Derrida, and Derrida's readers into the dynamic of the story itself:

> But into my miserable brain, always concerned with looking for noon at two o'clock . . . there suddenly came the idea that such conduct on my friend's part was excusable only by the desire to create an event in this poor devil's life, perhaps even to learn the varied consequences, disastrous or otherwise, that a counterfeit coin in the hands of a beggar might engender. Might it not multiply into real coins? Could it also not lead him to prison?[39]

Like the beggar himself, the reader does not know the status of the event, whether it is counterfeit or real and thus how to spend it, how to use it, how to make good on it. At the same time, the prose poem, presented as a literary work, leaves us with the project of interpretation, an interminable endeavor, each avenue dependent on the status of the literary secret *as* that which cannot be disclosed. As literature, as a part of what Derrida refers to as the institution of literature, it also suspends the question of its reality and thus indeed the very possibility of a dissimulation.

> For the secret remains guarded as to what Baudelaire, the narrator, or the friend meant to say or do . . . Such a secret enters literature, it is constituted by the possibility of the literary institution in its possibility of the secret only to the extent to which it loses all interiority, all thickness, all depth. It is kept absolutely inviolate only to the extent to which it is formed by a non-psycho-logical structure. This structure is not subjective or subjectible, even though it is responsible for the most radical effects of subjectivity or subjectivation. It is superficial, without substance, infinitely private because public through and through.
>
> (*DT* 215; *GT* 170)

Between these two discourses, the pamphlet as criticism and the poem, which tells the same story, there is also a fold and a repetition. As criticism, the pamphlet models a method for participating in the tradition of critique while, at the same time, ironizing it. We can thus read the text as modeling how Derrida situates himself both with and against the lineage of thinkers who have themselves written into the history of philosophy the possibility of a "religion without religion" (*DLM* 74; *GD* 50). Like Baudelaire, he is staging his criticism but, in so doing, implicating himself in it.

Nietzsche is pivotal here as well, and Derrida introduces him in the following paragraph as an example of the same dynamic, the same strategy of upping the ante on the Christian critique of economy. Nietzsche, of course, generated his own discourse on money and truth, one that equally upsets the relation between dissimulation, philosophy, and literature: "What, then, is truth? A mobile army of metaphors, metonyms and anthropomorphisms . . . truths are illusions about which one has forgotten that this is what they are; metaphors which are worn out and without sensuous power: coins which have lost their pictures and now matter only as metal, no longer as coins."[40] Just as this image both plays on the possibility of inverting value and yet thwarts even the structure of inversion, so too, Derrida suggests, does the "demystifying" function of *On the Genealogy of Morals*. If Nietzsche ultimately believed that he could ask the question, "How can one *believe* this history of *credence* or *credit*?" then his own text is a kind of survival or Christian remnant as demystifying, as critique. "Nietzsche must indeed believe he knows what believing means, unless he means to make-believe [à moins qu'il n'entende le faire accroire]" (*DLM* 157; *GD* 116). In the fold of these two options, which is really three—with a certain indiscretion between making someone believe and make-believe—Derrida allows Nietzsche to remain, but it is itself the hinge or the fold between religion and literature and ultimately a site of undecidability between the two, which opens the question whether a discourse on religion that is not of it is possible. Even as Derrida himself would seem to perpetuate the tradition here by demystifying Nietzsche, exposing Nietzsche's own dependence on faith, and thus indeed his own, he opens up the possibility that such a discourse could function differently, could perform its own dissimulation, expose it, hide right out in the open. This is a possibility that depends upon a religious legacy, upon the specter of a theological logic that one can return to the source, make good on the promise by perpetuating its effects. But, in exposing this logic, it becomes, Derrida writes, quoting Baudelaire, a "homicidal and suicidal literature" (*DLM* 150; *GD* 110).[41] We return thus to the image of the grenade, to the idea that literature can function something like a suicide bomb.

IRONY AND SECRECY

To speak of Baudelaire's "L'École païenne" and Nietzsche's *On the Genealogy of Morals* as two examples of a "homicidal and suicidal literature" is to return to the issue of the ironic dimension of these texts. As we have explored in the first chapter, irony often depends on a dissimulation. If one can say the opposite of what one means, then the discourse must have two levels, the level of the overt discourse and the level of the covert message. This is also the assumption of esotericism and the representation of the position of truth within traditions of mystical reading. The difference between religion and literature hinges on the way in which the two levels of meaning are maintained or exploited.

Like Derrida, Frank Kermode has also talked about this dynamic in both literature and religion in terms of secrecy. Kernode's 1979 work *The Genesis of Secrecy* treats the link between religious esotericism and the persistence of the secret in literature, particularly the ways in which the literary critic does and does not take up a position analogous to the religious exegete and thus helps flesh out how literature as a modern institution can resist the modern dogma of transparency and accountability without retheologizing mystery as the site of transcendence.[42] Kermode, too, argues that the discipline of literary criticism is a particular inheritance handed down from "men who studied a specific kerygma."[43] The assumption of an insider and outsider position, of a carnal versus a spiritual reading, an esoteric versus plain sense, has left its impact in the study of literature, Kermode argues, as a legacy of the Christian tradition. What emerges in Kermode's book is the distinction between literary and religious readings, but also the ways in which examining the dynamics in a text that give rise to literary interpretation can shed a different light on religious interpretation. What, in terms of the exegete of the biblical text, is still the expectation of fullness or presence, the prophetic promise of pleroma, is the attenuated expectation by the secular reader and critic for a satisfying ending.[44] Mystery stories are appealing because they promise to solve the case and then they deliver. And yet what we recognize as literature is that which resists our desire. We demand of the literary text that it continue and sustain the desire for fullness. We read works of literature as though they will fulfill that desire, but we equally demand that they thwart it.

We can add to Kermode's analysis here by considering it in terms of irony or in terms of how the concealed level and the revealed level of meaning function in relation to one another. In the parables from Mark that Kermode treats, or with any religious text assumed to have an esoteric or secret meaning, for the text to do its work, for it to bind together a community of readers, the assumption must be maintained that the outward shell conceals a secret, a truth of which God is the guarantor. They relate to that truth as an external covering to an internal treasure, "like apples of gold in settings of silver."[45] A text like the Gospel of Mark pursues the ironic dimension of esotericism by showing us the failure of the disciples themselves to comprehend the parables and by enticing the reader to be among those who share the secret, among those who know.

The modern institution of literature works similarly with the desire of the reader to penetrate the text, to locate the truth that grounds the difference between the overt and the covert meaning and holds them apart. If literature is, as Derrida suggests, "homicidal and suicidal," it has to do with the instability that it introduces into this dynamic by removing the position of the one who sees in secret, yet enticing the reader to take up that position only to thwart his or her access to it.

As György Lukács suggested in his reading of the novel as the quintessentially modern literary form, this is not merely a ruse on the part of the author but an irony itself consequent to the author's position, his capacity through the novel to give form to idea, to take up the Godlike position of creator, but without being able to take up the position of actual transcendence, being bound by the limits of his own experience. He calls it "the writer's irony," a "negative mysticism to be found in times without a God, a "doctrine of *docta ignoranta* toward meaning,"[46]

Whereas for Lukács this is a historical insight that follows from the modern alienated condition of the subject, if we think with Derrida that the secret itself is produced in and through textuality, then the experience of literature's ironic dimensions can equally reflect back on the reading of sacred texts as well. When the radiance of the literary text emerges as something produced by the textual dynamics themselves, by the impossibility of translating singularity into discourse, then the radiance of the biblical text can also appear as a consequence of the same dynamic. As Kermode points out, the very pleasures of modern interpretation "are henceforth linked to loss and disappointment."[47] There is thus a demythologizing function to literature that participates in and yet thwarts the dynamics that sustain the interpretation of the biblical canon.

We can think about this demythologizing function as a layering of ironies that in effect collapses the distinction between surface and depth. In the case of the Nietzsche's and Baudelaire's texts and Derrida's readings of them, they invite the reader into a dynamic similar to that invoked by the gospels, to be the one who recognizes the difference between what the authors claim to be doing and what they are actually doing. We can think of this in terms of historical irony, an irony that relies on the supposedly clear vision of a perspective other than the actors', one with the privilege of seeing clearly where the actors do not.[48] In the case of these two texts, one might argue that there is an irony in the fact that Nietzsche and Baudelaire both participate in a dynamic they claim to critique: Nietzsche critiques the dynamic of debt and credit in Christianity while depending on a notion of credibility; Baudelaire critiques the counterfeiter for his deceit while being deceitful. But, as Derrida reads them, they include the further move of advertising their own hypocrisy, their own dissimulation, of inviting one to call their bluff. In this sense they seem to be implicated in both senses of irony, but with the outcome that they invite the critical gaze of their readers and thwart criticism by collapsing the distinction between the concealed and the revealed. It is in this sense that these two texts participate in a "homicidal and suicidal literature." More specifically, it is by collapsing the distance between hypocrisy and the critique of hypocrisy, playing the role of the Jew and Paul or the Catholic and the reformer simultaneously, that they perform this operation.

But Derrida seems to want to go further, not merely to speak of these texts as serving this function but to identify this tendency as endemic to the very institution of literature. "One among its [literature's] traits from out of the strange and impossible filiation that we detect in it, in memory of so many fathers and sons. . . . This institution retains the feature that we would characterize after Baudelaire as that of appearing always as a 'homi-cidial and suicidal literature'" (*DLM* 150; *GD* 110). Literature, he argues in "Literature in Secret," following the reading of Baudelaire and Nietzsche in *Gift of Death*, is present anytime "a text is consigned to public space that is relatively legible or intelligible, but whose sense, referent, signatory, and addressee are not fully determinable *realities*" (*DLM* 175; *GD* 131). In other words, literature hides right out in the open. Certainly it cannot be said that everything that falls under the name of *literature* works with irony in a form analogous to Baudelaire and Nietzsche, especially given that these texts are on the margins of what we recognize as literature. But the claim would fol-low from Derrida's assertion that literature is the inheritor of an Abrahamic legacy. If we understand literature as both living on the lure of the secret and exposing it as crypt "without depth, with no other basis than the abyss of the call or address, without any law other than the secret of the event called work," then it too would share in what Derrida, quoting Baudelaire, calls "homicidal suicidal literature" (*DLM* 206; *GD* 157). If literature inherits from the Abrahamic tradition the structure of a secret, as the ciphering of a source that delivers through the promise of reception and proliferation but simultaneously exposes that structure itself as a fiction, as the illusion of a verticality that cannot be exposed, then indeed literature can be said to participate in a dynamic it also calls into question.

LITERARY TERRORISM

The relation between literature and terror is itself an artifact of twentieth-century literary criticism, particularly as it came to be associated with Blan-chot and his reading of Jean Paulhan's *Les Fleurs de Tarbes ou la Terreur dans les lettres* in the essay "Comment la littérature est-elle possible?" published in 1942, at a moment in which Blanchot was himself switching political sides from the royalist right to the communist left.

Jean Paulhan's book first appeared in 1936 as a series of articles in the *Nouvelle Revue Française*, of which Paulhan was the editor, and then again as a small book in 1941.[49] The reference to terror in the title refers both to the French Revolution's Reign of Terror in the 1790s and more generally to the Hegelian philosophy of history and the French Revolution's role in it. But Paulhan ultimately defines it more generally, writing that terror "refers to those moments in the history of nations when "purity of the soul, and the freshness of a communal innocence" are valued over and above cultural production, the citizen over his activity.[50] Terror involves a critique of literary practice and the degradation of literature to mere artifice. While the critique of the terrorists presupposes an opposition between literature and politics, reframed by Paulhan in light of current circumstances and the rhetoric of Vichy, which itself embraced commitment over know-how, purity of soul over skill, the resistance to this "terrorism" repoliticized literature as a rejection of a certain form of politics tied to authenticity. Paulhan also finds fault with the expressionist trend of thought, with those who see language as betraying the inner life, as "a crust of words that very quickly hardens."[51] Bergson is his primary exemplar for such an attitude, for promoting a dualism between the purity of heart and the limits of expression. The more comprehensive claim of the expressionists, according to Paulhan, was that commonplace phrases lead to laziness or complacency. Commonplace phrases, according to this argument, make use of us rather than our making use of them. The terrorist would thus council a kind of vigilance in regard to these terms. But Paulhan's argument, in response, is finally that those concerned for the purity of thought are ultimately more dependent on language than anyone else. *"Run away from language and it will come after you. Go after language, and it will run away from you,"* Paulhan concludes, thus arguing for a new method that seems, on the face of it, to acknowledge the critique of the "terrorists" but reject its efficacy.[52] He argues that one needs to deal with the anxiety produced by language by putting those clichés, and those commonplace terms that most enslave us and make us victim to their connotations, into circulation *as commonplaces*, to repeat them in sum as quotations. In other words, Paulhan's solution was to ironize language in order to free us from the anxiety that ensues when we realize that the inner is indeed inextricably bound to the outer.

The irony implicit in Paulhan's argument is most clearly announced in the trope that frames it.[53] The first title, *Les Fleurs de Tarbes* refers to a sign at the Tarbes Park reading, "It is forbidden to enter the Park carrying flowers."[54] The sign is meant to keep people from picking flowers in the park and then claiming they came with them. Already the sign is ironic.

These flowers, Paulhan suggests, are analogous to the rhetorical conventions excluded from literature by recent terrorist critics. Paulhan's proposal is to reimagine the scene such that the sign would instead say, "It is forbidden to enter the garden without flowers." "When all was said and done it was an ingenuous measure," he writes, "because the visitors, already overburdened with their own flowers, were hardly likely to think of picking any others."[55]

But then Paulhan continues, unsettling in the last page of the treatise the very distinction he seemed to want to maintain between the inner and the outer. As soon as he has made his argument, announced his strategy, he adds an addendum: "A little while later, what happened was . . . "[56] At this moment the instability of the irony asserts itself, and it is clear that the very differentiation between the flowers inside the garden and those brought from the outside becomes impossible to maintain. And Paulhan concludes his treatise in italics, which is the style he uses for signaling his own employment of commonplace phrases, or his own ironizing of them. He suggests that the direction of his investigation has led him to the conclusion that one who follows this trajectory must ultimately reverse it. The language he has tried to use, to treat as an instrument by ironizing it, has, it seems, made use of him, He thus writes: *But what happened subsequently was that I was surprised by them for want of taking them by surprise, and (if I may say so) they dealt with me because I failed to deal with them. There are thus glimmers of light, visible to whomever sees them, hidden from whomever looks at them; gestures which cannot be performed without a certain negligence (like some stars, or stretching out your arm out to its full length). In fact, let's just say I have said nothing. The end of Terror in Literature.*[57] Blanchot responds in his essay, "Comment la littérature est-elle possible?" by reading Paulhan as having produced his own "Copernican revolution." What Paulhan exposed is that literature *is* terror, "when we put terror into question, refuting it or showing the frightening consequences of its logic, it is literature itself we are questioning and gradually annihilating."[58] What Paulhan did, argues Blanchot, was to reveal that the distinction between the inner and outer is itself an illusion. Instead of language revolving around thought, he exposes a "very subtle and very complex mechanism by which thought, in order to rediscover its authenticity, turns around language."[59] But Blanchot argues this by suggesting that Paulhan's overt text conceals an esoteric meaning, by arguing for a secret text underlying the proposed argument.

After having followed Derrida for all these pages, the technique on display here should be familiar. Paulhan and Blanchot both participate in an ironizing gesture that functions by exposing the relation of inner and outer, esoteric and real to be itself an illusion, yet perpetuating it in the performance of their own discourse.

Despite Blanchot's adoption of the language of terror and his later invocation of the language of revolution in relation to literature, critics have largely read this essay as a point of departure for Blanchot *away* from politics. Jeffrey Mehlman, in his 1983 book *Legacies of Anti-Semitism,* goes even further. He suggests, first, that the essay itself was meant to liquidate Blanchot's own terrorist past by following in the footsteps of Paulhan and reducing it to having said nothing.[60] But what Mehlman seems to miss here is that Blanchot advocates for a new kind of terrorism in Paulhan, the terrorism of literature, that functions by calling into question the logic and order of fascism, its invocations of purity, power, and indeed sovereignty. This was certainly a reversal of Blanchot's politics in the late 1930s; however, it was not a rejection of politics but rather a transferal of the value of revolution and nihilating action to literature itself.[61] Blanchot thus subsequently wrote in "La littérature et le droit à la mort" that

> the Terrorists are those who desire absolute freedom, are fully conscious that this constitutes a desire for their own death. . . . Literature contemplates itself in revolution, it finds its justification in revolution, and if it has been called the reign of Terror, this is because its ideal is indeed that moment in history, that moment when "life endures death and maintains itself in it" in order to gain from death the possibility of speaking and the truth of speech. This is the "question" that seeks to pose itself in literature, the "question" that is its essence.[62]

Literature is thus a form of freedom and a form of dying without action and without violence. It is nihilating as inaction, as unworking. In the late 1950s, in response to the war in Algeria, Blanchot began to speak of this as a power of refusal. "There is a kind of reason that we will no longer accept, there is an appearance of wisdom that horrifies us, there is an offer of agreement and compromise that we will not hear."[63] Like Bartleby's, this refusal was not one of overt protest, but an unwillingness *even* to resist as an active force, to find an alternative to forms of political expression that reify agency as something transparent, that accept a version of the subject who can be invoked and convoked by the political law. Thus one had to resist even what was reasonable, even what one could accept as having value, of being in one's self-interest. For Blanchot, May 1968 offered the best possibility for such a politics to appear in the public sphere. In his commitment to anonymity, the tracts that he authored, according to Dionysius Mascolo, were published anonymously, and it was the political force of such an unlocalizable resistance that he saw realized in the protests. As he put it in the postscript to a representative of Yugoslav radio-television: "In a few days, an entire modern society fell into dissolution; the great Law was shattered; the great Theory collapsed; the Transgression was accomplished; and by whom? By a plurality of forces escaping all the frames of contestation, coming literally from nowhere, unlocalized and unlocalizable. This is what I believe is decisive."[64] It is this possibility of finding within politics a space that cannot be recuperated, cannot be made to answer for itself, that Derrida most clearly adopted from Blanchot. As he said in an interview with Maurizio Ferraris, he felt fear or terror in "the public space that makes no room for the secret."[65]

LITERATURE AND THE RIGHT TO PRIVACY

It was in this endeavor that Derrida and Levinas were also most closely aligned in resistance to the transparent subject, in a concern to think the consequences of the other's secrecy. But for Levinas that secrecy itself was secured by a site of transcendence, by an absent God. What if, Derrida asks, that absent God now registers only as an inheritance? What if in and through literature one could resist the modern dogma of the transparent subject without the one who sees in secret? What if one could invoke a suspension of the factical without invoking the miracle? What if one could hear a demand or a call that trumps the law without it being attributed to a sovereign power that stands above the law itself? What if one could do this without even the demand for absolute disruption or revolution? And what if all that were required was the the lure of a literary text?[66]

Literature's suspension of the factual may make it look like a form of escape, like a politics without commitment, and this, as we've seen, was one of Levinas's most visceral charges against Derrida: he refused to commit; instead he played. The politics announced by this view of the literary text is certainly not one of militancy, and it isn't a method for taking up a particular cause. But it is an intervention into the democratic sphere, one that reminds us that there is a freedom more radical than autonomy, that the construction of the subject as self-transparent, an object of empirical analysis, is already a violation. It reminds us that language gives us access to something perhaps more important than its referents, it secures our fundamental privacy, and that privacy may not be what keeps us from one another but is in fact the condition we share. At the same time, the literary text implies an ethic of sacrifice and indeed of a kind of exposure, a space where privacy and exposure coincide.

In *Time and Narrative* Paul Ricoeur responds to Kermode's *Genesis of Secrecy*, through the paradigm of Mimesis 3. He responds to the provocation of thinking the relation between the secrecy of the text and the secrecy of the subject:

> Is there not a hidden complicity between the "secrecy" engendered by the narrative itself—or at least by narratives like those of Mark and Kafka—and the as yet untold stories of our lives that constitute the prehistory, the background, the living imbrication from which the told story emerges? In other words, is there not a hidden affinity between the secret of *where* the story emerges from and the secret *to which* it returns.[67]

This is one way of thinking about the exemplarity of literature, the way in which it instantiates a feature of experience and in so doing teaches us about that feature. Derrida himself says that wherever there is some lack of distinction between use and mention, between the "I" as speaking and the "I" as representing speech, there is something of literature. But, as the inability to master this distinction infects all language, wherever there is a speaking subject there is something of literature. Literature would thus teach us to see language itself as simultaneously exposure and masking, yet it would also teach us how to recognize its features at play and how to reread religious texts in light of them, to be aware of the power dynamics that follow each time an authority and a hierarchy of insiders is invoked, each time a secret is attributed to an agent, to one who sees and one who knows, each time a guard is stationed at the door.[68]

When Blanchot withdrew completely from public life, he did so to affirm his commitment to what Derrida calls "donner la mort" as it is embodied in literature, the sacrifice of sovereignty over one's own words.[69] Derrida did not follow suit. Instead, he suggested, presence was itself the ruse. One has no other choice but to submit to the other's response. And so he rewrote philosophy as literature and welcomed the scavengers to the corpse.[70] This was Derrida's own performance of the passion, a way of giving one's body, and yet it is secured through the text's absolute nonresponsiveness, an exposure that, like the act of killing itself, will never yield up the agency of the other, "a passion without martyrdom" (*P* 71; *OTN* 31).

This could be the principle of a politics, Derrida's late writings affirmed, indeed a kind of Levinasian politics, in which the heteronomy of the other needs no transcendent reference but only the leaving behind of an artifact for the other—a trace, a word, a broken tablet—not so that its code might someday be cracked, its author known, its truth revealed. But rather so that its secret, in never being told, never being able to be told, might itself make possible a sociality of desire, secured in the meridians, the lines that connect us not through sharing the same space or the same time but in the act of reception *across* space and across time.

EPILOGUE

"There Is Not a Pin to Choose Between Us"

Ten pages into *Gift of Death* there is an intriguing note to Derrida's 1991 seminar on the secret: "Literature concerning the secret is almost always organized around scenes and intrigues that deal with death," it begins. This is a theme, he adds, that he had attempted to demonstrate in the seminar, "referring most often to 'American' examples."[1] His list includes Poe's "The Purloined Letter," Melville's "Bartleby the Scrivener," and Henry James's *The Aspern Papers* and "The Figure in the Carpet." There are numerous traces of Derrida's readings of the first two stories in his published works, but, as far as I have been able to discover, there are no other significant references to Henry James in Derrida's corpus.[2] And yet there are few writers for whom the secret plays a greater role and whose treatment of it has been as thoroughly thematized. The reference was thus too enticing to ignore.

On the face of it, James's 1896 story, "The Figure in the Carpet," which follows a series of critics on their quest to discover the submerged secret at the heart of a famous writer's successful literary oeuvre, would seem particularly relevant to Derrida's own project. The story is told by an unnamed critic offered the chance by his friend Corvick to review the prominent writer Vereker's latest work for *The Middle*. Corvick was originally commissioned to do the review for the journal, but has passed it along to the narrator after receiving a telegram calling him to Paris to come to the aid of a Miss Gwendolen Erme, whom Corvick would clearly like to marry, her ailing mother being the only remaining obstacle. The narrator produces his review with pride, knowing that he will meet "the great man" himself at an upcoming weekend party.[3] At the party, when he discovers that the narrator has overheard him refer to the review as "the usual twaddle," Vereker makes a point of coming by the critic's room to apologize (127). In trying to explain himself, Vereker reveals that his work contains a secret, "the passion of his passion" that every critic had thus far failed to see (129). Between the two of them, they trade a series of metaphors to describe the nature of this secret, calling it "an exquisite scheme," "a bird in a cage," "a piece of cheese in a mousetrap," "the organ of life," "a sort of buried treasure," "the very string that my pearls are strung on," and "a complex figure in a Persian carpet" (131, 132, 136). When asked if it is a "kind of esoteric message," Vereker replies that "it can't be described in cheap journalese" (131). He eggs on the narrator with potential clues, only then to tell him to "give it up, give it up" (132). He worries and hopes that the secret will be revealed, but then follows this up by adding, "But I needn't worry—it won't." This oscillation only motivates the narrator further, and he shares his story of the encounter with Corvick upon his return in hopes that the more senior critic might have better luck unlocking the secret. Corvick tells Gwendolen, and between the two lovers it becomes a shared project—an obsession even.

From there the story proceeds through a series of enticements and deferrals, and a string of deaths. Corvick removes himself to India on a journalistic assignment and supposedly solves the riddle while he's there, but refuses to reveal what it is until he's confirmed it with Vereker himself. He ultimately returns and supposedly has it verified, but the narrator is himself called away from England by an ailing brother and thus fails to hear the news from Corvick. In the meantime, Corvick marries Miss Gwendolen Erme, but on their honeymoon they have a carriage accident and he dies. Mrs. Corvick then becomes the supposed possessor of the secret, but refuses to share it. "I've heard everything," she tells the narrator, "and I mean to keep it to myself" (148). Gwendolen seems ennobled by her knowledge, practically glowing from its impact, and produces a novel herself in its wake. The narrator considers pursuing her hand in hopes that the secret would come out with such intimacy. Meanwhile, Vereker dies six months later, and his wife follows. The narrator fails in his quest for Gwendolen, and she marries another critic, Drayton Deane from *TheMiddle,* but dies in childbirth. The story ends with the narrator soliciting Deane for the secret, only to find that he knew nothing of it. The story thus closes, of course, without the secret revealed, and the narrator's only satisfaction comes from Deane's shared ignorance. "I may say that to-day as victims of unappeased desire there isn't a pin to choose between us. The poor man's state is almost my consolation; there are really moments when I feel it to be quite my revenge" (156). Deane here is himself also the stand-in for the reader, for as a consequence of the narrator's telling, a telling that fails to reveal the secret even as it shares it, the narrator extends both the awareness of the state of ignorance and the concomitant desire to penetrate the secret.

Not surprisingly the story has itself elicited tremendous speculation and served as a testing ground for the critical enterprise, especially as criticism came in the second half of the twentieth century to engage the very mechanics of literature's meaning-making process. In the first edition of *Poétique*, a journal inaugurated in France by Hélène Cixous, Gérard Genette, and Tzvetan Todorov to develop a notion of "la littérarité," which "exceeds the boundaries of literature," Cixous wrote on "The Figure in the Carpet" among other stories and novels written by James.[4] In the essay she develops a reading of James, but clearly of narrative art more generally, as a kind of magic lantern projection in which "the theatricality of the shadow of the real is underlined," where knowledge is always dangerous either as too much or too little, "too violent and insufficient."[5] As the only literary author besides Balzac treated in this French journal's first issue, James is a striking choice for the journal's task, but the role of the enigma in his work was clearly attractive to those working out a structuralist method of literary criticism in France. Cixous's own reading followed analyses by Phillipe Sollers and by Todorov.[6]

In 1978, in *The Act of Reading*, Wolfgang Iser used the story to work out his model for reader-response theory, arguing that the meaning of literature can never be a formula, or an object to be grasped, but only emerges through the reader's engagement with a text, thus taking the critic Corvick's discovery of the meaning of Vereker's work as a paradigm for how literature generates meaning.[7] Corvick is staged as the insider, and the narrator as the outsider. Corvick models the "right" way to read, and the narrator is misguided. But what Iser fails to point out is that, as readers, we are not with Corvick, but with Vereker. Iser seems to propose that by judging Vereker a failure we move closer to Corvick's position. No doubt the story's ironic dimension functions to solicit this move, but the alignment fails, for James gives us no access to Corvick or his "knowledge," and such a reading risks making the real critic himself play the alazon. Shlomith Rimmon-Kenan, in her 1977 book *The Concept of Ambiguity: The Example of James,* used the story to work out the nature of literary ambiguity, revealing the elements that resist clarification, showing that the story is constructed to thwart the reader's desire to answer the question not only of what the secret is but also of whether or not there even is a secret. She counts the ambiguous pronouns and James's "doubly directed clues" and shows the story to function like a maze made up only of dead ends.[8] At the same time, she too reads it as "metaliterary," duplicating in the reader the same search for a solution that Vereker, with his clues, elicits from his readers. Most readings of "The Figure in the Carpet", she points out, tend to choose a side, either affirming the existence of the secret or denying it. J. Hillis Miller, in 1980, formulated his reading method in explicitly *deconstructive* terms. Like a number of others, he too reads the story as an allegory on the very process of narration, on its promise of representation as order, and order as representation, as a narrative about the fact that realistic representation is already a kind of catachresis, which James reveals through mechanisms of obscuration and deferral. According to this reading, "The Figure in the Carpet" is a story about the fact that succumbing to the lure of saying what a narrative is about is already to have taken the bait, which implies, of course, as Miller already knows, that he himself has swallowed the hook.[9]

In all these readings there is a kind of unacknowledged theological echo, resonant in the role of the unknown and unknowable that animates the story.[10] But even as every critic who reads it is fascinated by the dynamic of the unrevealed and unrevealable, the lure of knowledge and its danger, only Miller notes the way in which the "figure" in the carpet as an image plays on the notion of logos, as that which is evident in every surface, in every manifestation of the creator, and yet necessarily remains veiled insofar as it can only appear *as* something else and thus cannot be grasped in itself. The story flirts with the trope of the mystery cult; Vereker balks at the possibility of an esotericism, but speaks of the ideal of a group of potential "initated."[11] And the story unfolds as a group of the initiated is formed, but to whose insight the narrative provides no access. The fact of their subsequent demise mimics the link in various mystical literatures between esoteric knowledge and death. Of course, in the Christian tradition, with mystics such as Catherine of Siena, Marguerite Porete, and Meister Eckhart, union and annihilation of the soul is followed by a resurrection back into the world, but here, in our literary counterpart, their deaths serve merely as another obstacle to knowledge.[12] James himself describes the story as about "the quality and play of an ironic consciousness in the designer left wholly alone, amid a chattering unperceiving world."[13] Yet this God's-eye view is not that of the story itself. James can only tell this story through the consciousness of one who doesn't see and who blocks the reader's access to sight. Whether or not the "designer" is himself all-knowing, whether the secret is something that he could reveal or even articulate, is itself impossible to discern. Vereker's clues are only more metaphors, "figures" for the secret and often at odds with one another in their description. Even James, in his preface to the story, describes the secret as "undiscovered, not to say undiscoverable."[14] This is itself an ambiguous phrase. The double negative seems only to further suspend our comprehension. Why should he *not say* "undiscoverable," because it is discoverable or because one shouldn't avow its undiscoverability? The very preface itself thus extends the game, taking it to a metalevel, inciting the urge to find graspable insight, but only furthering speculation.

Derrida's own interest in the James story may have come from Miller, but it could easily also have arisen from the extensive French interest in the story ten years earlier.[15] Given its themes and its role in criticism, at least in conversation with Derrida, if not inspired by him, it is notable that Derrida never published on it.[16]

Like Corvick and the story's narrator, upon realizing this, I too began to play the role of tormented critic. Like James and Vereker, this is a role that Derrida solicits. How many hours had I spent combing his texts, looking for references to Levinas, tracing out shared metaphors, trying to discern a meaning running through layers of obfuscating prose? If Corvick and the narrator were duped, so was I. Was this really any way to be spending my time? Yet there I was, wondering if a story itself about this dynamic had some special significance for Derrida's own project. *Had it served as an unacknowledged inspiration? Providing him perhaps with the rubric of the secret as the means to think about the link between literature and religion. It certainly fit his model as a story about the relation between secrecy and death, but also about the relationship between revelation and betrayal.*

With all these questions in mind, and an awareness of the fact that I was behaving like an overzealous "initiate," I made my own pilgrimage to the Derrida archive at UC Irvine where the manuscripts for Derrida's seminars are housed under impressive security: an attendant monitors the researchers at all times; no photographs are allowed. Only ten pages of photocopies can be made in any reader's lifetime and from only one session of one seminar. The files themselves come with a large laminated legal-size marker printed with the archive's rules and decorated with a photograph of Derrida's face in its characteristically wry smile. This was certainly not what Levinas had in mind when he spoke of the face to face.

While I was there a couple of scholars, a husband and wife in black leather and designer eyeglasses, asked to see the papers. They had traveled a long way, they told the librarian, just to be there. When the librarian asked what in particular they wanted to see, they said it didn't matter. They taught Derrida, they told her, and just wanted to *see* the handwriting, finger the pages. That was fine, she said, but they had to wear gloves. They sat in silence over Derrida's indecipherable handwriting for fifteen minutes, returned the files, and then left.

How could it be, given Derrida's own concern in *Archive Fever* that the archive is patriarchal in its restrictions as the site of the intersection of law and singularity in *privilege*, that we were in this anonymous room, in a state school library, behaving as though we had entered the inner sanctum? The irony was indisputable, but it was also exemplary.[17] Nonetheless, with all these dynamics in mind, I confess, it was with a kind of zealous curiosity and a wild heartbeat that I opened the first session of the seminar entitled "Repondre au secret" and began searching for the reference to James.

The course begins with an extensive reading of "Bartleby," the reading I had supposed was behind the essay "Passions," but moves quickly to a more general theorizing of the role of secrecy in literature.[18] About midway through the first session, Derrida looks up from the reading of "Bartleby," Bartleby as character and "Bartleby" as story, to suggest the character himself as an emblem for literature. "It is also this statute of the literary récit of which the secret is not divulged and never will be . . . revealing the ultimate essence without essence of the secret. . . . It says 'I am a secret,' without unveiling anything, without saying anything, and without showing."[19] Such a line could, of course, serve as a reading of "The Figure in the Carpet," but

James does not appear until the fourth session of the seminar, when Derrida turns his attention to Heidegger and to a disruption of the proper and the improper in Heidegger's own construction of care and being toward death.

"The Figure in the Carpet" and *The Aspern Papers* first appear only as references in the opening of the session, as examples of texts in which death "comes to bring a secret that has never existed."[20] Then Derrida raises the possibility that James's accounts might disrupt the very distinction between authenticity and "falling" (*Verfallen*), between the anticipation of something futural and what Heidegger refers to as "the running away from waiting" manifest in curiosity.[21] What interests Derrida in the stories is the relation between curiosity, as the approach to something "provisionally" hidden, and death, the fact that the stories themselves disrupt the distinction between a secret with content and death as that secret which cannot be uncovered. Citing Heidegger's own degraded modalities of Dasein, Derrida writes, "Literature is above all curiosity, for the curious, it cultivates curiosity, these secrets are not real secrets, these are the secrets to excite *Gerede, bavardage* (talk or idle chatter) and one could say advertising, for fleeing anxiety, for . . . distracting one from death."[22] Unlike poetry, novels and stories are the object of Heidegger's disdain. But it is literature, perhaps most acutely in its narrative form, that disrupts the very distinction between the proper and the improper, Derrida suggests. Yet, in offering this analysis, he does not exactly provide a reading of the James stories, although he anticipates his reading at least three times. Instead he provides a provisional postscript, a postscript to his lecture in the conditional tense: "My second anticipated postscript would concern that which Heidegger would think or would have thought finally of this literature of the secret in secret, of this American literature that occupies us here. One could imagine that before it, but particularly before James he would have, if he had, read him (did he read him? I don't know, I don't believe so) severely or disdainfully like police novels or detective novels as opposed to poetry [*Dichtung*]."[23] He then goes on to compare Heidegger to Miss Tina Bordereau, the dowdy niece in James's *The Aspern Papers,* at the moment when she discovers with her aunt that the narrator is, as the aunt declares, "a publishing scoundrel."[24] In the story Miss Bordereau plays something of the author figure herself when she says that indeed the papers of the great poet Aspern do exist, but she cannot show them. Instead she holds them out as a kind of lure or promise for the narrator. If he were to become "a relation," however, things would be different.[25]

Derrida's suggestion with the comparison to Miss Bordereau is that Heidegger himself can't keep up the distinction between the secret as ruse and the profundity of the true secret or mystery, even as he condemns the former in favor of the latter. There is thus a parallel between the argument that Derrida makes here between Henry James and Heidegger and that which he makes in *Gift of Death* between the biblical secret and the literary secret. Derrida's larger political point here brings us back to the relationship between literature and democracy. What Heidegger condemns as curiosity and idle talk, he condemns as well a kind of "vulgar" democracy that venerates surface over depth, distraction over authenticity, the movement of the crowd over the contemplation of the individual. What Derrida suggests is that literature disenables the possibility of holding fast to such distinctions. Literature exposes its mysteries as a mere lure and advertises its own seductive devices. It calls the reader to impute depth to the story, to speculate on the characters' motivations, their backstory, their secrets, but when the reader tries to look behind the story to locate that depth, there are no people there, no depth of consciousness, only another sheaf of paper.

Literature does indeed belong to the throngs, to democracy, Derrida suggests, but among the crowds one's exposure can be a form of privacy. If, in a monarchy, power depends upon the secret of the monarch, secured by the secrecy of God, literature recalls for us that in democracy secrecy remains, despite the endless efforts to evacuate it from the public sphere; it remains, but it hides right out in the open.

Another important point worth mentioning about the seminar is that the note points us toward its most explicit content. The majority of the sessions concern the comparison between literature's relation to secrecy and Heidegger's *Sein zum Tode.* The central content of *Gift of Death,* the reading of Patočka, Kierkegaard, and Levinas, is itself something of a digression in the course, and it interrupts Derrida's very promise to offer a reading of the relation between Heidegger and James. Session 4 of the seminar closes with the suggestion that Derrida will return to the topic of James and Heidegger in the next session, but session 5 opens with the announcement of a digression. The digression, it turns out, is the reading of Patočka that becomes the central focus of *Gift of Death.* James does not again make an appearance.

My first reaction to this fact was of course grave disappointment. I had come in search of a reading of "The Figure in the Carpet" and found none. It was as though I had finally laid my hands on the Aspern papers themselves, only to discover that they were insignificant sheaves of paper. Why, I asked myself, had he even mentioned this story as a "subject" of a recent seminar when it appeared in title alone? And then I noticed a passage before the postscript in the seminar notes in which "The Figure in the Carpet" appeared again.

> We could naturally, I do not dare say get bogged down [*enliser*] or get stuck, but rather remain to infinity, or rather up to death in the text of *Being and Time* as we could or ought to do in "Bartleby" or Baudelaire, much later in *The Aspern Papers* or "The Figure in the Carpet." I could show if I had the time that it is a question of two ways, indiscernible, despite every effort, of discerning, of determining being for death [*l'etre pour la la mort*] (l'etre with l' and not lettre in a word like dead letters) as relation to the secret of the secret. My only consolation consequently, given that I may not or ought not do it here, is to content myself in marking the pages, I can hope that you can do the work and *you will see for yourselves*.[26]

This was a strange moment for me in the archive. My heart again began to race. Was this a setup, or what I had been looking for all along? I was tempted to look behind me or even up. Instead I looked over at the goofy bookmark, at the laminated page with Derrida's face on it. There was no transcendent presence in the room, no real face of the other to call to me, no encounter to be had, just words on a page and no one behind them. What I felt distinctly was absence—the sense in which death separates. I saw that Derrida's own death was already foreshadowed in these letters, in the type on the page. I saw that, like the writers he discussed, he too linked curiosity and death, used it to lure his readers. It was both cheese in a mousetrap *and* the strand to string his pearls on. It had already been predicted: of course, I would arrive and initiate my own repetition of the story. I would arrive with the passion to see for myself. There would be no reading of "The Figure in the Carpet," but he would set in motion its very dynamics. Like Vereker, he would "leave" the interpretation "to somebody else."[27]

And so there in the archive I sat. I came convinced that I would find in the course Derrida's definitive reading, that it would serve as the perfect capstone for my book, that I would be the one to unearth this new insight, to make the discovery. Was I just the victim of curiosity, one more voracious critic, one more publishing scoundrel? Or, even worse, was I another devotee, setting in motion the very dynamics of initiation and esotericism?

Or could I see things otherwise?

I thought about the last scene in the James story when the narrator finally manages to corner Drayton Deane and demand of him the secret, only to discover that Deane does not possess it. It is a scene that is consistently read as an indication of the superficiality of the story's narrator. Despite all his searching, he has come to understand nothing. For those critics who see themselves as having fathomed the story's secret, it is a moment when the irony of the story seems to be that they are on the inside while the narrator is on the outside. They understand. James has cleverly managed to write the story so that they can indeed be among the initiated while our poor narrator remains on the threshold with his new victim.

But who indeed is the alazon in this scenario?

"I may say that to-day as victims of unappeased desire there isn't a pin to choose between us. The poor man's state is almost my consolation; there are really moments when I feel it to be quite my revenge," the story concludes.[28] The phrase the narrator uses to describe his relation to Deane is striking: "there isn't a pin to choose between us." It recalls the old Norse folktale "There is Not a Pin to Choose Between Them." The story is about an old man whose silly wife is taken by a con man when she tries to sell their cow. In trying to better the situation, the man marches off in anger, goes out, and behaves a little like a con man himself, taking money from other silly women. When he finally returns home, he tells his wife how silly she is, but concedes, "that is all one now, for the rest are not a bit wiser than you. There is not a pin to choose between you."

We could take the reference to the folktale here as a sign that the narrator knows he's been conned and thus, perhaps, so have we along with him. But it is significant that the phrase is now inclusive, indeed that literature allows such a stance, not so much the con itself but the awareness of it. One can know that it is all a trick and nonetheless read on, indeed desire on without the possibility of eternal life or even the promise of truth on the distant horizon. We can know that the very possibility of penetrating the secret is a ruse, that Vereker's secret is indeed undiscoverable, and yet we read on and we read again. For Heidegger this was a sign that we seek distraction, that we're always running from the possibility of our impossibility. Perhaps it is less a distraction and more like the virtual space of a collective wake.

In the end, the narrator and Deane are there as readers—critics even— together in their ignorance and their desire, as are we, the readers. They are also there as mourners and survivors. The scene takes place in the smoking room of a small club of which both are members. Alone in the room, in high-backed chairs, the story that the narrator has been telling unfolds before his new audience. "I told him in a word just what I've written out here, and I became aware" the narrator continues, "to my surprise, by his ejaculations, by his questions, that he would have been after all not unworthy to be trusted by his wife."[29] It is, in fact, the first real insight the narrator has had in the story and perhaps the first real insight James has allowed us, his readers. But, for all that, it remains in the past conditional, a hypothesis untested and untestable. In their mutual ignorance, the narrator and Deane form their own club, a club of the *uninitiated*.

The final line of the story, one might assume, suggests otherwise. The "poor man's state" is almost the narrator's consolation, and there are moments, he concludes, when he feels it to be his revenge. But revenge against what? It is certainly not revenge against Deane, for they are now together in their shared ignorance. Perhaps it is against death? Against the secret? Can the two be differentiated, one from the other?

In reading for myself these last lines of the story and knowing that I don't know, I thought of Derrida after the death of his own friend. I thought of him standing at Levinas's graveside and then two years later at the colloquium, a stranger, indeed, at a club to which he *did not* belong. And I thought of a sentiment I had encountered often in reading Derrida, which I had come across again in the archive, reading the seminar's previous session, "the only secret that remains," Derrida wrote in his notes, "is that of the encounter, the chance of the encounter that crosses two signatures, what Celan in the Meridian calls *Geheimnis der Begegnung*—the secret of the encounter in which the poem consists."[30]

I have throughout this book referred to Derrida as misreading, perverting, betraying Levinas, but I have also described this as an act of fidelity and a gesture of friendship, one *as* the other. It was, in the end, also the drawing of a meridian and a means of survival. It was the beginning of a constellation that would continue to be forged after both were gone and only the words on the page remained, soliciting us, resisting our desire to produce the last word.

NOTES

PREFACE

1. See Derrida's *Politics of Friendship*, trans. George Collins (London: Verso, 2006) for exploration of this theme. Here Derrida meditates on Aristotle's "Oh, my friends, there is no friend." Levinas is not mentioned extensively in the text, but Derrida does consider what it would mean to think of him as a third to Blanchot and Bataille. Already there is an invocation of the friend/enemy distinction in this grouping. For Levinas and Bataille had a hostile relationship in print, while Blanchot made his friendship with both a theme of his work.

2. Robert Bernasconi, Simon Critchley and Jill Robbins have all secured a place for Derrida as a philosopher of ethics by emphasizing the relationship between Derrida's conception of justice and Levinasian ethics, reading Derrida thus as primarily a philosopher of alterity.

3. Critchley and de Vries make a case for a narrative of Derrida's work moving toward Levinas and thus toward ethics. In *Minimal Theologies* de Vries in his epilogue explicitly makes the case that "it is no accident that Derrida 'increasingly' turned to Levinas for ways to 'deformalize' his thinking." Hent de Vries, *Minimal Theologies: Critiques of Secular Reason in Adorno and Levinas* (Baltimore: Johns Hopkins University Press, 2005), 587. Simon Critchley's *Ethics of Deconstruction* (Edinburgh: Edinburgh University Press, 1992) argues for deconstruction's ethical importance through "a rapprochement with the work of Emmanuel Levinas" (3). Nicole Anderson's *Ethics Under Erasure* (London: Continuum, 2012) does an admiral job of critiquing Critchley's alignment of Levinas and Derrida and describing his motivation in articulating that alignment as a matter of protecting Derrida from charges of nihilism (27). For Michael Naas, in "The Phenomenon in Question," *Taking on the Tradition: Jacques Derrida and the Legacies of Tradition* (Stanford: Stanford University Press, 2003), the relationship hinges on the position of philosophical discourse in Levinas's work,

which Naas associates with the issue of the question in the discipline of philosophy. My argument differs somewhat from his insofar as I see philosophical discourse and the question of the phenomenon as a shared issue and I see their responses diverging along the lines of religion and literature.

4. See Jacques Rancière's essay "Should Democracy Come? Ethics and Politics in Derrida," in *Derrida and the Time of the Political* (Durham: Duke University Press, 2009), 274–88; and Slavoj Žižek, "Neighbors and Monsters," in *The Neighbor: Three Inquiries in Political Theology* (Chicago: University of Chicago University Press, 2005), 154–55. See also Sarah Hammerschlag, "Poetics of the Broken Tablet" in *The Trace of God: Derrida and Religion*, ed. Peter Gordon and Edward Baring (New York: Fordham University Press, 2014) and "Bad Jews, Authentic Jews, Figural Jews," in *Judaism, Liberalism, and Political Theology*, ed. Randi Rashkover and Martin Kavka (Bloomington: Indiana University Press, 2014), 221–40.

5. See Alain Badiou, *Saint Paul: la fondation de l'universalisme* (Paris: Presses universitaires de France, 1997); Slavoj Žižek, *The Puppet and the Dwarf: The Perverse Core of Christianity* (Cambridge: MIT Press, 2003); Simon Critchley, *The Faith of the Faithless: Experiments in Political Theology* (London: Verso, 2014); and Ward Blanton, *A Materialism for the Masses: Saint Paul and the Philosophy of Undying Life* (New York: Columbia University Press, 2014). Blanton does a nice job of treating these as constituting together a phenomenon, even as he offers his own rereading as one more reclamation of the apostle.

6. Hent de Vries, *Philosophy and the Turn to Religion* (Baltimore: Johns Hopkins University Press, 1999), 38.

7. Ibid.

8. In making this claim, I am contesting Edward Baring's argument that Derrida's philosophical position arises out of his early relation to Christian existentialism. See Edward Baring, *The Young Derrida and French Philosophy, 1945–1968* (Cambridge: Cambridge University Press, 2011).

9. See the introduction to Mark Bevir, Jill Hargis, and Sara Rushing, eds., *Histories of Postmodernism* (New York: Routledge, 2007), for a discussion of the relation between historicism and postmodern philosophy. Both Peeters and Baring acknowledge their historical/biographical projects as somewhat in tension with the deconstructive method.

10. Jacques Derrida, *Positions*, trans. Alan Bass (Chicago: University of Chicago Press, 1982), 56–57.

11. See Edward Baring, *The Young Derrida and French Philosophy, 1945–1968;* and Benoît Peeters, *Derrida, A Biography*, trans. Andrew Brown (Cambridge: Polity, 2013).

12. For a book-length treatment of the theme of legacy and inheritance in Derrida's work as a political principle, see Samir Haddad, *Derrida and the Inheritance of Democracy*, (Bloomington: Indiana University Press, 2013). Haddad treats Derrida's approach to literature as a minor element in this strategy, whereas I would argue that it is indispensable to any consideration of Derrida's politics, especially

as we understand his politics as a means of negotiating his own philosophical and religious inheritance. See also J. Hillis Miller, *For Derrida* (New York: Fordham University Press, 2009).

13. See *Derrida and Negative Theology*, ed. Toby Foshay (Albany: SUNY Press, 1992) for the terms of the debate and Derrida's response. I am also thinking of Kevin Hart's *Trespass of the Sign: Deconstruction, Theology and Philosophy* (New York: Fordham University Press, 2000); and John Caputo's *The Prayers and Tears of Jacques Derrida: Religion Without Religion* (Bloomington: Indiana University Press, 1997). Caputo is ultimately more focused on reappropriating the notion of messianicity. Finally, I have referenced Edith Wyschogrod's influential early work on postmodern philosophy and religion, *Saints and Postmodernism: Revisioning Moral Philosophy* (Chicago: University of Chicago, 1990), which helped establish "postmodern ethics" as a field built from an interweaving of Levinas, Lyotard, Derrida, Kristeva, and others.

14. Martin Hägglünd's *Radical Atheism: Derrida and the Time of Life* (Stanford: Stanford University Press, 2008) does important work toward refuting the theological interpretations of Derrida, but goes perhaps too far. Hägglünd simplifies the theological playing field by assuming that Derrida's concept of survival and its dependence on finitude is itself a rebuttal of *any* theological reading, as though religion were itself reducible to a belief in the afterlife.

15. The correlation of literary studies with religious studies, however, has many other important theorists, including T. S. Eliot, Eric Auerbach, Northrop Frye, Frank Kermode, Paul Ricoeur, and others. My point is not to delimit the field here, but merely to explain the fact that Derrida has not yet found his proper reception within this subfield of North American religious studies.

16. Scott's 1993 work is framed as a rebuttal to Derrida's deconstruction of the metaphysics of presence. Derrida's work is not, however, engaged in any detail. Rather Scott approaches his adversary through George Steiner as intermediary. Nathan Scott, *Visions of Presence in Modern American Poetry* (Baltimore: Johns Hopkins University Press, 1993), 1.

17. See, for example, Eric Ziolkowski, "History of Religions and the Study of Religion and Literature: Grounds for Alliance," *Literature and Theology* 12.3 (1998): 305–25.

18. The *Encyclopedia of Religion* entry for "Literature and Religion" by Anthony Yu and Larry Bouchard does give consideration in its final section to "Deconstruction and Religion," and there an oscillation similar to the one we've been tracking is evident. Insofar as Derrida owes a debt to Emmanuel Levinas in his thinking of alterity, he is credited as a constructive force for the field, but Derrida's method is also criticized as ahistorical. According to Bouchard and Yu, Derida's relevance seems to arise in and through Hent de Vries's own appropriation of Derrida and de Vries's claim that deconstruction and negative theology can function as "silent companions in an attempt to declare new discursive forms and practices of philosophical and cultural analysis, of ethical deliberation and political engagement." *Encyclopedia of Religion*, 2d ed. (Detroit: MacMillan, 2005), 8:5476.

19. Critchley, in *The Faith of the Faithless,* also speaks of politics as a kind of fiction, but the model he uses is very much at odds with the one I am presenting here. His method arises out of Wallace Stevens's "fiction of an absolute" and is a means of enabling belief and thus motivating action. As I employ the term here, following Derrida's analysis, it is about reinserting irony into politics and cultivating exposure to others. It is a means of relating to the legacy of a religious past while disengaging the structures of power that maintain belief.

1. "WHAT MUST A JEWISH THINKER BE?"

1. Marie-Ann Lescourret, *Emmanuel Levinas* (Paris: Flammarion, 1994), 170 (emphasis and translation mine).
2. This is assuming that Derrida is correct about the year. Records (CZA 3713) indicate that he actually attended in 1964 when the theme was "the Jewish temptation."
3. For an alternative response to this question, see Simon Critchley, *The Ethics of Deconstruction* (Edinburgh: Edinburgh University Press, 1992), 107–41. Critchley suggests that Derrida's betrayals are a kind of loyalty to the principle of dissymmetry at the heart of Levinas's ethics, such that gratitude would only reinvoke a kind of reciprocity with which Levinas, in countering the tale of Ulysses with the tale of Abraham, would want to break. I don't dispute this reading, but I think it fails to contend with the more fundamental disagreement between the two over the workings of signification.
4. Jacques Derrida and Élisabeth Roudinesco, *For What Tomorrow . . . a Dialogue,* trans. Jeff Fort (Stanford: Stanford University Press, 2004), 111.
5. See François Poirié, *Emmanuel Levinas: Qui êtes-vous?* (Paris: La Manufacture, 1987), 69–70.
6. Benoît Peeters, *Derrida: A Biography* (London: Polity, 2012), 30.
7. Jacques Derrida, *Sur parole* (Paris: Editions de l'Aube, 2003), 19.
8. Emannuel Levinas, "Être Juif," *Confluences,* nos. 15–17 (1947): 64, translated by Mary Beth Mader and republished in *Continental Philosophical Review* 40.3 (2007): 205–10.
9. See Jacques Derrida, "Abraham, l'autre" in *Judéitiés: Questions pour Jacques Derrida,* ed. Joseph Cohen and Raphael Zagury-Orly (Paris: Galilée, 2003). I have treated this dynamic elsewhere in *The Figural Jew* (Chicago: University of Chicago Press, 2010), 201–60 and "Poetics of the Broken Tablet," 59–71, in *The Trace of God: Derrida and Religion,* ed. Peter Gordon and Edward Baring (New York: Fordham University Press, 2014). Also in that volume, Ethan Kleinberg, in "Not Yet Marrano," ibid., 39–58, takes up the relation between Sartre's essay and Derrida's own response in his 2001 essay "Abraham, l'autre."
10. *Gift of Death* was published first in English in 1995 without the essay "Literature in Secret." It was then published in 1999 as *Donner la mort* in French with the final

essay and then republished in a second edition in English in 2008, see Jacques Derrida, *Donner la Mort* (Paris: Galilée, 1999) and *Gift of Death and Literature in Secret,* trans. David Wills (Chicago: University of Chicago, 2008).

11. Derrida is fairly vague in "Literature in Secret" about which texts constitute the modern institution of literature, but the place of Kafka in the essay indicates that Kafka's work is a prime exemplar of the category. Elsewhere other writers—Melville, Henry James, Poe—function similarly.

12. See Paul Ricoeur and André LaCoque, *Thinking Biblically: Exegetical and Hermeneutical Studies* (Chicago: University of Chicago Press, 1998), xvi. Also Moshe Halbertal, *People of the Book Canon, Meaning, and Authority* (Cambridge: Harvard University Press, 1997), 7–8.

13. Jonathan Lear, *A Case for Irony* (Cambridge: Harvard University Press, 2011).

14. Wayne Booth, *A Rhetoric of Irony* (Chicago: University of Chicago Press, 1974), 10.

15. Ibid., 14.

16. Linda Hutcheon, *Irony's Edge: Theory and Politics of Irony* (New York: Routledge, 1994), 29, citing R. G. Elliott, *The Power of Satire* (Princeton: Princeton University Press, 1960), 273.

17. Northrop Frye, *The Educated Imagination and Other Writings on Critical Theory* (Toronto: University of Toronto Press, 1996), 49. For more on satire's destructive and constructive elements, see also Gilbert Highet, *Anatomy of Satire* (Princeton: Princeton University Press, 1962), 235–41.

18. Peeters, *Derrida*, 139.

19. Stéphane Mosès, "Au Coeur d'un chiasme" in *Derrida, La Tradition de la Philosophie,* ed. Marc Crepon and Frédéric Worms (Paris: Galilée, 2008), 111.

20. I am depending on Peeters's account here, and Peeters doesn't specify which essays Derrida sent to Levinas, but we can presume at least that Derrida gave Levinas "Force and Signification" and "Edmond Jabès and the Question of the Book," given the dates of this exchange.

21. Letter from Emmanuel Levinas to Derrida, 22 October 1964, in Peeters, *Derrida*, 140.

22. Ibid.

23. Booth, *A Rhetoric of Irony,* 59.

24. Derrida himself references Joyce's *Ulysses,* 622, but does not provide the edition.

25. See Jacques Derrida, "A Word of Welcome" (*AEL* 40, 18) and my treatment of it in Hammerschlag, *The Figural Jew,* 249–50.

26. "Entretien avec Henri Atlan," *Cahiers d'Etudes Lévinassiennes,* no. 6 (2007): 144.

27. First published in *Evidences* 20 (October 1951): 302–8.

28. Søren Kierkegaard, *The Concept of Irony,* trans. Howard V. Hong (Princeton: Princeton University Press, 1992), 261.

29. Ibid., 49.

30. Originally published in *Information Juive* 131 (June 1961): 1–4.

31. Lear, *A Case for Irony,* 25.

32. Ibid., 38.

33. Paul de Man, *Aesthetic Ideology* (Minneapolis: University of Minnesota, 1996), 165.

34. See Alexander Nehamas's analysis of irony in *Euthyphro* in *The Art of Living: Socratic Reflections from Plato to Foucault* (Berkeley: University of California Press, 1998), 19–69.

35. Booth, *The Rhetoric of Irony*, 18.

36. De Man, *Aesthetic Ideology*, 184 and *Allegories of Reading: Figural Language in Rousseau, Nietzsche, Rilke, and Proust* (New Haven: Yale University Press, 1979), 17.

37. See Richard Rorty, *Contingency, Irony, and Solidarity* (Cambridge: Cambridge University Press, 1989), 122–37.

38. Hayden White, *Tropics of Discourse: Essays in Cultural Criticism* (Baltimore: Johns Hopkins University Press, 1978), 281.

39. See also the version of this argument published independently as Hayden White, "The Absurdist Moment in Contemporary Literary Theory," *Contemporary Literature* 17.3 (Summer 1976): 378–403.

40. Rorty, *Contingency, Irony, and Solidarity*, 133. See also Simon Critchley's essay "Deconstruction and Pragmatism," in *Ethics, Politics, Subjectivity* (London: Verso, 1999), 83–121. Critchley opposes Rorty's claim that deconstruction is apolitical by arguing that, insofar as Derrida is loyal to Levinas's ethics and produces a politics out of a dedication to the idea of infinite responsibility to the other, he gains political cogency. I differ from Critchley here by arguing that it is by his subversive reading of Levinas, through his destabilizing irony—that element of Derrida's texts which for Rorty disqualifies them as political—that Derrida's work gains its political force.

41. For Derrida's response to Rorty, see Simon Critchley, Jacques Derrida, Ernesto Laclau, and Richard Rorty, *Deconstruction and Pragmatism,* ed. Chantal Mouffe (London: Routledge, 1996), 81–82.

42. We can also associate this fear with Habermas's critique of the postmodern; see Jürgen Habermas, "Modernity Versus Postmodernity," *New German Critique* 22 (Winter 1981): 3–14. This fear is described in relation to irony by Rorty in *Contingency, Irony, and Solidarity,* 67.

43. See Sarah Hammerschlag, "Another, Other Abraham," *Shofar: An Interdisciplinary Journal of Jewish Studies* 26, no. 4 (2008): 74–96.

44. See Emmanuel Levinas, "L'autre dans Proust" (*NP* 117–24; *PN* 99–105). This essay, which will be discussed further in chapter 3, echoes reflections that Levinas recorded in his journals during the war. Proust was clearly a source for Levinas's conception of the subject, particularly his descriptions of eros. At the same time, in the final paragraph of the essay he includes a disclaimer: "But Proust's most profound teaching—if indeed poetry teaches—consists in situating the real in a relation with what forever remains other" (*NP* 123; *PN* 104–5).

45. Emmanuel Levinas, *Basic Philosophical Writings*, ed. Adriaan Peperzak, Simon Critchley, and Robert Bernasconi (Bloomington: Indiana University Press, 1996), 40. Originally published as "La Signification et le sens" in *Revue de Métaphysique et de Morale* 69 (1964): 125–56.

46. Ibid, 52. Levinas is also here addressing Merleau-Ponty's *Signs* (1960).
47. Ibid., 62.
48. I have not followed Lingis's translation here.
49. See the opening pages of Jacques Derrida, "A Word of Welcome," particularly (*AEL* 40, 18).
50. Critchley, *The Ethics of Deconstruction*, 141.
51. See Llewelyn's reading of the dialogue in John Llewelyn, *Appositions of Jacques Derrida and Emmanuel Levinas* (Bloomington: Indiana University Press, 2002). Llewelyn reads it as a poem, modeled on the Song of Songs, also discussed by Derrida in the essay, a kind of liturgical gesture whose function is to "question *viva voce* every fisible anatomic atom" (162–63).
52. I have not followed Aronowicz's translation here.
53. On Levinas's communitarian tendencies, see Hammerschlag, *The Figural Jew*, 154–65. On Levinas's work in Jewish education, see Claire Katz, *Levinas and the Crisis of Humanism* (Bloomington: Indiana University Press, 2013). On the renaissance of Jewish education in postwar Paris, see Johanna Lehr, *La Thora dans la Cité* (Lormont: Le Bord de l'eau, 2013).
54. Given that the majority of the text is itself on Kierkegaard, one has to wonder whether Derrida had Kierkegaard's own image of the vampire from *The Concept of Irony* (261) in mind here.
55. Søren Kierkegaard, *Fear and Trembling and Sickness Unto Death,* trans. Walter Lowrie (Princeton: Princeton University Press, 2013), 213.
56. Jacques Derrida, *Glas,* trans. John P. Leavey Jr. (Lincoln: University of Nebraska Press, 1990), 190.
57. Critchley et al., *Deconstruction and Pragmatism*, 83.
58. Ibid., 84.

2. LEVINAS, LITERATURE, AND THE RUIN OF THE WORLD

1. Derrida's "Literature in Secret" ends with a cascade of descriptions and definitions for literature, as "the place of all secrets without secrecy," "as a religious remainder," religion's inheritor and forgiver (*DLM* 203–8; *GD* 154–58). This from a thinker who had spent years of his earlier career obscuring the distinction between literature and philosophy, even as he never ceased to make claims for one against the other. In "Faith and Knowledge," Derrida treats the "emergence and semantics" of the noun *religion* both in terms of its historical Latin root but also as a kind of quasi-transcendental with its own formal and philosophical demands—suspended between a notion of the holy or the unscathed and a notion of faith, a response to a call (FK 44, 64). The later notion was itself formulated to reflect a debt to Levinas, who defines religion in *Totality and Infinity* rather idiosyncratically as "the bond

198 ɞ 2. LEVINAS, LITERATURE, AND THE RUIN OF THE WORLD

that is established between the same and the other without constituting a totality"
(*TI* 30; 40).

2. See Léon Brunschvicg, "Religion et philosophie de l'esprit," in *Écrits Philosophiques III* (Paris: Presses Universitaire de France, 1958), 209–19.

3. And in his refusal to accept the exemption from anti-Semitic legislation offered to him by the Vichy government.

4. See Léon Brunschvicg, "L'Humanisme de l'occident," in *Écrits philosophiques I* (Paris: Presses Universitaire de France, 1951), 8–9.

5. Ibid.

6. François Poirié, *Emmanuel Levinas, Qui etes-vous?* (Paris: La Manufacture, 1987), 70.

7. Gary Gutting, *French Philosophy in the Twentieth Century* (Cambridge: Cambridge University Press, 2001), 3–4.

8. See Robert J. Smith, *The Ecole Normale Supérieure and the Third Republic* (Albany: SUNY Press, 1982).

9. Hubert Bourgin, *De Jaurès a Léon Blum: l'École normale et la politique* (Paris: Fayard, 1938), 233.

10. Ibid., 216, 232.

11. Ibid., 516.

12. Paul Nizan, *Les Chiens de garde* (Paris: F. Maspero, 1969), 24.

13. Ibid., 53.

14. Ibid.

15. Ibid., 110.

16. Pierre Birnbaum, *Les Fous de la République: histoire politique des juifs d'Etat, de Gambetta à Vichy* (Paris: Fayard, 1992).

17. The editorial committee consisted of Alexandre Koyré, the Russian immigrant to France who led the first Hegel seminars in Paris, Albert Spaier, an immigrant from Romania who taught philosophy of science at Caen, and the French historian of religions Henri-Charles Puech.

18. *Recherches Philosophiques* 1 (1931–1932): 7.

19. Jean Wahl, "Vers le concret," *Recherches Philosophiques* 1 (1931–1932): 3.

20. Jean Wahl, "Subjectivité et Transcendence" in *Bulletin de la Société française de philosophie* 37.5 (October-December 1937): 63. Levinas referred to this lecture as his "fameuse communication" in his homage to Wahl. Emmanuel Levinas, *Jean Wahl et Gabriel Marcel* (Paris: Beauchesne, 1976), 28.

21. Ibid.

22. Jean Wahl, "Subjectivité et Transcendence" in *Existence humaine et transcendance*, (Neuchatel: Baconnière, 1944), 41.

23. Ibid., 41.

24. Ethan Kleinberg, *Generation Existential: Heidegger's Philosophy in France, 1927–1961* (Ithaca: Cornell University Press, 2005), 86.

25. Cited in Bruce Baugh, *French Hegel* (New York: Routledge, 2003), 42.

26. The list includes Jacques Lacan, Henri Corbin, Raymond Aron, Maurice Merleau-Ponty, George Bataille, and indeed Levinas. See Judith Butler's account in *Subjects of Desire* (New York: Columbia University Press, 1999). She sees Wahl as a premature exception in the history of French Hegel's reception (viii). Bruce Baugh, to the contrary, argues, "it would be hard to overemphasize the importance of Wahl's criticism of Hegel or his interpretation of Kierkegaard" (*French Hegel,* 41).

27. Emmanuel Levinas, "De l'évasion," *Recherches Philosophiques* 5 (1935–1936): 373–92.

28. David Carroll, *French Literary Fascism: Nationalism, Antisemitism, and the Ideology of Culture* (Princeton: Princeton University Press, 1995), 40. Carroll identifies Maurice Barrès as the origin of such a notion, citing in particular the deification of Hugo in *Les Déracinés*. "The role of the national poet, of the master of the French words . . . is to facilitate the return to the origin, to the moment before division when perfect communion was a natural state, when the 'race; was born not of blood but *in and as words*." As I will show, there is a countertradition that develops in the twentieth century, particularly through the work of Blanchot and Sartre, picked up by Derrida that reorients the relation of literature and politics.

29. Bergson provides an interesting case in this story. While he is cited frequently in Levinas's work, it is rarely to form an association with him. Levinas does at one point speak of himself as "Bergsonian," but only insofar as Bergson established his own concept of evolution through a remodeling of Spencer's. In that sense Levinas would seem to be Bergsonian insofar as he developed his characterization of being as a countermodel to Heidegger's. It seems that, for the most part, Bergson's endorsement of the Christian tradition and his negative characterization of Judaism in "Les Deux Sources" pushed him beyond the pale. Thus Levinas groups him with Simone Weil as an assimilated Jew, one of those who "accused themselves," that is to say the tradition, for lacking comprehension of supernatural salvation (*DL* 244; *DF* 161). Even here, it is striking how Levinas refuses, in fact, to free either Weil or Bergson from the tradition, even as they both resisted identifying *as* Jews. That is itself a sign that the terms of Jewish identification had shifted as a consequence of the Nazi race laws.

30. The essay "De l'evasion" was published in a section of *Recherches Philosophiques* entitled 'De l'existence et de l'être" and followed Bataille's "Le Labrynthe." The trend to treat being as insufficient is evident itself in Bataille's essay and thus marks a contrast with Levinas's approach.

31. See for example Lam. R II.9 (56b) and Sifre Deuteronomy 34. See also Sarah Hammerschlag, "'A Splinter in the Flesh': Levinas and the Resignification of Jewish Suffering, 1928–1947," *International Journal of Philosophical Studies* 20.3 (2012): 389–419.

32. Among Levinas's barrack mates were at least two Catholic clerics.

33. Only 2.5 percent of French prisoners of war died during their captivity. See Christopher Lloyd, "Enduring Captivity: French POW Narratives of World War II," *Journal of War and Culture Studies* 6.1(February 1, 2013): 24–39; and Adrian Gilbert, *POW: Allied Prisoners in Europe, 1941–1945* (London: John Murray, 2006).

34. In the seventh notebook, Levinas quotes Baudelaire's poem "Spleen": "L'ennui, fruit de la morne incuriosité, prend les proportions de l'immortalité." This becomes the final line of *Totality and Infinity*. Thanks to Martin Kavka for pointing this out to me. For mention of Macbeth see *CC* 174 and *TI* 155, 146; and *AQE* 14; *OTB* 3.

35. Some of this may have had to do with access. The International Committee of the Red Cross distributed packages of books to POW camps. Some lagers even had libraries, but all books were censored. Anything that might seem to disparage Germany was banned, as were works by emigrés, Communist, and Jewish authors. Gilbert, *POW,* 186–87. See also Y. Durand, *La vie quotidienne des Prisonniers de guerre dans les stalags, les oflags et les Kommando, 1939–1945* (Paris: Hachette, 1987), 186–87, cited by Rodolphe Calin and Catherine Chalier in the preface to *CC* 24.

36. Seán Hand, "Salvation Through Literature," *Levinas Studies* 8.1 (2013): 45–65. Bloy is the most cited source of the notebooks. More than half of the sixth notebook is taken up with citations from Bloy's *Lettres à sa fiancée.* Levinas's interest in Bloy is, on one level, not surprising. Bloy's 1892 *Salvation by the Jews* had revived the notion that the suffering of the Jews was redemptive, a carrying on of the work of Christ. While such a view functioned to justify Dreyfus's suffering in such a way that it was itself a redemptive event, it was, nonetheless, for some a powerful counteraccount to Drumont's. See Stephen Schloesser, *Jazz Age Catholicicism: Mystic Modernism in Postwar Paris, 1919–1933* (Toronto: University of Toronto Press, 2005), 65–66.

37. Alfred de Vigny, *Stello* (Paris: Calman Levy, 1882), 174. Translated in English by Irving Massey (Montreal: McGill University Press, 1963), 132. For more on Maistre's influence in nineteenth- and twentieth-century French thought, see Françoise Meltzer's chapter "Beliefs" in *Seeing Double: Baudelaire's Modernity* (Chicago: University of Chicago Press, 2011), 11–74. Bataille can be understood to have developed his interest on sacrifice from Maistre analogously, by reversing the dynamic such that sacrifice is rethought as erotic self-loss. See Jesse Goldhammer, *The Headless Republic: Sacrificial Violence in Modern French Thought* (Ithaca: Cornell University Press, 2005), 152–91.

38. Levinas explicitly relates his notion of substitution to the Christian paradigm in "Un Dieu homme?" published in 1968. "How can I deal philosophically with a notion that belongs to the intimate sphere of hundreds of millions of believers—the mystery of mysteries of their theology—that for nearly twenty centuries has united people whose fate I share along with most of their ideas, with the exception of the very belief in questions here this evening?" writes Levinas in the essay's opening paragraph (*EN* 64, 53). It concludes, "Messianism is that apogee in Being—a reversal of being 'persevering in this being'—which begins in me" (*EN* 71, 60).

39. I want to distinguish my argument here from the kind of argument Samual Moyn makes in *Origins of the Other: Emmanuel Levinas Between Revelation and Ethics* (Ithaca: Cornell University Press, 2005). I critique the kind of causality he asserted in my review of his book. See Sarah Hammerschlag, "Samuel Moyn's *Origins of the Other*," *Journal of Religion* 87.1 (January 2007): 127–28.

40. Marcel Proust, *À l'ombre des jeunes filles* (Paris: Nouvelle Revue Française, 1920), 74; Proust, *Remembrance of Things Past*, trans. C. K. Scott Moncrieff (New York: Random House, 1981), 1:545.

41. Levinas says this most explicitly in "La réalité et son ombre" in *Les Temps Modernes* 38 (1948): 771–89. He is not explicit about what method "criticism" should take, but only that art criticism and literary criticism redeem the object from silence and stillness. He also makes this point in his essay on Michel Leiris, "The Transcendence of Words." See Seàn Hand, ed., *The Levinas Reader* (Cambridge: Blackwell, 1989), 144–49. "All the arts, even the sonorous ones, create silence," he writes. He calls it oppressive and frightening and suggests that in this silence there is a need and a demand "for critique" (*HS* 201; *OS* 147).

42. Dating of one set of fragments indicates the years of 1959–1960. See Emmanuel Levinas, *Eros, littérature et philosophie inédits,* ed. Jean-Luc Nancy and Danielle Cohen-Levinas (Paris: Imec/Grasset, 2013), 62. This volume also includes early poetry Levinas wrote in Russian.

43. Later published as "Nameless" in *NP* 177–82; *PN* 119–23.

44. The language is nearly identical in the essay "Sans Nom" (*NP* 177; *PN* 119). This image is also in the novel (*ELP* 52, 85).

45. This is a play on the joke that the barber hangs a sign outside his door that says, "Demain on rase gratis" (*NP* 67; *PN* 56).

46. Jean Wahl, "Présentation," *Deucalion* 1.1 (1946): 9.

47. In *Ésprit,* Edouard Mounier, the leading figure of personalism, described the appearance of *Deucalion* as probing the borders of rationalism, "here by literature, there by religion." Emmanuel Mounier, in *L'Orientation des sciences humaines en France* 128.12 (December 1946): 877.

48. Jean Wahl, *Poésie, pensée, perception* (Paris: Calman-Lévy, 1948).

49. See Christopher Benfey and Karen Remmler, eds., *Artists, Intellectuals and World War II: The Pontigny Encounters at Mount Holyoke College, 1942–1944* (Amherst: University of Massachusetts Press, 2006).

50. For a take on this period that focuses on the debates over humanism, see Stephanos Geroulanos, *An Atheism That Is Not Humanist Emerges in French Thought* (Stanford: Stanford University Press, 2010).

51. Simone de Beauvoir, *The Force of Circumstance* (New York: Putnam, 1965), 13.

52. Suzanne Guerlac, *Literary Polemics: Bataille, Sartre, Valéry* (Stanford: Stanford University Press, 1997), 56–57.

53. Jean-Paul Sartre, *Qu'est-ce que la litterature* (Paris: Gallimard, 1948), *What Is Literature,* trans. Steven Ungar (Cambridge: Harvard University Press, 1988).

54. Ibid., 219, 151.

55. Ibid., 279, 189.

56. Ibid., 254–57, 173–74.

57. Guerlac convincingly argues for the influence of Bataille's ideas in *Qu'est-ce que la littérature*. Bataille himself seems to call attention to that influence in his response to Sartre's *Saint Genet,* "Genet et l'étude de Sartre sur lui," published in *La littérature et le Mal* (Paris: Gallimard, 1957).

58. Georges Bataille, *Oeuvres Completes V* (Paris: Gallimard, 1973), 156, and *Inner Experience* (Albany: SUNY Press, 1988), 135.

59. Sartre takes up Bataille's conception of poetry in *What Is Literature?* but without mentioning Bataille's name. Instead he uses the same example—the words *butter* and *horse*—to argue against Bataille's notion of poetry as sacrifice, even as he makes Bataille's denigrated conception of discourse as project, where words are tools, the very basis of his defense of literature. Ibid.

60. Ibid., 170, 147.

61. For an excellent and in-depth account of this relationship, see Amy Hollywood, *Sensible Ecstasy: Mysticism, Sexuality, and the Demands of History* (Chicago: University of Chicago Press, 2001), 25–89.

62. Georges Bataille, "De l'age de pierre a Jacques Prévert," *Critique* 1.3–4 (1946): 195–214, here 198–99.

63. Bataille, *Inner Experience*, 106.

64. Levinas had already published in 1947 the essay on Proust in *Deucalion* in which he used terms very close to Bataille's own in describing Proust in *Inner Experience*. Bataille describes the relation between communication, knowledge, and love in these terms:

> But the unknown (seduction) becomes elusive if I want to possess it, if I attempt to know the object; while Proust never tired of wanting to use, to abuse objects which life proposes. Such that he knew hardly anything of love but was impossible jealousy . . . If the truth which a woman proposes to the one who loves her is the unknown (the inaccessible), he can neither know her nor reach her, but she can break him; if he is broken, what does he himself become, if not the unknown, the inaccessible, which lay dormant in him? But neither lover could at will grasp anything from such a game, nor immobilize it, nor make it last. That which communicates (which is penetrated in each one by the other) is the measure of blindness which neither knows nor knows of itself.
>
> (BATAILLE, *INNER EXPERIENCE*, 139)

Levinas, in terms that seem to be responding to Bataille's, writes in 1947 of the same relation, "But if communication thus bears the sign of failure or inauthenticity, it is because it is sought as fusion. One sets out from the idea that duality should be transformed into unity . . . this is the last vestige of a conception identifying being and knowing... One does not see that the success of knowledge would in fact destroy the nearness, the proximity of the other. A proximity that, far from meaning something less than identification, opens up the horizon of social existence, brings out all the surplus of our experience of friendship and love and brings to the definitiveness of our identical existence all the virtuality of the non-definitive."

    Both thus see the virtue of the relation as one revealing the failure of fusion, but while for Levinas this seems to lead to a model of sociality, in which proximity is defined in terms of difference, for Bataille the encounter with the mystery of the other seems to return one to the mystery of the self. Whether Levinas was explicitly responding to Bataille's reading we can't say for certain, but the proximity of their two readings reveals their intellectual proximity and fundamental points of difference.

65. Bataille, "De l'existentialisme au primat de l'économie," *Critique* 5.3, no. 21 (1948): 129; trans. Jill Robbins and reprinted as an appendix in Jill Robbins, *Altered Reading: Levinas and Literature* (Chicago: University of Chicago Press, 1999), 167–68.

66. Ibid., 131, 170.

67. Ibid., 132, 171.

68. Ibid., 141, 180. I made minor changes to Jill Robbin's translation here.

69. Ibid., 140, 179.

70. *Les Temps Modernes* 4.38 (November 1948): 771–89.

71. Martin Jay, *Downcast Eyes: The Denigration of Vision in Twentieth-Century French Thought* (Berkeley: University of California Press, 1994), 554.

72. *Les Temps Modernes* 4.38 (November 1948): 769.

73. Translation mine.

74. Translation mine.

75. "There is something nasty, selfish, and cowardly in artistic pleasure. There are times when one could be ashamed of it, as if carousing in a town struck by the plague" (*IH* 125; *UH* 90). There is a striking resonance between this line and his depiction of Derrida's work in "Wholly Other" as a no-man's land and his comparison of it to the emptiness of French cities and town after the 1940 exodus south (*NP* 66; *PN* 56).

76. See Sarah Hammerschlag, *The Figural Jew: Politics and Identity in Postwar French Thought* (Chicago: University of Chicago Press, 2010), 166–200.

77. Later published as a single essay under the name of the latter in Maurice Blanchot, *La Part du feu* (Paris: Gallimard, 1949), 291–331.

78. Ibid., 294 and Maurice Blanchot, *Work of Fire*, trans. Charlotte Mandell (Stanford: Stanford University Press, 1995), 302. This claim is tied also to Blanchot's essay "How Is Literature Possible" on Paulhan's *The Flowers of Tarbes*. See chapter 5, this volume.

79. Sartre, *Qu'est-ce que la litterature*, 27, *What Is Literature?* 35.

80. Blanchot, *La Part du feu*, 316, *Work of Fire*, 327.

81. See Kevin Hart, *The Dark Gaze: Maurice Blanchot and the Sacred* (Chicago: University of Chicago Press, 2004) for a detailed consideration of the relation between literature and the sacred in Blanchot.

82. Blanchot, *La Part du Feu,* 317, *Work of Fire,* 328.

83. Ibid.

84. Leiris was also on the editorial board of *Les Temps Modernes,* thus Levinas was once again publishing a critique of a figure closely tied to the journal in which he was publishing.

85. See Philippe Lacoue-Labarthe, *Heidegger and the Politics of Poetry,* trans. Jeff Fort (Urbana: University of Illinois, 2007).

86. Martin Heidegger, "Der Ursprung des Kunstwerkes," *Holzwege,* 6th ed. (Frankfurt: Klostermann, 1980), 60. Quoted in Lacoue-Labarthe, *Heidegger and the Politics of Poetry,* 10.

87. Martin Heidegger, *Elucidations of Hölderlin's Poetry,* trans. Keith Hoeller (Amherst, NY: Humanity, 2000), 48.

88. For more on the reception of Sartre's "Existentialism Is a Humanism," see Geroulanos's *An Atheism That Is Not Humanist,* 222–50.

89. For more on the early postwar response to Heidegger in Paris, see Kleinberg, *Generation Existential,* 168–78.

90. *Les Temps Modernes* 1.4 (January 1946): 713.

91. Ibid., 716.

92. Dominique Janicaud, *Heidegger en France* (Paris: Albin Michel, 2001), 94–97; Jean Wahl, *Introduction à la pensée de Heidegger* (Paris: Livre de poche, 1998).

93. Geroulanos points out that Wahl was the first to publicly report that Heidegger had barred Husserl from the library at the University of Freiberg and that his engagement with Heidegger always maintained its critical elements.

94. Heidegger, "Why Poets?" in *Off the Beaten Track,* trans. Julian Young (Cambridge: Cambridge University Press, 2002), 200.

95. Ibid., 204.

96. Marie-Ann Lescourret, *Emmanuel Levinas* (Paris: Flammarion, 1994), 268.

97. *Critique* 1.1 (1946).

98. Mircea Eliade, "Science, Idéalisme et phénomenes paranormaux," *Critique* 4.23 (April 1948): 315–23.

99. Bataille, "L'Ivresse des Tavernes et la Religion," *Critique* 4.25 (June 1948): 534.

100. Aime Patri, "Proudhon et Dieu," *Critique* 1.3–4 (August-September 1946): 267–71.

101. See Michael Kelly, "Catholicism and the Left in Twentieth-Century France," in Kay Chadwick, ed., *Catholicism, Politics and Society in Twentieth Century France* (Liverpool: Liverpool University Press, 2000), 141–69; and Adrian Dansette, *Destin du catholicism français, 1926–1956* (Paris: Flammarion, 1957).

102. In 1946 in *Ésprit,* in an essay situating personalism in relation to other postwar movements, Mounier articulated his relation to Péguy this way. "We not only took up again the word of Péguy, 'The revolution will be moral or it will not be.' We specified, 'The moral revolution will be economic or it will not be.' The economic movement will be 'moral' or it will be nothing." Emmanuel Mounier, "Situation du Personalisme," *Ésprit* 118.1 (January 1946): 7.

103. Mounier's relationship to the Vichy regime is complex. The rhetoric of Mounier's personalism shared much with the Vichy language of national revolution. Mounier too critiqued the sickness of individualism and capitalism and sympathized with the language of national renewal. He even collaborated on early Vichy movements oriented around the regeneration of France's youth. But as Vichy moved toward a more collaborative stance with Germany, Mounier distanced himself from the regime and publicly distanced his own movement's values from Nazi principles. After the war, *Ésprit* was the first journal to begin publication in December of 1944 and to recraft its relation to the past. Its first issue retold the story of the journal during the war as a narrative of resistance and began with the story of its "clandestine history," how its important leaders suffered in prison, internment camps, and fought in the Maquis. *Ésprit* 105.1 (December 1944): 1. See John Hellman, *Emmanuel Mounier and the New Catholic Left, 1930–1950* (Toronto: University of Toronto Press, 1981), 158–203. See also Michel Winock, *Histoire politique de la revue Esprit, 1930–1950* (Paris: Seuil, 1975). Sternhell describes Mounier's journey as paradigmatic of "all those protesting intellectuals of the 1930's who in search of a revolution that was not Marxist, rejected by definition the liberal and social-democratic consensus. Mounier rejected fascism, but could not deny the fact that its violent critique of 'désordre établi' was in line with the fascists. The proposed solutions were different but the critiques were practically identical." Zeev Sternhell, *Ni droite ni gauche: l'idéologie fasciste en France* (Paris: Seuil, 1983), 299.

104. See Michael Kelly, *The Cultural and Intellectual Rebuilding of France After the Second World War* (Chippenham: Palgrave, 2004), 145–54.

105. Hellman, *Emmanuel Mounier and the New Catholic Left,* 231.

106. Christine Daigle, *Existentialist Thinkers and Ethics* (Montreal: McGill University Press, 2006), 5.

107. Gabriel Marcel, *The Philosophy of Existence* (London: Harvill, 1948).

108. Ibid., 96.

109. Ibid.

110. Emmanuel Mounier, "Introductions aux Existentialismes," *Ésprit* 121.4 (April 1946): 97, 102.

111. Tony Judt, *Past Imperfect: French Intellectuals, 1944–1956* (Berkeley: University of California Press, 1992), 88; Baring, *The Young Derrida,* 93–96; Geroulanos, *An Atheism That Is Not Humanist,* 252–58.

112. Michael Kelly, *The Cultural and Intellectual Rebuilding of France After the Second World War,* 147.

113. Kelly, "Catholicism and the Left in Twentieth-Century France," 160.

114. Jean Lacroix, *La Crise intellectuelle du Catholicisme français* (Paris: Fayard, 1970), 50.

115. Emmanuel Levinas, "Philosophie et Religion," *Critique* 27.289 (June 1971): 537.

116. Levinas footnotes *frémissement* as a translation of φρικη (although he mistakenly in *Critique* writes φρενυ). Ibid.

3. BETWEEN THE JEW AND WRITING

1. Baring dates the exchange to 1961 based on the fact that it would have had to take place before Levinas's *soutenance de thèse*. I have nonetheless preserved the indeterminacy here with which Derrida himself recollected the moment to Ricoeur. See Edward Baring, *The Young Derrida and French Philosophy, 1945–1968* (Cambridge: Cambeidge University Press, 2011), 269.

2. Benoît Peeters, *Derrida, a Biography*, trans. Andrew Brown (Cambridge: Polity, 2013), 137.

3. As both Baring and Peeters describe it, among Derrida's peers at the École normale supérieure, Derrida represented a mostly uninhabited middle ground between the Marxists and the Catholic *Talas*, a term that supposedly arose from "ils von[t à la] messe" (they go to mass). Baring, *Young Derrida*, 93. While Baring emphasizes Derrida's relation to the Christians, Peeters concerns himself with Derrida's negotiations with the communists. See Peeters, *Derrida*, 63.

4. Peeters, *Derrida*, 133.

5. Ibid., 139. Already Derrida was employing a certain doublespeak. But at least on the first reading the irony of his referring to his own work as "dead leaves" would not yet have been apparent to Levinas. By 1963 Levinas had not relied explicitly on a dead letter/living spirit distinction in his work or worked out the distinction between the saying and the said, but he had already described the face as a living presence.

6. He used it in multiple essay titles in *Writing and Difference* and again in 1967 for *Voice and Phenomenon*, where part of the aim is to reverse and unsettle the priority of the living voice as a marker of presence. Again in 1996 for "Foi et Savoir," in a gloss on Bergson's "Les deux sources," Ed Baring points to the play between *et* and *est* in *L'ecriture et la différence*, but of course the play applies each and every time Derrida uses the form *x et x* in a title, even without the direct article. Baring, *The Young Derrida*, 220.

7. See Steven Shakespeare, *Derrida and Theology* (London: T&T Clark, 2009); Harold Coward and Toby Foshay, *Derrida and Negative Theology* (Albany: SUNY Pres, 1992); Kevin Hart, *The Trespass of the Sign: Deconstruction, Theology, and Philosophy* (Cambridge: Cambridge University Press, 1989).

8. Baring, *The Young Derrida*, 62, quoting Derrida, "Les Dieux et Dieu: les Dieux existent-ils?" Irvine I.12.

9. Baring, *The Young Derrida*, 139.

10. Marcel quotes this passage from *Etre et Avoir* in his Gifford Lectures, *The Mystery of Being* (London: Harvill, 1950), 212.

11. Ibid.

12. Richard Kearney, *Dialogues with Contemporary Continental Thinkers* (Manchester: Manchester University Press, 1984), 107.

13. Among these essays, collected in the order of their publication, is also Derrida's scathing treatment of Foucault's *Folie et déraison*, "Cogito and the History of Madness,"

which precedes the other three in composition, but nonetheless shares in some of their preoccupations. Particularly, all three share a common recourse to the language of dreams, as does *De la Grammatologie* published in 1967, the same year as *L'Écriture et la différence*.

14. Heidegger, "Letter on Humanism" in *Pathmarks*, ed. William McNeill (Cambridge: Cambridge University Press, 1998), 249.

15. See *TI* 205, 189; "The Poet's Vision" in *PN* 128; *SB* 12.

16. Derrida's essay on Bataille in *Writing and Difference*, "From Restricted to General Economy," offers a reading of Bataille which makes Bataille a practitioner of *écriture* in the Derridean sense.

17. Derrida uses this metaphor often to indicate both the power and the danger of a certain kind of thinking. It becomes explicitly a trope in *Mal d'archive*. See my analysis in Sarah Hammerschlag, *The Figural Jew* (Chicago: University of Chicago Press, 2010), 235.

18. I have altered Bass's translation slightly. The use of "dream" language also pervades *Of Grammatology*. There it is clear that the function of "dreaming" for Derrida is tied to the role of the dream in Freud's *Interpretation of Dreams*. The argument is that philosophical discourse is pervaded by evidence of its own expressions of an unattainable wish fulfillment, and this is evident, as in dreams, where we see the operations of dreaming—transposition, displacement, overdetermination, etc. In *Of Grammatology* Derrida is also explicit about the fact that in reading Rousseau his rhetoric will often mirror the rhetoric of psychoanalysis, but without reverting to an explanation that "takes us outside of the writing toward a psychobiographical signified" (*DLG* 221; *OG* 159).

19. Friedrich Nietzsche, *Birth of Tragedy*, trans. Douglas Smith (Oxford: Oxford University Press, 2000), 30.

20. See footnote on Derrida and the apophatic in chapter 1.

21. Friedrich Nietzsche, *Thus Spoke Zarathustra*, trans. Graham Parkes (Oxford: Oxford University Press), 172.

22. Ibid., 170.

23. UC Irvine Derrida Archive, box 95, folder 1.

24. Levinas only uses this term *le creux* once in *Totality and Infinity* (*TI* 32), but the verb *creuser* is frequently used to describe the function of desire in relation to the other.

25. "We share the same traditional heritage," he told an interviewer in 1986, "even if Levinas has been engaged with it for a much longer time and with greater profundity. Therefore, the difference is not there either. This is not the only example, but I often have difficulty in placing these discrepancies otherwise than as differences of 'signature,' that is of idiom, of ways of proceeding, of history, and of inscriptions connected to the biographical aspect, etc. These are not philosophical differences." *Altérités: Jacques Derrida et Pierre-Jean Labarièrre. Avec des études de Francis Guibal et Stanislas Breton* (Paris: Osiris, 1986), 75.

26. Here he sides with Blanchot, of whom he writes, "Blanchot could probably extend over all of Levinas's propositions what he says about the dissymetry within the space of communication: 'Here I believe, is what is decisive in the affirmation which we must hear, and which must be maintained independently of the theological context in which it occurs.' But is this possible?" Derrida answers this question in the essay not by rejecting the theological project but by arguing for God as an effect of the trace (*ED* 151–52; *WD* 102–3).

27. Jacques Schérer, in *Le Livre de Mallarmé* (Paris: Gallimard, 1978), explores the Mallarmean thesis of treating the relation between poetry and music and thus "giving vis-à-vis language the same freedom that the composer gives to the noises of nature," to exercise this freedom within the architecture of the book, such that the book could itself be played by different voices (77).

28. See John Llewlyn's chapter, "Derrida, Mallarmé, Anatole" in his *Appositions of Jacques Derrida and Emmanuel Levinas* (Bloomington: Indiana University Press, 2002), 39–50.

29. Derrida Archive, "Literature et verité: le concept de mimesis," box 10, folder 1, 1968–1969.

30. There seems to be some uncertainty about what year Jabès came to Paris. In *Le Livre des Questions* (Paris: Gallimard, 1988), 1957 is given as the date, so I have preserved that here, but multiple other sources list it as 1956.

31. "Book of the Dead" in Edmond Jabès, *The Sin of the Book* (Lincoln: University of Nebraska Press, 1985), 4.

32. In the forward to *The Book of Margins,* Mark Taylor tells the story that when he referred to Jabès as "a Jewish writer," Jabès, irritated, interrupted him and clarified, "I am not a Jewish writer; I am a writer and a Jew." Edmond Jabès, *The Book of Margins* (Chicago: University of Chicago Press, 1993), ix.

33. Peeters, *Derrida,* 134–40.

34. Derrida, "Countersignature," trans. Mairéad Hanrahan, *Paragraph* 27. 2 (2004): 38. Originally published in *Poétiques de Jean Genet: La traversée des genres* (Actes du Colloque Cérisy-la-Salle, 2000). Ed. Albert Dichy Patrick Bougon (Paris: IMEC, 2004).

35. Ibid.

36. In the version published in *Writing and Difference,* Derrida adds, "It does not negate itself any more than it affirms itself: it differs from itself, defers itself, and writes itself as différance," thus inserting the concept of *différance,* which dates from the 1966 essay "Freud and the Scene of Writing." On the history of this term, see Baring, *The Young Derrida,* 190–220.

37. The linking of these two questions, the theological and the Jewish, points as well to the position of Judaism as exemplary, both particular nation and universal.

38. *Revue de métaphysique et de morale,* nos. 3 and 4 (1964).

39. Derrida concludes with a note that draws attention to Levinas's attempt to distinguish an Abrahamic mode from *Ulysses.* Pointing out that the notion of errance

here puts Levinas closer to Heidegger than Levinas would like and asking as well if the theme of return isn't itself a bit Hebraic. He also announces in this note the topic that becomes one of the primary themes of "En ce moment," the masculinity of Levinas's philosophy. Does not this align him with the "essential virility of the metaphysical language?" he asks (*ED* 228; *WD* 321).

40. I have not followed Seàn Hand's translations here.

41. The essay can be read—as Derrida does—as an engagement with Rosenzweig's own project for Jewish learning and indeed as a commitment to reenact it in France after the war. The use of the flame metaphor evokes Rosenzweig's own model of Jewish temporality in *The Star of Redemption*. Derrida, in his original parenthetical citation of the essay in *Revue de Métaphysique,* also refers the reader to "Entre deux Mondes," Levinas's essay on Rosenzweig, first given at the 1959 Colloque des intellectuels juifs de langue française. Emmanuel Levinas, "Entre deux Mondes," *Revue de Métaphysique et de Morale* 4 (October-December1964): 472.

42. Rosenzweig himself referred to *The Star* as project of translation, of translating Judaism into German. For more on this theme, see Dana Hollander, "Franz Rosenzweig on Nation, Translation and Judaism," *Philosophy Today* 38.4 (Winter 1994): 380–89.

43. Derrida is quoting Levinas in *Totality and Infinity* (*TI* 9, 24).

44. Maurice Blanchot, *L'Entretien infini* (Paris: Gallimard, 1969), 73, *The Infinite Conversation,* trans. Susan Hanson (Minneapolis: University of Minnesota, 1993), 51.

45. Maurice Blanchot, *La Part du feu* (Gallimard: Paris, 1949), 299, translated by Charlotte Mandell as *The Work of Fire* (Stanford: Stanford University Press, 1995), 307. The essay was originally published in two parts in 1947 and 1948.

46. In this essay it seems clear that Derrida has not himself reached the mature concept of the freedom of writing. The closest we get to a formulation that has hints of his later definition is the claim that it is by being "enregistered . . . entrusted to an engraving, a groove" that inscription acquires its infinite transmissibility and "the play of meaning" can "overflow signification" (*ED* 23; *WD* 12).

47. See also Hammerschlag, *The Figural Jew,* 248–49.

48. On the theme of freedom in Judaism in Levinas, see also Jean Halperin's essay "Liberté et responsibilité" in *Textes pour Emmanuel Levinas,* ed. François Laruelle (Paris: J-M Place, 1980), 61–70. Halperin was president of the preparatory committee for the Colloque des intellectuels juifs de langue française and the editor of the volumes that were produced by the colloquium.

49. *DL* (1963) 9.

50. Emmanuel Levinas, "Judaism privée," *Évidences,* no. 14 (November 1950): 19, *DL* (1963) 295.

51. Ibid.

52. Ibid.

53. I slightly altered Lingis's translation here.

54. Jacques Derrida and Élisabeth Roudinesco, *For What Tomorrow,* trans. Jeff Fort (Stanford: Stanford University Press, 2004), 111.

55. For more on Derrida's reformulation of "being-Jewish," see Hammerschlag, *The Figural Jew,* 201–67.

56. See Peeters, 85–123.

57. Hammerschlag, *The Figural Jew,* chapter 6. See also "Poetics of the Broken Tablet" in *The Trace of God: Derrida and Religion,* ed. Peter Gordon and Edward Baring (New York: Fordham University Press, 2014).

58. *DL* (1963) 310.

59. Emmanuel Levinas, "Religion and Revolution," *Annals of International Studies* 5, no. 11 (1980): 63.

4. TO LOSE ONE'S HEAD

1. UC Irvine Archive, box 10, folder 1.

2. Richard Beardsworth, *Derrida and the Political* (London: Routledge, 1996), xv.

3. At least the analysis focuses less on the literary dynamics of his texts and more on their political implications. I would include here Samir Haddad's *Derrida and the Inheritance of Democracy* (Bloomington: Indiana University Press 2013); and A. J. P. Thomson's *Deconstruction and Democracy; Derrida's Politics of Friendship* (London: Continuum, 2005).

4. Jacques Derrida and Maurizion Ferraris, *A Taste for the Secret* (New York: Wiley, 2001), 50.

5. Benoît Peeters, *Derrida, a Biography,* trans. Andrew Brown (Cambridge: Polity, 2013), 197. Jacques Derrida *Points, Interviews, 1974–1994,* ed. Elisabeth Weber (Stanford: Stanford University Press, 1995), 347–48.

6. My own interview with Solomon Malka, August 2008.

7. Marie-Ann Lescourret, *Emmanuel Levinas* (Paris: Flammarion, 1994), 242.

8. Derrida is a particularly complicated case on this question. Both Peeters and Baring describe the complex relationship between Derrida and Althusser and his followers at ENS in the mid 1960s. Peeters, *Derrida,* 150–51. After May 1968, Derrida was pressed on the "enigma of his silence on Marx." His response ultimately became *Specters of Marx,* an attempt to follow "this or that unnoticed vein in the Marxist text" (Peeters, *Derrida,* 220–21). Levinas's invocations of Marx usually function to align himself with the demand for social justice, but most often by insisting that there is a "materialist and realist" tradition that long precedes Marx. Often this refers to Judaism (*NTR* 131), but sometimes to certain strands in Western philosophy as well (*NP* 134; *PN* 112).

9. See also *AE* 214 and 273; *OTB* 136 and 177 on "the play of being and nothingness."

10. Prophecy is still maintained as a category of witnessing, but is relegated to the final chapter, whereas it appears in the preface of *Totality and Infinity.* In *OTB* prophecy is a model for speech in which the primary locus is not in the statement "I believe" but as the making of oneself a sign in being for the other.

11. "Strictly speaking the other is the end" (*AE* 203; *OTB* 128).
12. I altered the syntax of Lingis's translation here slightly to match the original.
13. See also Jill Robbins, *Altered Readings: Levinas and Literature* (Chicago: University of Chicago Press, 1999) on this point.
14. I am oversimplifying here for the sake of the point, as Derrida maintains the undecidability here between the a priori and the empirical, refusing to decide which precedes.
15. Michael Naas, *Miracle and Machine: Jacques Derrida and the Two Sources of Religion, Science, and the Media* (New York: Fordham University Press, 2012), 227–29. Samuel Weber, "Once and for All" *Grey Room* 20 (Summer 2005): 110.
16. Paul Celan, *Meridian* (Stanford: Stanford University Press, 2011), 15–48.
17. Ibid., 185.
18. Emmanuel Levinas, *Levinas Reader*, ed. Séan Hand (London; Blackwell, 1989), 294.
19. Judith Butler, *Parting Ways* (New York: Columbia University Press, 2013), 39. Howard Caygill, *Levinas and the Political* (London: Routledge, 2002), 191–193.
20. Levinas, *Levinas Reader*, 298.
21. Derrida, "Countersignature," trans. Mairéad Hanrahan, *Paragraph* 27.2 (2004): 29. Originally published in *Poétiques de Jean Genet: la traversée des genres* (Actes du Colloque Cérisy-la-Salle 2000), ed. Albert Dichy Patrick Bougon (Paris: IMEC, 2004).
22. The pomegranate is, according to Jewish tradition, supposed to have 613 seeds, symbolizing the 613 commandments of Torah.
23. In an interview with Maurizio Ferraris, Derrida compares deconstruction to terrorism, to a childhood fantasy of his that he planted bombs on railways and watched the explosion from a distance. "I see very well that this image, which translates a deep phantasmatic compulsion, could be illustrated by deconstructive operations, which consist in planting discretely, with delayed-action mechanism, devices that all of a sudden put a transit route out of commission, making the enemy's movements more hazardous. But the friend, too, will have to live and think differently, know where he's going and tread lightly." Derrida and Ferraris, *A Taste for the Secret*, 52.
24. Ibid., 57–58.
25. Derrida's systematic use of the "secret" emerges with his more explicit references to religion in his work, thus with "Of an Apocalyptic Tone" (1980) and forward. He already uses the term frequently, however, in *Writing and Difference*, particularly in relation to Levinas.
26. Søren Kierkegaard, *Fear and Trembling* (Radford: Wilder, 2008), 88.
27. This number includes himself among the twelve as commentator on himself for the volume to which his essay was a contribution.
28. This later phrase appears for the first time in *L'Autre cap*, published one year prior.
29. Herman Melville, *Bartleby the Scrivener: A Story of Wall Street* (New York: Hesperus, 2007), 19.
30. Ibid., 32, 34.
31. Ibid., 27.

32. Ibid., 26.

33. For Derrida's clearest formulation of this "poetico-literary" function, see "This Strange Institution Called Literature," in *Acts of Literature*, ed. Derek Attridge (New York: Routledge, 1992), 45–46.

34. This phrase becomes important in *L'Autre cap* (1991) and remains important through *Voyous* (2003).

35. Immanuel Kant, *Groundwork of the Metaphysics of Morals*, trans. Mary Gregor (Cambridge: Cambridge University Press, 2012), 4:438.

36. Immanuel Kant, *Critique of Pure Reason*, trans. Paul Guyer and Allen W. Wood (Cambridge: Cambridge University Press, 1998), 339.

37. Jan Patočka, *Heretical Essays in the Philosophy of History*, trans. Erazim Kohák (New York: Carus, 1996).

38. For the importance of inheritance to Derrida's political thought, see Haddad, *Derrida and the Inheritance of Democracy*. Haddad does not address the importance of literature to this structure.

39. My emphasis.

40. Walter Benjamin, *Selected Writings*, vol. 1: *1913–1926* (Cambridge: Harvard University Press 1996), 250.

5. LITERATURE AND THE POLITICAL-THEOLOGICAL REMAINS

1. Claude Lefort, *Democracy and Political Theory*, trans. David Macey (Minneapolis: University of Minnesota, 1988), 226.

2. Ibid., 255.

3. Eric Santner, in *The Royal Remains: The People's Two Bodies and the Endgames of Sovereignty* (Chicago: University of Chicago Press, 2011), thinks through the fleshly aspect of this remainder, what he calls "the *biopolitical* pressures generated by the shift from royal to popular sovereignty" (xi). Santner articulates another powerful model for thinking about literature as a religious legacy and its consequent political function, particularly his analysis of comedy as a means of negotiating and coping with the effects of life after sovereignty. In the epilogue he goes as far as saying that "in Beckett's universe . . . 'scripture' becomes life by way of a unique kind of convergence of *language* and *physical comedy*" (251).

4. See my discussion of *Rogues* (*Voyous*) in the last chapter.

5. See John Milbank, *Theology and Social Theory: Beyond Secular Theory* (Oxford: Blackwell, 1990).

6. In this group we could include Gianni Vattimo as well as John Caputo as the two most clear-cut and vocal candidates. But one could also include Jean-Luc Nancy's *Dis-Enclosure: The Deconstruction of Christianity* (New York: Fordham University

Press, 2008), which is a subtler argument for the critical function of Christianity, but also more supersessionist.

7. For many of these recent thinkers championing the return to religion, Derrida has played a crucial role, either as a foil, in the case of John Milbank, Graham Ward, and Kevin Hart, or as a model, in the case of John Caputo and Hent de Vries. For a succinct treatment of theological responses to Derrida, see Steven Shakespeare, *Derrida and Theology* (London: T&T Clark, 2009), 175–215. For de Vries, what he sees as Derrida's own turn toward Levinas and what he calls the *à Dieu*, thus toward a religious idiom, implies the embrace of a vocabulary more suitable than that of "writing" to address ethical and political matters. De Vries, *Minimal Theologies: Critiques of Secular Reason in Adorno and Levinas* (Baltimore: Johns Hopkins University Press, 2005), 265, 434. This book has tried to counter that claim through an alternative account of their relationship.

8. Hent de Vries, *Philosophy and the Turn to Religion* (Baltimore: Johns Hopkins University Press, 1999), 435.

9. Simon Critchley, *Faith of the Faithless: Experiments in Political Theology* (London: Verso, 2014), 4.

10. De Vries mostly treats the literary figures his authors read either as interlocutors, whose statements in their work can be compared to philosophical statements, or he considers the readings of Celan, Kafka, or Jabès by Derrida, Adorno, or Levinas as a means to developing his argument about the theological valence of their thought. Occasionally, though, he does briefly address what the "poem" does (de Vries, *Minimal Theologies,* 570) or how the status of fiction affects our conception of the law (de Vries, *Philosophy and the Turn to Religion,* 385).

11. Paul Ricoeur, in *Rule of Metaphor* and *Time and Narrative,* is the standard-bearer for conceptualizing the epistemological function of literature. What is clear in Ricoeur is that his interest is in the disclosive function of rhetorical tropes and narrativity. Both of his major projects on literature seek to show how the literary features of languages allow for ways of knowing and seeing unique to their instruments. I have not sought to foreclose that avenue, but rather to think, following Derrida, how literature's resistances to disclosure and clarification can also supplement the philosophical and political fields.

12. Where one marks the boundary between the old and the new is certainly a point of debate. With Lacoue-Labarthe and Nancy we can locate it in early romanticism with the view that the written word could be an end in itself "isolated from the surrounding world and complete in itself like a porcupine." *Atheneum* fragment 206, Philippe Lacoue-Labarthe and Jean-Luc Nancy, *The Literary Absolute: The Theory of Literature in German Romanticism,* trans. Philip Barnard (Albany: SUNY Press, 1988), 13. Lacoue-Labarthe and Nancy, however, also point out that the eighteenth-century novel is itself the primary reference point for their own theorization of the genre. Thomas Pavel's recent *The Lives of the Novel: A History*

(Princeton: Princeton University Press, 2013), in tracing the origins of the novel, shows how difficult it is even with this one genre to mark a point of beginning. He begins with ancient Greek examples going back to the fourth century BC, but the eighteenth century English novel remains a key point of reference for the shifting place of these long prose narratives in European cultural history. I have chosen not to prioritize any particular genre in my own engagement with the category but only to treat it as a category constituted by other theorists, and particularly as it developed in the postwar French context in the conversation between Sartre and his interlocutors.

13. As the subtitle of *Monolingualism of the Other: The Prosthesis of Origin,* already asserts, speaking a language that is not one's own is in fact the condition of every speaker. As a concept for Derrida, "the prosthesis of origin" can be traced to Heidegger's own concept of "thrownness" in *Being and Time.*

14. See Pascale Casanova, *The World Republic of Letters,* trans. M. B. DeBevoise (Cambridge: Harvard University Press, 2004). See also Amir Mufti's response: "Orientalism and the Institution of World Literature," *Critical Inquiry* 36.3 (Spring 2010): 458–93.

15. Casanova, *The World Republic of Letters,* 24. Paul Valéry is central to her argument and equally central to Derrida's account of Europe's political role. In *L'autre cap,* Derrida equally privileges Valéry, particularly the essay "Notes sur la grandeur et décadence de l'Europe." For Derrida, Valéry's description of Europe as avant-garde, out in front, can serve as the basis for rethinking Europe in terms of hospitality to what is other, a Europe "that consists precisely in not closing itself off in its own identity and in advancing itself in an exemplary way toward what it is not" (*AC* 33; *OH* 29).

16. Casanova quoting Valery Larbaud. Casanova, *The World Republic of Letters,* 21.

17. Here I follow Said in understanding literature and criticism as moving in modernity from a model of filiation to one of affiliation. No doubt literature and criticism can nonetheless reify cultural hegemony, as Said points out, but it is also important not only to see the way in which literature and criticism support traditional cultural hierarchies, but also how they make possible and enable the secular as Said understands it, as "situated, skeptical, reflectively open to its own failings." Edward Said, *The World, the Text, and the Critic* (Cambridge: Harvard University Press, 1983), 25–27.

18. Judith Butler, *Gender Trouble: Feminism and the Subversion of Identity* (New York: Routledge, 2006), xv, 215*n*1. Butler's analysis of the role of repetition and parody as a means to denature gender norms owes a tremendous amount to Derrida's conception of the force of repetition as a means to reveal the "limitless displacement" of referentiality, but she does not consider the role that Derrida ascribes to literature in that process.

19. Judith Butler, *Parting Ways: Jewishness and the Critique of Zionism* (New York: Columbia University Press, 2013), 1.

20. Ibid., 39.

21. It is arguable whether these sources should themselves be considered Jewish. Levinas and Buber are the only thinkers heavily invoked who understood themselves as working within the tradition. By including Arendt, Benjamin, and Primo Levi, Butler is certainly expanding the canon and trying to understand it inclusively.

22. Butler, *Parting Ways*, 12, 14.

23. See Sarah Hammerschlag, *The Figural Jew: Politics and Identity in Postwar French Thought* (Chicago: University of Chicago Press, 2010), 267.

24. Alain Badiou, *Circonstances III: portées du mot "Juifs"* (Paris: Lignes, 2005), and then with Eric Hazan, *L'antisémitisme partout aujourd'hui en France* (Paris: La Fabrique, 2011).

25. Badiou, *Circonstances III,* 51.

26. The title of the book itself recalls the right-wing newspaper *Je Suis Partout,* which published issues in the 1930s on "les Juifs" and "Les Juifs et la France."

27. David Nirenberg, *Anti-Judaism* (New York: Norton, 2014), 1–12.

28. Ward Blanton, *A Materialism for the Masses: Saint Paul and the Philosophy of Undying Life* (New York: Columbia University Press, 2014), 5.

29. See Ryan Coyne's *Heidegger's Confessions: Augustine's Remains in Being and Time and Beyond* (Chicago: University of Chicago Press, 2015) for a model account of modernity's theological legacy, one that does not deduce from the persistence of theological remainders a set of normative theological claims.

30. Walter Benjamin, *Illuminations,* trans. Harry Zohn (New York: Schocken, 1969), 263.

31. Ward Blanton, for all his sensitivity to the effects of the Pauline resurgence, nonetheless argues for a recovery, for the possibility of imagining that we can unburden Paul of all his historical baggage and thus make him a resource for a new materialism. His central image of having unearthed "a sacred corpse all fitted up with concrete slippers" at least calls attention to the design of these recovery efforts and, in its irony, exposes the artificiality of its own claims (187).

32. The reference is to *The Aspern Papers,* in which the narrator jokingly raises the prospect of "violating the tomb" to uncover the letters and thus the secret of the fictional poet Jeffrey Aspern. Henry James, *The Aspern Papers and Other Stories* (Oxford: Oxford University Press, 2013), 82. One of James's stories on the theme of the secret, the story follows the logic laid out by Derrida, in "Passions" and elsewhere, whereby literature invokes the possibility of a secret that can be revealed, but functions as a genre on the principle that it cannot be.

33. Genesis 22:17.

34. Auerbach also privileges this moment as key to the history of literature as "one of the most famous examples of the realistic type of figural interpretation." Erich Auerbach, "Figura" in *Scenes from the Drama of European Literature* (Minneapolis: University of Minnesota Press, 1984), 36.

35. One could argue for the connection of literature to religion as arising out of the rabbinic tradition as well. Pirke Avot, the ninth tractate of the Mishna, would be a case in point. It simultaneously establishes a line of transmission from the second century back to the giving of the Torah at Mount Sinai and creates a proliferation of its meaning through a multiplication of interpretations that increase and are carried forward with each generation. Yet, as Moshe Halbertal argued in *The People of the Book: Canon, Meaning, and Authority* (Cambridge: Harvard University Press, 1997), the freedom of interpretation is maintained and structured through maintenance of the community. There is thus a political form that correlates to the proliferation of effects, a form that must instantiate the order of dissemination. Proliferation must radiate out from the center as a series of these concentric circles, and thus the circles themselves must be politically sustained.

36. The paragraph in which Derrida introduces literature is a later addition to *Gift of Death,* only appearing in the French publication and the second edition of the English.

37. Charles Baudelaire, *Oeuvres Completes* (Paris: Gallimard, 1975), 2:49.

38. Jacques Derrida, *Given Time I: Counterfeit Money,* trans. Peggy Kamuf (Chicago: University of Chicago University Press, 1992). For more on the relation between these two articulations of the story, see Francoise Meltzer, *Seeing Double: Baudelaire's Modernity* (Chicago: University of Chicago Press, 2011), 192–95.

39. Baudelaire, *Oeuvres Completes,* 1:323.

40. Friedrich Nietzsche, *Kritische Gesamtausgabe Werke* (Berlin: de Gruyter, 1999), 3:2.373, *Portable Nietzsche,* ed. Walter Kaufman (New York: Penguin 1977), 42.

41. Quoting "The Pagan School."

42. While Derrida certainly referenced the secret in texts before the 1980s, the connection he makes between secrecy and literature postdates Kermode's book. The two were at a conference together at the University of Chicago in 1980 in which Kermode gave a paper on secrecy and literature that followed from his 1979 work, originally given as a series of lectures at Harvard, *The Genesis of Secrecy* (Cambridge: Harvard University Press, 1979).

43. Ibid., 2.

44. Ibid., 65.

45. Proverbs 25:11. This metaphor is crucial to Maimonides in the introduction to *The Guide to the Perplexed* as a means to securing his hierarchy of biblical meaning.

46. Georg Lukács, *The Theory of the Novel,* trans. Anna Bostock (Cambridge: MIT Press, 1971), 90.

47. Kermode, *The Genesis of Secrecy,* 123.

48. For a synopsis of debates on historical irony, see Martin Jay, "Intention and Irony: The Missed Encounter Between Hayden White and Quentin Skinner," *History and Theory,* February 1, 2013, 32–48. One could argue that the irony itself is Christian, if we follow Reinhold Neibhur's interpretation of biblical irony as "the fanaticism of

all good men, who do not know that they are not as good as they esteem themselves." Reinhold Neibhur, *The Irony of American History* (Chicago: University of Chicago Press, 1952), 160.

49. The review has been historically linked to French fascism because of Drieu La Rochelle's involvement with the journal during the Nazi Occupation. Paulhan, however, preceded La Rochelle as editor, and under his directorship the journal published everyone from Paul Nizan and Sartre to Emmanuel Mounier and Thierry Maulnier. See Steven Ungar, *Scandal and Aftereffect: Blanchot and France Since 1930* (Minneapolis: University of Minnesota 1995), 102–36.

50. Jean Paulhan, *Les Fleurs de Tarbes ou La Terreur dans les lettres* (Paris: Gallimard, 1945), 47; Jean Paulhan, *The Flowers of Tarbes, or Terror in Literature*, trans. Michael Syrotinski (Urbana: University of Illinois Press, 2006), 24.

51. Ibid., 70, 30.

52. Ibid., 148, 82.

53. For more on irony in Paulhan and Blanchot, see Kevin Newmark, *Irony on Occasion: From Schlegel and Kierkegaard to Derrida and de Man* (New York: Fordham University Press, 2012), 203–41.

54. Paulhan, *Les Fleurs de Tarbes*, 166, *The Flowers of Tarbes*, 93.

55. Ibid., 166, 94.

56. Ibid.

57. Ibid.

58. Maurice Blanchot, *The Blanchot Reader*, ed. Michael Holland (Cambridge: Blackwell, 1995), 56.

59. Ibid., 59.

60. Jeffrey Mehlman, *Legacies of Antisemitism in France* (Minneapolis: University of Minnesota, 1983), 13.

61. The most recent take on Maurice Blanchot's writings from the 1930s is Michel Surya's *L'autre Blanchot: L'écriture de jour, l'écriture de nuit* (Paris: Gallimard, 2015).

62. Maurice Blanchot, *La Part du feu* (Paris: Gallimard, 1949), 310–11, *The Work of Fire* (Stanford: Stanford University Press, 1995), 320–21.

63. Maurice Blanchot, *Écrits politiques, 1953–1993* (Paris: Gallimard, 1993), 29, *Political Writings, 1953–1993*, trans. Zakir Paul (New York: Fordham University Press, 2010), 7.

64. The correspondent was later identified as Ilija Bojovic; Blanchot, *Écrits politiques*, 175, *Political Writings*, 84.

65. Jacques Derrida, *A Taste for the Secret*, interviews with Maurizio Ferraris (New York: Wiley, 2001), 59.

66. This is a paraphrasing of the principles set forth at the close of "Litterature au secret," principles Derrida attributes to literature and that make it an heir to the Abrahamic promise (*DLM* 206–7; *GD* 156–57).

67. Paul Ricoeur, *Time and Narrative*, vol. 1, trans. Kathleen Mclaughlin and David Pellauer (Chicago: University of Chicago Press, 1983), 1:75.

68. "That happens every day [cela ce produit tous les jours]," Derrida writes in "Passions" (*P* 69; *OTN* 30).

69. The idiom itself refers to suicide. And Blanchot's disappearance was a form of suicide, an embodiment of the death of the author.

70. In "Passions" Derrida suggests this as a description of his method when discussing what he would bring with him to read on a desert island. He says that despite his taste for literature, it is not what he would bring with him on a desert Island, but rather history or memoirs "perhaps to make literature out of them" (*P* 64; *OTN* 28).

EPILOGUE

1. The quotes around American are a curious inclusion, and I take it as an opposition to Patočka's construction of Europe and "European responsibility," but also as a tacit reference to the fact that their Americanness is important to Derrida. He uses it in the course to counter Heidegger's parsing of authenticity and falling. Heidegger's disdain for America makes this category doubly important. It stands as well for a "superficiality" that Derrida wants to rehabilitate.

2. In "Justices," an essay written for a conference on J. Hillis Miller, Derrida mentions James, but only as a subject of interest to Miller. Barbara Cohen and Dragan Kujundzic, eds., *Provocations to Reading: J. Hillis Miller and the Democracy to Come* (New York: Fordham University Press, 2005), 252. "Bartleby" appears in *Gift of Death* and functions, as I argued in chapter 4, as an oblique reference elsewhere. *La Carte Postale* includes the section "Le facteur de la verité" on Lacan's reading of "The Purloined Letter," Derrida, *La Carte Postale: de Socrate à Freud et au-delà* (Paris: Flammarion, 1980), 441–524. First published in English as "The Purveyor of Truth" in *Yale French Studies* 52 (1975): 31–113. "Passions" further footnotes this discussion (*P* 73; *OTN* 131). What Lacan misses in his analysis, according to Derrida, is the fact of the Dead Letter Office. That is to say, that the letter does not always reach its destination. This is the hypothesis that Lacan misses, according to Derrida, because he misses that the ritual is laid bare in the narrative frame of Poe's "The Purloined Letter." It is this exposure, this repetition, that characterizes the institution of literature.

3. Henry James, *The Aspern Papers and Other Stories* (Oxford: Oxford University Press, 2013), 124.

4. The journal describes "la littérarité" as a concern "with any sort of language game and writing, any rhetoric in act, any obliteration of verbal transparency," "Presentation," *Poetique* 1.1 (1970).

5. Hélène Cixous, "Henry James: L'écriture comme placement ou De l'ambiguité de l'intérêt," in *Poetique* 1.1 (1970): 35–50.

6. Phillipe Sollers, in *Logiques* (1968), reads it as a treatment of narrative formation, the making into figure of the function of withholding in fiction, but also thus for the confluence between fiction and life, for the fact that death serves the same role in life

and that in and through death, one's life passes into narrative form. Phillipe Sollers, *Logiques* (Paris: Seuil, 1968), 122. In his essay "Le secret du récit" (1969), Todorov reads the story as a structuralist map to James's oeuvre, noting that almost all his important works, whether explicitly or implicitly, function according to the logic of the secret, the obscured cause that sets the events in motion. He thus read the story as an incitement to find the figure in James's carpet and then schematized it into three variants. Even as he concedes that at the end of the story the reader is as ignorant as he was in the beginning, he declared himself triumphant in having solved both Vereker's and James's riddle by declaring the key to be the very "existence of a secret, of an absolute and absent cause . . . by definition inviolable, because it *is* its existence." Tzvetan Todorov, *Poétique de la Prose* (Paris: Seuil, 1969), 183.

7. Wolfgang Iser, *The Act of Reading: A Theory of Aesthetic Response* (Baltimore: Johns Hopkins University Press, 1978), 10.

8. Shlomith Rimmon-Kenan, *The Concept of Ambiguity: The Example of James* (Chicago: University of Chicago Press), 104.

9. See J. Hillis Miller, "The Figure in the Carpet," *Poetics Today* 1.3 (Spring 1980): 107–18 and *Reading Narrative* (Norman: University of Oklahoma Press, 1982), 84–106.

10. Mussil takes up the challenge of trying to think about how the meaning-making process of literature in a secular context replaces the appeal to transcendence of religious texts in Stephan Mussil, "A Secret in Spite of Itself," *New Literary History* 39.4 (2008): 769–99.

11. James, *The Aspern Papers and Other Stories*, 130.

12. A similar paradigm is present in the rabbinic PaRDeS parable in which four men enter the orchard: the first dies, the second goes mad, the third mutilates the shoots— each one who hears the secret experiences a disastrous fate, but at least Rabbi Akiva enters in peace and departs in peace. One could ask whether "The Figure in the Carpet" offers any positive model.

13. James, *The Aspern Papers and Other Stories,* 219.

14. Ibid., 218.

15. J. Hillis Miller's move to Irvine was clearly one of Derrida's motivations for his own shift to Irvine. Miller mentions Derrida's course sequence on the secret in his essay "The Other's Other: Jealousy and Art in Proust," *Qui Parle* 9.1 (1995): 119–40. In his *For Derrida* (New York: Fordham University Press, 2009), Miller often makes reference to Henry James as a means of elucidating certain principles in Derrida. One can imagine that this was a source of conversation between the two.

16. Miller is explicit about Derrida's influence on his reading. Rimmon-Kenan engages the differences between structuralism and deconstruction. Mussil references the relation between his reading and what would be a Derridean reading, and Sollers and Cixous were among Derrida's most important interlocutors in the late 1960s and early 1970s. See Benoît Peeters, *Derrida, a Biography,* trans. Andrew Brown (Cambridge: Polity, 2013), 141–42, 198–99.

17. See Derrida, "Archive Fever: A Freudian Impression," *Diacritics* 25.2 (Summer 1995): 10.

18. I have referenced these in chapter 4.

19. Box 21, folder 4 (session 1), 11. All translations of archive materials are mine. For the last fifteen years of his seminars at UCI, Derrida gave the seminars in English, but from French lectures. He improvised the translations in class. According to Miller, he refused to tape the English sessions. See Miller, *For Derrida,* 75.

20. 21.5 (session 4), 4.

21. Heidegger, *Sein and Zeit* (Tübingen: Max Niemeyer, 1967), 2.4:347.

22. 1.5 (session 4), 17.

23. Ibid., 19.

24. James, *The Aspern Papers and Other Stories,* 72.

25. Ibid., 82.

26. The emphasis is mine here. This could be taken both as a reference to the dynamics of curiosity as that which one can see, but also as a reference to what Vereker says to the narrator, that the secret is for the critics to articulate.

27. James, *The Aspern Papers and Other Stories,* 130.

28. Ibid., 156.

29. Ibid.

30. Box 21, folder 4 (session dated November 27, 1991), 17.

BIBLIOGRAPHY

ARCHIVES CONSULTED

Central Zionist Archive (CZA). World Jewish Congress Folders on Colloque des intellectuels Israélite de langue française.
University of California–Irvine. Derrida Collection. Boxes 10, 21, and 95.

WORKS BY DERRIDA

"Abraham, l'autre." In *Judéités: questions pour Jacques Derrida,* 11–42. Ed. Joseph Cohen
and Raphael Zagury-Orly. Paris: Galilée, 2003.
"Abraham, the Other." In *Judeities: Questions for Jacques Derrida,* 1–35. Ed. Bettina Bergo,
Joseph Cohen, and Raphael Zagury-Orly. Trans. Bettina Bergo and Michael B. Smith.
New York: Fordham University Press, 2007.
Adieu à Emmanuel Lévinas. Paris: Galilée, 1997.
Adieu to Emmanuel Levinas. Trans. Pascale-Anne Brault and Michael B. Naas. Stanford:
Stanford University Press, 1999.
*Altérités: Jacques Derrida et Pierre-Jean Labarièrre. Avec des études de Francis Guibal et
Stanislas Breton.* Paris: Osiris, 1986.
"Avouer—L'impossible: <<retours>>, repentir et réconcilation." In *Comment vivre ensem-
ble? Acts du XXXVIIe Colloque des intellectuels juifs de langue française* (1998), 181–221.
Ed. Jean Halpérin and Nelly Hansson. Paris: Albin Michel, 2001.
"Avowing—the Impossible: "Returns," Repentance, and Reconciliation." Trans. Gil Andi-
jar. In *Living Together: Jacques Derrida's Communities of Violence and Peace,* 18–41. Ed.
Elisabeth Weber. New York: Fordham University Press, 2013.
Archive Fever: A Freudian Impression. Trans. Eric Prenowitz. Chicago: University of Chi-
cago Press, 1996.

"Archive Fever: A Freudian Impression." *Diacritics* 25.2 (Summer 1995): 9–63.
"Before the Law." In *Acts of Literature,* 181–220. Ed. Derek Attridge. New York: Routledge, 1992.
"Countersignature." Trans. Mairéad Hanrahan. *Paragraph* 27.2 (2004): 7–42.
De la Grammatologie. Paris: Minuit, 1967.
"Devant la loi." In *La Faculté de juger.* Paris: Minuit, 1985.
Dissemination. Trans. Barbara Johnson. Chicago: University of Chicago Press, 1981.
Donner la Mort. Paris: Galilée, 1999.
Donner le temps: 1. La fausse monnaie. Paris, Galilée, 1991.
"Faith and Knowledge." In *Acts of Religion,* 40–101. Ed. Gil Andijar. New York: Routledge, 2002.
Foi et Savoir: suivi de *Le siecle et le pardon.* Paris: Seuil, 2000.
For What Tomorrow . . . a Dialogue. With Élisabeth Roudinesco. Trans. Jeff Fort. Stanford: Stanford University Press, 2004.
"Force of Law." In *Acts of Religion,* 228–98. Ed. Gil Andijar. New York: Routledge, 2002.
Glas. Trans. John P. Leavey Jr. Lincoln: University of Nebraska Press, 1990.
Gift of Death and Literature in Secret. Trans. David Wills. Chicago: University of Chicago, 2008.
Given Time I: Counterfeit Money. Trans. Peggy Kamuf. Chicago: University of Chicago Press, 1992.
La Carte Postale: de Socrate à Freud et au-delà. Paris: Flammarion, 1980.
L'Autre cap: suivi de *La Démocratie ajournée.* Paris: Minuit: 1991.
La Voix et le phénomène. Paris: Presses Universitaires de France, 1967.
L'Écriture et la différence. Paris: Seuil, 1967.
Mal d'archive: une impression freudienne. Paris: Galilée, 1995.
Monolinguisme de l'autre ou, La prothèse d'origine. Paris: Galilée, 1996.
Monolingualism of the Other or, The Prosthesis of Origin. Trans. Patrick Mensah. Stanford: Stanford University Press, 1998.
Of Grammatology. Trans. Gayatri Spivak. Baltimore: Johns Hopkins University Press, 1974.
On the Name. Ed. Thomas Dutoit. Trans. David Wood, John P. Leavey Jr., and Ian Mcleod. Stanford: Stanford University Press, 1995.
The Other Heading: Reflections on Today's Europe. Trans. Pascale-Anne Brault and Michael B. Naas. Bloomington: Indiana University Press, 1992.
Passions: "L'offrande oblique." Paris: Galilee 1993.
Points, Interviews, 1974–1994. Ed. Elisabeth Weber. Stanford: Stanford University Press, 1995.
Politics of Friendship. Trans. George Collins. London: Verso, 2006.
Positions. Trans. By Alan Bass. Chicago, University of Chicago Press, 1982.
Le problème de la genese dans la philosophie de Husserl. Paris: Presses Universitaires de France, 1990.
The Problem of Genesis in Husserl's Philosophy. Trans. Marian Hobson. Chicago: University of Chicago Press, 2003.

Psyché: Inventions de l'autre 1. Paris: Galilée, 1998.

Psyche: Inventions of the Other, vol. 1. Ed. Peggy Kamuf and Elizabeth Rottenberg. Stanford: Stanford University Press, 2007.

"The Purveyor of Truth." *Yale French Studies,* no. 52 (1975): 31–113.

Rogues: Two Essays on Reason. Trans. Pascale-Anne Brault and Michael Naas. Stanford: Stanford University Press, 2005.

Sauf le nom. Paris: Galilée, 1993.

Schibboleth: pour Paul Celan. Paris: Galilée, 2003.

"Shibboleth: For Paul Celan." In *Sovereignties in Question: The Poetics of Paul Celan.* Ed. Thomas Dutoit and Outi Pasanen. New York: Fordham University Press, 2005.

Sur parole. Paris: De l'Aube, 2003.

A Taste for the Secret. Interviews with Maurizio Ferraris. New York: Wiley. 2001.

"This Strange Institution Called Literature." In *Acts of Literature,* 45–46. Ed. Derek Attridge. New York: Routledge, 1992.

Voice and Phenomenon: Introduction to the Problem of the Sign in Husserl's Phenomenology. Trans. Leonard Lawlor. Evanston: Northwestern University Press, 2011.

Voyous: deux essais sur la raison. Paris: Galilée, 2003.

Writing and Difference. Trans. Alan Bass. Chicago: University of Chicago Press, 1978.

WORKS BY EMMANUEL LEVINAS

Au delà du verset. Paris: Minuit, 1982.

Autrement qu'être ou au delà de l'essence. The Hague: Martinus Nijhoff, 1978.

Basic Philosophical Writings. Ed. Adriaan Peperzak, Simon Critchley, and Robert Bernasconi. Bloomington: Indiana University Press, 1996.

"Being Jewish." *Continental Philosophical Review* 40 (2007): 205–10.

Beyond the Verse: Talmudic Readings and Lectures. Trans. Gary D. Mole. Bloomington: Indiana University Press, 1994.

Carnets de Captivité. Ed. Rodolphe Calin and Catherine Chalier. Paris: Imec/Grasset, 2009.

"De l'évasion," in *Recherches philosophiques* 5 (1935–1936): 373–92.

De l'existence à l'existant. Paris: J. Vrin, 1993.

Derrida and Negative Theology. Ed. Toby Foshay. Albany: SUNY Press, 1992.

Difficile liberté: essais sur le judaïsme. Paris: Albin Michel, 1963, 1967.

Difficult Freedom: Essays on Judaism. Trans. Seán Hand. Baltimore: Johns Hopkins University Press, 1990.

Du sacré au saint: cinq nouvelles lectures talmudiques. Paris: Minuit, 1977.

Entre Nous: essais sur le penser-à-l'autre. Grasset & Fasquelle, 1991.

Entre Nous: Thinking-of-the-Other. Trans. Michael B. Smith and Barbara Harshav. New York: Columbia University Press: 1998.

Eros, Littérature et Philosophie inédits. Ed. Jean-Luc Nancy and Danielle Cohen-Levinas. Paris: Imec/Grasset, 2013.

"Être Juif." *Confluences* 15–17 (1947): 253–64.

Existence and Existents. Trans. Alphonso Lingis. Dordrecht: Kluwer, 1978.

Hors Sujet. Montpelier: Fata Morgana, 1997.

Jean Wahl et Gabriel Marcel. Paris: Beauchesne, 1976.

Les Imprévus de l'histoire. Montpelier: Fata Morgana, 1994.

Levinas Reader. Ed. Séan Hand. London: Blackwell, 1989.

Noms Propres: Agnon, Buber, Celan, Delhomme, Derrida, Jabès, Kierkegaard, Lacroix, Laporte, Picard, Proust, Van Breda, Wahl. Montpelier: Fata Morgana, 1976.

Nine Talmudic Readings. Trans. Annette Aronowicz. Bloomington: Indiana University Press, 1990.

On Escape. Trans. Bettina Bergo. Stanford: Stanford University Press, 2003.

Otherwise Than Being or Beyond Essence. Trans. Alphonso Lingis. Pittsburgh: Duquesne University Press, 1998.

Outside the Subject. Trans. Michael B. Smith. Stanford: Stanford University Press, 1994.

Parole et Silence et autres conférences inédites au Collège philosophique. Ed. Rodolphe Calin and Catherine Chalier. Paris: Imec/Grasset, 2009.

"Philosophie et Religion." *Critique* 27.289 (June 1971): 532–42.

Proper Names. Trans. Michael B. Smith. Stanford: Stanford University Press, 1996.

"La Signification et le sens." In *Revue de Métaphysique et de Morale* 2 (April-June 1964): 125–35.

Sur Blanchot. Montpelier: Fata Morgana, 1975.

Totalité et Infini: essai sur l'extériorité. The Hague: Martinus Nijhoff, 1961.

Totality and Infinity: an essay on exteriority. Trans. Alphonso Lingis. Pittsburgh: Duquesne University Press, 1969.

Quatre lectures talmudiques. Paris: Minuit, 1968.

"Religion and Revolution" in *Annals of International Studies* 5.11 (1980): 50–67.

Unforseen History. Trans. Nidra Poller. Urbana: University of Illinois Press, 2004.

OTHER TEXTS

Anderson, Nicole. *Ethics Under Erasure.* London: Continuum, 2012.

Atlan, Henri. "Entretien avec Henri Atlan." *Cahiers d'Etudes Lévinassiennes,* no. 6 (2007): 137–60.

Auerbach, Eric. *Mimesis: The Representation of Reality in Western Literature.* Trans. Willard Trask. Princeton: Princeton University Press, 2003.

——. *Scenes from the Drama of European Literature.* Minneapolis: University of Minnesota Press, 1984.

Badiou, Alain. *Circonstances 3: portées du mot "Juifs."* Paris: Lignes, 2005.

——. *Saint Paul: la fondation de l'universalisme*. Paris: Presses universitaires de France, 1997.

——, with Eric Hazan. *L'antisémitisme partout aujourd'hui en France*. Paris: La Fabrique, 2011.

Baring, Edward. *The Young Derrida and French Philosophy, 1945–1968*. Cambridge: Cambridge University Press, 2011.

Bataille, Georges. "De l'age de pierre a Jacques Prévert." *Critique* 3–4 (1946): 195–214.

——. "De l'existentialisme au primat de l'économie." *Critique* 3.21 (1948): 127–41.

——. *Inner Experience*. Trans. Stuart Kendall. Albany: SUNY Press, 1988.

——. *La littérature et le Mal*. Paris: Gallimard, 1957.

——. "L'Ivresse des Tavernes et la Religion." *Critique* 4.25 (June 1948): 531–39.

——. *Oeuvres Completes V*. Paris: Gallimard, 1973.

Baudelaire, Charles. *Oeuvres Completes*. Paris: Paris: Pléïade, 1975.

Baugh, Bruce. *French Hegel*. New York: Routledge, 2003.

Beardsworth, Richard. *Derrida and the Political*. London: Routledge, 1996.

Beauvoir, Simone de. *The Force of Circumstance*. New York: Putnam, 1965.

Benfey, Christopher, and Karen Remmler, eds. *Artists, Intellectuals, and World War II: The Pontigny Encounters at Mount Holyoke College, 1942–1944*. Amherst: University of Massachusetts Press, 2006.

Benjamin, Walter. *Illuminations*. Trans. Harry Zohn. New York: Schocken, 1969.

——. *Selected Writings, 1913–1926*, vol. 1. Cambridge: Harvard University Press 1996.

Bevir, Mark, Jill Hargis, and Sara Rushing, eds. *Histories of Postmodernism*. New York: Routledge, 2007.

Birnbaum, Pierre. *Les Fous de la République: histoire politique des juifs d'Etat, de Gambetta à Vichy*. Paris: Fayard, 1992.

Blanchot, Maurice. *The Blanchot Reader*. Ed. Michael Holland. Cambridge: Blackwell, 1995.

——. *Ecrits politiques, 1953–1993*. Paris: Gallimard, 1993.

——. *The Infinite Conversation*. Trans. Susan Hanson. Minneapolis: University of Minnesota, 1993.

——. *La Part du feu*. Paris, Gallimard, 1949.

——. *L'entretien infini*. Paris: Gallimard, 1969.

——. *Political Writings, 1953–1993*. Trans. Zakir Paul. New York: Fordham University Press, 2010.

——. *Work of Fire*. Trans. Charlotte Mandell. Stanford: Stanford University Press, 1995.

Blanton, Ward. *A Materialism for the Masses: Saint Paul and the Philosophy of Undying Life*. New York: Columbia University Press, 2014.

Booth, Wayne. *A Rhetoric of Irony*. Chicago: University of Chicago Press, 1974.

Bouchard, Larry, and Anthony Yu. "Literature and Religion." *Encyclopedia of Religion*, vol. 8. 2d ed. Detroit: MacMillan, 2005.

Bourgin, Hubert. *De Jaurès a Léon Blum: l'École normale et la politique*. Paris: Fayard, 1938.

Brunschvicg, Léon. *Écrits Philosophiques I–III*. Paris: Presses Universitaire de France, 1951–1958.

Butler, Judith. *Gender Trouble: Feminism and the Subversion of Identity*. New York: Routledge, 2006.

——. *Parting Ways: Jewishness and the Critique of Zionism*. New York: Columbia University Press, 2013.

Caputo, John. *The Prayers and Tears of Jacques Derrida: Religion Without Religion*. Bloomington: Indiana University Press, 1997.

Carroll, David. *French Literary Fascism: Nationalism, Antisemitism, and the Ideology of Culture*. Princeton: Princeton University Press, 1995.

Casanova, Pascale, *The World Republic of Letters*. Trans. M. B. DeBevoise. Cambridge: Harvard University Press, 2004.

Caygill, Howard. *Levinas and the Political*. London: Routledge, 2002.

Celan, Paul. *Meridian: Final Version—Drafts—Materials*. Trans. Pierre Joris. Ed. Bernhard Böschenstein and Heino Schmull. Stanford: Stanford University Press, 2011.

Cixous, Hélène. "Henry James: l'écriture comme placement ou de l'ambiguité de l'intérêt." *Poetique* 1.1 (1970): 35–50.

Cohen, Barbara, and Dragan Kujundzic, eds. *Provocations to Reading: J. Hillis Miller and the Democracy to Come*. New York: Fordham, 2005.

Coyne, Ryan. *Heidegger's Confessions: Augustine's Remains in* Being and Time *and Beyond*. Chicago: University of Chicago Press, 2015.

Critchley, Simon. "Deconstruction and Pragmatism." In *Ethics, Politics, Subjectivity*. London, Verso, 1999.

——. *The Ethics of Deconstruction*. Edinburgh: Edinburgh University Press, 1992.

——. *The Faith of the Faithless: Experiments in Political Theology*. London: Verso, 2014.

——, Jacques Derrida, Ernesto Laclau, and Richard Rorty. *Deconstruction and Pragmatism*. Ed. Chantal Mouffe. London: Routledge 1996.

Daigle, Christine. *Existentialist Thinkers and Ethics*. Montreal: McGill University Press, 2006.

Dansette, Adrian. *Destin du catholicism français, 1926–1956*. Paris, Flammarion, 1957.

Durand, Yves. *La vie quotidienne des prisonniers de guerre dans les stalags, les oflags et les Kommando, 1939–1945*. Paris: Hachette, 1987.

Eliade, Mircea. "Science, Idéalisme et phénomenes paranormaux." *Critique* 4.23 (April 1948): 315–23.

Elliott, R. G. *The Power of Satire*. Princeton: Princeton University Press, 1960.

Frye, Northrop. *The Educated Imagination and Other Writings on Critical Theory*. Toronto: University of Toronto Press, 1996.

Geroulanos, Stephanos. *An Atheism That Is Not Humanist Emerges in French Thought*. Stanford, Stanford University Press, 2010.

Gilbert, Adrian. *POW: Allied Prisoners in Europe, 1941–1945*. London: John Murray, 2006.

Goldhammer, Jesse. *The Headless Republic: Sacrificial Violence in Modern French Thought*. Ithaca: Cornell University Press, 2005.

Guerlac, Suzanne. *Literary Polemics: Bataille, Sartre, Valéry*. Stanford: Stanford University Press, 1997.

Gutting, Gary. *French Philosophy in the Twentieth Century*. Cambridge: Cambridge University Press, 2001.

Habermas, Jurgen. "Modernity Versus Postmodernity." *New German Critique* 22 (Winter 1981): 3–14.

Haddad, Samir. *Derrida and the Inheritance of Democracy*. Bloomington: Indiana University Press, 2013.

Hägglünd, Martin. *Radical Atheism: Derrida and the Time of Life*. Stanford: Stanford University Press, 2008.

Halbertal, Moshe. *People of the Book: Canon, Meaning, and Authority*. Cambridge: Harvard University Press, 1997.

Halperin, Jean. "Liberté et responsibilité." In *Textes pour Emmanuel Levinas*, 61–70. Ed. François Laruelle. Paris: J.-M. Place, 1980.

Hammerschlag, Sarah. "Another, Other Abraham." *Shofar: An Interdisciplinary Journal of Jewish Studies* 26.4 (2008): 74–96.

——. "Bad Jews, Authentic Jews, Figural Jews: Badiou and the Politics of Exemplarity." In *Judaism, Liberalism, and Political Theology*, 221–40. Randi Rashkover and Martin Kavka. Bloomington: Indiana University Press, 2014.

——. *The Figural Jew: Politics and Identity in Postwar French Thought*. Chicago: University of Chicago Press, 2010.

——. "Poetics of the Broken Tablet." In *The Trace of God: Derrida and Religion*, 59–71. Ed. Peter Gordon and Edward Baring. New York: Fordham University Press, 2014.

——. "Samuel Moyn's *Origins of the Other*." *Journal of Religion* 87.1 (2007): 127–28.

——. "'A Splinter in the Flesh': Levinas and the Resignification of Jewish Suffering, 1928–1947." *International Journal of Philosophical Studies* 20.3 (2012): 389–419.

Hand, Seàn. "Salvation Through Literature." *Levinas Studies* 8.1 (2013): 45–65.

Hart, Kevin. *The Dark Gaze: Maurice Blanchot and the Sacred*. Chicago: University of Chicago Press, 2004.

——. *Trespass of the Sign: Deconstruction, Theology, and Philosophy*. New York: Fordham University Press, 2000.

Heidegger, *Being and Time*. Trans. John Macquarrie and Edward Robinson. New York: Harper and Row, 1962.

——. "Der Ursprung des Kunstwerkes." In *Holzwege*, 6th ed. Frankfurt: Klostermann, 1980.

——. *Elucidations of Hölderlin's Poetry*. Trans. Keith Hoeller. Amherst, NY: Humanity, 2000.

——. *Pathmarks*. Ed. William McNeill. Cambridge: Cambridge University Press, 1998.

——. *Sein und Zeit*. 11th ed. Tübingen: Max Niemeyer, 1967.

——. "Why Poets." In *Off the Beaten Track*, 200–41. Trans. Julian Young. Cambridge: Cambridge University Press, 2002.

Hellman, John. *Emmanuel Mounier and the New Catholic Left, 1930–1950*. Toronto: University of Toronto Press, 1981.

Highet, Gilbert. *Anatomy of Satire*. Princeton: Princeton University Press, 1962.

Hollander, Dana. "Franz Rosenzweig on Nation, Translation, and Judaism." In *Philosophy Today* 38.4 (Winter 1994): 380–89.

Hollywood, Amy. *Sensible Ecstasy: Mysticism, Sexuality, and the Demands of History.* Chicago: University of Chicago Press, 2001.

Hutcheon, Linda. *Irony's Edge: Theory and Politics of Irony.* New York: Routledge, 1994.

Iser, Wolfgang. *The Act of Reading: A Theory of Aesthetic Response.* Baltimore: Johns Hopkins University Press, 1978.

Jabès, Edmond. *The Book of Margins.* Chicago: University of Chicago Press, 1993.

——. "Book of the Dead." Interview with Paul Auster in Paul Auster, *Collected Prose,* 571–79. London: Bloomsbury, 2011.

——. *Le Livre des Questions.* Paris: Gallimard, 1988.

James, Henry. *The Aspern Papers and Other Stories.* Oxford: Oxford University Press, 2013.

Janicaud, Dominique. *Heidegger en France.* Paris: Albin Michel, 2001.

Jay, Martin. *Downcast Eyes: The Denigration of Vision in Twentieth-Century French Thought.* Berkeley: University of California Press, 1994.

——. "Intention and Irony: The Missed Encounter Between Hayden White and Quentin Skinner." *History and Theory,* February 1, 2013, 32–48.

Judt, Tony. *Past Imperfect: French Intellectuals, 1944–1956.* Berkeley: University of California Press, 1992.

Kant, Immanuel. *Critique of Pure Reason.* Ed. and trans. Paul Guyer and Allen W. Wood. Cambridge: Cambridge University Press, 1998.

——. *Groundwork of the Metaphysics of Morals.* Trans. Mary Gregor. Cambridge: Cambridge University Press, 2012.

Katz, Claire. *Levinas and the Crisis of Humanism.* Bloomington: Indiana University Press, 2013.

Kearney, Richard. *Dialogues with Contemporary Continental Thinkers.* Manchester: Manchester University Press, 1984.

Kelly, Michael. "Catholicism and the Left in Twentieth-Century France." In *Catholicism, Politics, and Society in Twentieth-Century France,* 141–69. Ed. Kay Chadwick. Liverpool: Liverpool University Press, 2000.

——. *The Cultural and Intellectual Rebuilding of France After the Second World War.* Chippenham: Palgrave, 2004.

Kermode, Frank. *The Genesis of Secrecy: On the Interpretation of Narrative.* Cambridge: Harvard University Press, 1979.

Kierkegaard, Søren. *The Concept of Irony.* Trans. Howard V. Hong. Princeton: Princeton University Press, 1992.

——. *Fear and Trembling and Sickness Unto Death.* Trans. Walter Lowrie. Princeton: Princeton University Press, 2013.

Kleinberg, Ethan. *Generation Existential: Heidegger's Philosophy in France, 1927–1961.* Ithaca: Cornell University Press, 2005.

——. "Not Yet Marrano." In *The Trace of God,* 39–58. Ed. Peter Gordon and Edward Baring. New York: Fordham University Press, 2014.

Lacroix, Jean. *La Crise intellectuelle du Catholicisme Francais*. Paris: Fayard, 1970.

LaCocque, André, and Paul Ricoeur. Trans. David Pellauer. *Thinking Biblically: Exegetical and Hermeneutical Studies*. Chicago: University of Chicago Press, 1998.

Lacoue-Labarthe, Philippe. *Heidegger and the Politics of Poetry*. Trans. Jeff Fort. Urbana: University of Illinois, 2007.

—— and Jean-Luc Nancy. *The Literary Absolute: The Theory of Literature in German Romanticism*. Trans. Philip Barnard. Albany: SUNY Press, 1988.

Lear, Jonathan. *A Case for Irony*. Cambridge: Harvard University Press, 2011.

Lefort, Claude. *Democracy and Political Theory*. Trans. David Macey. Minneapolis: University of Minnesota, 1988.

Lehr, Johanna. *La Thora dans la Cité*. Lormont: Le Bord de l'eau, 2013.

Lescourret, Marie-Ann. *Emmanuel Levinas*. Paris: Flammarion, 1994.

Llewelyn, John. *Appositions of Jacques Derrida and Emmanuel Levinas*. Bloomington: Indiana University Press, 2002.

Lloyd, Christopher. "Enduring Captivity: French POW Narratives of World War II." *Journal of War and Culture Studies* 6.1 (February 2013): 24–39.

Lukacs, George. *The Theory of the Novel*. Trans. Anna Bostock. Cambridge: MIT Press, 1971.

Maimonides, Moses. *The Guide to the Perplexed*. Trans. Shlomo Pines. Chicago: University of Chicago Press, 1963.

Mallarmé, Stéphane, and Jacques Schérer. *Le Livre de Mallarmé*. Paris: Gallimard, 1978.

Man, Paul de. *Aesthetic Ideology*. Minneapolis: University of Minnesota Press, 1996.

——. *Allegories of Reading: Figural Language in Rousseau, Nietzsche, Rilke and Proust*. New Haven: Yale University Press, 1979.

Marcel, Gabriel. *The Mystery of Being*. London, Harvill, 1950.

——. *The Philosophy of Existence*. Trans. Manya Harari. London: Harvill, 1948.

Mehlman, Jeffrey. *Legacies of Antisemitism in France*. Minneapolis: University of Minnesota, 1983.

Meltzer, Françoise. *Seeing Double: Baudelaire's Modernity*. Chicago: University of Chicago University Press, 2011.

Melville, Herman. *Bartleby the Scrivener: A Story of Wall Street*. New York: Hesperus, 2007.

Milbank, John. *Theology and Social Theory: Beyond Secular Theory*. Oxford: Blackwell, 1990.

Miller, J. Hillis. "The Figure in the Carpet." *Poetics Today* 1.3 (Spring 1980): 107–18 and *Reading Narrative*, 84–106. Norman: University of Oklahoma Press, 1982.

——. *For Derrida*. New York: Fordham University Press, 2009.

——. "The Other's Other: Jealousy and Art in Proust." *Qui Parle* 9.1 (1995) 119–40.

Mosès, Stéphane. "Au Coeur d'un chiasme." In *Derrida, La Tradition de la Philosophie*, 109–33. Ed. Marc Crepon and Frédéric Worms. Paris: Galilée, 2008.

Mounier, Emmanuel. "Introduction aux Existentialismes." *Esprit* 121.4 (April 1946): 521–39.

——. "Situation du Personalisme." *Esprit* 118.1 (January 1946): 4–25.

Moyn, Sam. *Origins of the Other: Emmanuel Levinas Between Revelation and Ethics.* Ithaca: Cornell University Press 2005.

Mufti, Amir. "Orientalism and the Institution of World Literature." *Critical Inquiry* 36.3 (Spring 2010): 458–93.

Naas, Michael. *Miracle and Machine: Jacques Derrida and the Two Sources of Religion, Science, and the Media.* New York, Fordham University Press, 2012.

——. *Taking on the Tradition: Jacques Derrida and the Legacies of Tradition.* Stanford: Stanford University Press, 2003.

Nancy, Jean-Luc. *Dis-Enclosure: The Deconstruction of Christianity.* New York: Fordham University Press, 2008.

Neibuhr, Reinhold. *The Irony of American History.* Chicago: University of Chicago Press, 1952.

Newmark, Kevin. *Irony on Occasion: From Schlegel and Kierkegaard to Derrida and de Man.* New York: Fordham University Press, 2012.

Nietzsche, Friedrich. *Birth of Tragedy.* Trans. Douglas Smith. Oxford: Oxford University Press, 2000.

——. *Kritische Gesamtausgabe Werke.* Berlin: de Gruyter, 1999.

——. *Portable Nietzsche.* New York: Penguin 1977.

——. *Thus Spoke Zarathustra.* Trans. Graham Parkes. Oxford: Oxford University Press, 2008.

Nirenberg, David. *Anti-Judaism: The Western Tradition.* New York: Norton, 2014.

Nizan, Paul. *Les Chiens de garde.* Paris: F. Maspero, 1969.

Ofrat, Gideon. *The Jewish Derrida.* Trans. Peretz Kidron. Syracuse: Syracuse University Press, 2001.

Patočka, Jan. *Heretical Essays in the Philosophy of History.* Trans. Erazim Kohák. New York: Carus, 1996.

Patri, Aimé. "Proudhon et Dieu." *Critique* 3–4 (August-September 1946): 267–71.

Paulhan, Jean. *Les Fleurs de Tarbes, ou La Terreur dans les lettres.* Paris: Gallimard, 1945.

——. The *Flowers of Tarbes, or Terror in Literature.* Trans. Michael Syrotinski. Urbana: University of Illinois Press, 2006.

Pavel, Thomas. *The Lives of the Novel: A History.* Princeton: Princeton University Press, 2013.

Peeters, Benoît. *Derrida, a Biography.* Trans. Andrew Brown. Cambridge: Polity, 2013.

Poirié, François. *Emmanuel Levinas: Qui êtes-vous?* Paris: La Manufacture, 1987.

Proust, Marcel. *A l'ombre des jeunes filles.* Paris: Nouvelle Revue Francaise, 1920.

——. *Remembrance of Things Past*, Vol. 1. Trans. C. K. Scott Moncrieff. New York: Random House, 1981.

Rancière, Jacques. "Should Democracy Come? Ethics and Politics in Derrida." In *Derrida and the Time of the Political*, 274–88. Ed. Pheng Cheah and Suzanne Guerlac. Durham: Duke University Press, 2009.

Ricoeur, Paul. *Rule of Metaphor: Multidisciplinary Studies of the Creation of Meaning in Language.* Trans. Robert Czerny. Toronto: University of Toronto Press, 1977.

——. *Time and Narrative*, vol. 1. Trans. Kathleen Mclaughlin and David Pellauer. Chicago: University of Chicago Press, 1983.

Robbins, Jill. *Altered Readings: Levinas and Literature*. Chicago: University of Chicago Press, 1999.

Rimmon-Kenan, Shlomith. *The Concept of Ambiguity: Example of James*. Chicago: University of Chicago Press, 1977.

Roudinesco, Élisabeth, and Jacques Derrida, *For What Tomorrow*. Trans. Jeff Fort. Stanford: Stanford University Press, 2004.

Rorty, Richard. *Contingency, Irony, and Solidarity*. Cambridge: Cambridge University Press, 1989.

——. *Deconstruction and Pragmatism*. London: Routledge, 1996.

Said, Edward. *The World, the Text, and the Critic*. Cambridge: Harvard University Press, 1983.

Santner, Eric. *The Royal Remains: The People's Two Bodies and the Endgames of Sovereignty*. Chicago: University of Chicago Press, 2011.

Sartre, Jean-Paul. *Qu'est-ce que la litterature*. Paris: Gallimard, 1948.

——. *What Is Literature*. Trans. Steven Ungar. Cambridge: Harvard University Press, 1988.

Schloesser, Stephen. *Jazz Age Catholicicism: Mystic Modernism in Postwar Paris, 1919–1933*. Toronto: University of Toronto Press, 2005.

Scott, Nathan. *Visions of Presence in Modern American Poetry*. Baltimore: Johns Hopkins University Press, 1993.

Shakespeare, Steven. *Derrida and Theology*. London: T&T Clark, 2009.

Smith, Robert J. *The Ecole Normale Supérieure and the Third Republic*. Albany: SUNY Press, 1982.

Sollers, Phillipe. *Logiques*. Paris: Seuil, 1968.

Sternhell, Zeev. *Ni droite ni gauche: l'idéologie fasciste en France*. Paris: Seuil, 1983.

Surya, Michel. *L'autre Blanchot:L'écriture de jour, l'écriture de nuit*. Paris: Gallimard: 2015.

Thomson, A. J. P. *Deconstruction and Democracy: Derrida's Politics of Friendship*. London: Continuum, 2005.

Todorov, Tzvetan. *Poétique de la Prose*. Paris: Seuil, 1969.

Ungar, Steven. *Scandal and Aftereffect: Blanchot and France Since 1930*. Minneapolis: University of Minnesota 1995.

Vigny, Alfred de, *Stello*. Paris: Calman Levy, 1882.

——. *Stello*. Trans. Irving Massey. Montreal: McGill University Press, 1963.

Vries, Hent de. *Minimal Theologies: Critiques of Secular Reason in Adorno and Levinas*. Baltimore: Johns Hopkins University Press, 2005.

——. *Philosophy and the Turn to Religion*. Baltimore: Johns Hopkins University Press, 1999.

Wahl, Jean. *Existence Humaine et Transcendance*. Neuchâtel: Baconnière, 1944.

——. *Introduction à la pensée de Heidegger: cours donnés en Sorbonne de Janvier à Juin 1946*. Paris: Librarire générale française, 1998.

——. *Poésie, pensée, perception*. Paris: Calman-Lévy, 1948.

———. "Présentation." *Deucalion* 1.1 (1946): 9–11.

———. *A Short History of Existentialism*. Trans. Forrest Williams and Stanley Maron. Westport, CT: Greenwood, 1949.

———. "Subjectivité et Transcendence" in *Bulletin de la Société française de philosophie* 37, no. 5 (October-December 1937): 161–211.

———. *Vers le concret: études d'histoire de la philosophie contemporaine*. Paris: J. Vrin, 1932.

Weber, Sam. "Once and for All." *Grey Room* 20 (Summer 2005): 106–16.

Wehrs, Donald R. *Levinas and Twentieth Century Literature: Ethics and the Reconstruction of Subjectivity*. Newark: University of Delaware Press, 2013.

White, Hayden. "The Absurdist Moment in Contemporary Literary Theory" in *Contemporary Literature* 17.3 (Summer 1976): 378–403.

———. *Tropics of Discourse: Essays in Cultural Criticism*. Baltimore: Johns Hopkins University Press, 1978.

Winock, Michel. *Histoire politique de la revue Esprit, 1930–1950*. Paris: Seuil, 1975.

Wyschograd, Edith. *Saints and Postmodernism: Revisioning Moral Philosophy*. Chicago: University of Chicago, 1990.

Ziolkowski, Eric. "History of Religions and the Study of Religion and Literature: Grounds for Alliance," *Literature and Theology* 12.3 (1998): 305–28.

Žižek, Slavoj. Neighbors and Monsters," in *The Neighbor: Three Inquiries in Political Theology*, 154–55. Chicago: University of Chicago University Press, 2005.

———. *The Puppet and the Dwarf: The Perverse Core of Christianity*. Cambridge: MIT Press, 2003.

INDEX

intellectuels juifs de langue française
address, 1–6, 31–32; "comme si,"
6; on criticism, 82, 91, 167–68;
deconstruction for, xiv, 24, 84, 124–25;
eschatology for, 89–91; force for,
83–85; on freedom, 101–8; in French
intellectual scene, xi, 4; Heidegger and,
82, 185–86; history as critical force,
xiii; Husserl's critique by, 24; irony
for, 21–22, 33–34; Jabès's friendship
with, 92–93; on James, 185–87; Jewish
identity of, 2, 6, 30, 107, 160–61; Johns
Hopkins University seminar, 113–15;
on Judaism, 97–99; Judaism for, 31–32,
80, 95, 106–7; on Kafka, 143; language
for, 27; Levinas as ideal reader for,
76, 87; Levinas critiqued by, 17, 125;
Levinas's critique of, 22; Levinas's
eulogy by, 16, 18; Levinas's influence
on, 75–76, 85–86; Levinas's work
and, xiii, 75, 80; on literary criticism,
81; literary theory and, xiv; literature
and religion for, ix, xii, 11, 28, 33,
76–78, 94–95; on literature and truth,
113–14; literature for, 5, 29–32, 34–35;
on Mallarmé, 91–92; on metaphor,
86–88; military service, 107; mystery
for, 78–79; on Nietzsche, 168–69;
on Otherwise Than Being, 26–27, 118,
125–26; philosophical education of,
4; philosophical method, xiii; poetry
for, 58; politics for, 114–15; in postwar
period, xi; recognition of, 75–76;
on religion, 126; religion defined
by, 135; religion for, xi, 80, 206n3;
repetition and theology in, 79–80; as
revolutionary, 115–16; on Rousset, 82;
structuralism for, 81, 84, 91; subversion,
23; theology and, xiv, 79–80, 213n7;
Totality and Infinity and impact on,
7, 13, 75, 85–86; on the trace, xiv, 29,

34; transcendence for, 78; in United
States, xiv; vouloir dire, 9–10; writing
for, 99–100. See also Levinas-Derrida
alliance; specific works
Destabilization, irony for, 21–22
Deucalion (journal), 54–55
Dieu (God), 16, 29
Difference, concept of, 34, 208n36
Difficult Freedom (Difficile liberté,
Levinas), x, 67, 80, 97–99; freedom
in, 101; Judaism in, 103–4; politics in,
104–5
Disenchantment, 127–28
Dissemination (Derrida), 114
Dissemination, concept of, 159–60
Donner la mort. See Gift of Death
Doubt, as mode of questioning, 89
Dreams, 207n18
Dreyfus affair, 39
Durkheim, Emile, 39; as Levinas's
precursor, 44; Nizan's criticism of, 41;
religion for, 44

École normale israélite orientale, 107–8
"École païenne, L'" (Baudelaire), 167–68
Economy of death, 99
"Edmond Jabès and the Question of the
Book" (Derrida), 81, 95; Judaism in, 99
Eiron, 20–21
"Ellipsis" (Derrida), 111–12
"En ce moment même dans cet ouvrage me
voici" (Derrida), 7–8, 28–29, 208n39
Enlightenment, 156
Errance, concept of, 208n39
Eschatology, 89–90; in Writing and
Difference, 91
Esotericism, 136; secret in literature and
religious, 169–70
Ésprit (journal), 68–69
Ethics: Levinas and, 160; politics and,
131–32